SOCIAL JUSTICE IN ISLAM

AMERICAN COUNCIL OF LEARNED SOCIETIES
Near Eastern Translation Program
Number One

SOCIAL JUSTICE IN ISLAM

Sayed Kotb

Translated from the Arabic by
John B. Hardie

103217

OCTAGON BOOKS

A DIVISION OF FARRAR, STRAUS AND GIROUX

New York   1980

This work is a complete translation of
Al-'Adālah al-Ijtimā 'yah fi al-Islām by
Sayed Kotb, published by Maktabat Misr,
Cairo, n.d. (about 1945).

Reprinted 1970
by special arrangement with the American Council of Learned Societies

Second Octagon Printing 1979
Third Octagon Printing 1980

OCTAGON BOOKS
A DIVISION OF FARRAR, STRAUS & GIROUX, INC.
19 Union Square West
New York, N.Y. 10003

LIBRARY OF CONGRESS CATALOG CARD NUMBER: 75-96205
ISBN 0-374-94617-5

FOREWORD

The Near Eastern Translation Program as an operation
of the American Council of Learned Societies effected through
its Committee on Near Eastern Studies, was initiated in 1950
with the aid of a subsidy from The Rockefeller Foundation.
The aim of the program is the translation into English of significant works in all the important Near Eastern languages,
in the fields of the humanities and of the social sciences, to
provide an insight into local life and thought.

In the difficult problem of choosing books for translation,
the Committee has had the counsel and cooperation of scholars
throughout the United States and Canada, as well as in Europe
and the Near East generally. It is thought that the selections
will be of increasing use to readers interested in world affairs, and will also serve as collateral reading material for
courses in our colleges and universities.

The volumes translated are of various recent dates and
have been restricted by the fundamental aim of the program--
the discovery and selection of the best in contemporary
thought written by the various peoples of this region for themselves. Only in this way, it is believed, can American
readers be made aware of the concepts and ideologies by
which the thinking and attitudes of the various peoples of the
Near East are being molded. The translations are unabridged
English versions of the original text, made to represent the
closest approximation in the English language of what the
author said to his own readers.

It should, of course, be clearly understood that the views
expressed in the works translated are the opinions of the
writers and not of the American Council of Learned Societies
or the Committee on Near Eastern Studies. Both the Council
and the Committee, however, wish to express their appreciation for the generous service of the various authors who
have willingly facilitated translation and publication of their
work in this way.

iii

The American Council of Learned Societies
acknowledges with special gratitude
the cooperation of the author
Mr. Sayed Kotb
in this translation of his work
as an element in creating a better understanding
among American readers of the thinking and problems
of the Near Eastern peoples

CONTENTS

Translator's Preface

The subject matter of the Arabic work here rendered into English is of sufficiently universal interest to warrant an
appeal not merely to the Middle East specialist, but also to
the thoughtful man or woman to whom social conditions
throughout the world are of living concern. With this in mind
I have sought here primarily to produce a readable piece of
English. To this end academic accuracy has been in some
measure sacrificed, insofar as the English is frequently a
paraphrase rather than a literal rendering of the original;
though at the same time an effort has been made wherever
possible to preserve the robust flavor of language for which
Arabic is so notable. Thus, for example, I have made fresh
translations of the Qur'anic quotations which are such a
feature of the book, although the Arabic scholar will at once
perceive my indebtedness to the great translators, especially
Rodwell and Bell.

Similarly in the interests of a readable version for the
non-specialist no attempt has been made to use any of the
scientific systems of transliteration; such Arabic words as
have gained a measure of English currency, like "Caliph"
and "Medina" will be found in their familiar forms, while
others are represented by the simplest forms which approxi-
mate to the Arabic spelling, independent of modern pronun-
ciation, since this varies dialectically throughout the Middle
East.

Footnotes, again, have been restricted to a minimum,
but with the non-specialist reader in mind I have tried in
many cases to sketch in very briefly the historical, literary,
or religious background to the text. All such notes, as distinct from the author's own notes are clearly marked. For
the benefit of the same lay reader a short bibliography of
easily accessible works is appended; in these books may be
found the elements of knowledge without which any study of
Arabic literature, ancient or modern, must be largely abor-
tive.

One further comment requires to be made. Throughout

the translation I have conscientiously rendered the author's
own opinions and interpretations, and those alone. There
will be many points which the specialist and the non-specialist alike will feel like challenging. So much the better, for
this, from a Western point of view, is a provocative book.
But the aim of the present work has been neither to comment
nor to criticize, but simply to translate, as the author himself would have written it, had he written in English.

For those who are making their first acquaintance with
Islam and its beliefs, the following short statements may
prove helpful. The Prophet Muhammad ibn (son of) Abdullah was born in Mecca towards the end of the sixth century
A.D. At about the age of forty he became conscious of a
call to prophecy, and from that time forward was the recipient of frequent revelations. His preaching at Mecca was
based on the existence of only One Supreme God, Allah (THE
God), the demands of that God in the way of moral living, and
the reality of a final judgment on the Day of Resurrection.
The name of the faith was significant; Islam means commit-
ting oneself to God, and those who do so are Muslims. The
terms Muhammedanism and Muhammedan are frequently
used in the West, but are not popular among Muslims themselves, since they hold, and rightly, that they are not worshippers of Muhammad, who was simply the Messenger or
Apostle of Allah.

Islam made but slow progress at Mecca, and on July 16th,
622 A.D. there took place the Emigration (Hijra) of Muhammad to Medina. It is from this date that the Muslim era
starts; hence dates are given in two forms, the second of
which is A(nno) H(ijrae). The Muslim year, being lunar, is
some eleven days shorter than the solar, and hence the Muslim date cannot be found simply by subtracting 622 from the
Christian. The year 1371 A.H. should open in October 1951.

At Medina Muhammad and his Companions quickly became
influential, thanks to the willing support of the Medinese
Helpers (Ansar). In a series of engagements Muslim arms
conquered the Hejaz, the territory in which both Mecca and
Medina stand, though not without set-backs and difficulties.
Finally Mecca was captured, and all Arabia paid at least lip
service to the Messenger. After his death in 632 A.D. (111
A.H.) he was followed as head of the Muslim community by
a Successor or Caliph (Khalifa). The first four of these Caliph

the so-called Orthodox Caliphs, were all men who had been
Companions of the Prophet, but after them the power passed
successively to two dynasties, that of the Umayyads and that
of the Abbasids. Following a period of smaller independent
dynasties in various parts of the Muslim world, the hegemony
of that world fell to Turkey, where it remained until the time
of the first World War.

The sacred book of Islam is the Qur'an, which consists
of the revelations of Muhammad, collected after his death
by his followers. It is divided into chapters which are known
as Suras, and, together with the Sunna, or custom of the
Prophet during his life, forms the supreme authority of Muslim life. Hence the frequent reference to it in this work.

The resurgence of Islam as a living and influential faith
seeking to meet the needs of the present day with all its
perplexities, is one of the great features of this century.
The forces at work in and through Islam are more potent
than the West generally recognizes, and our greatest need
at the moment is a better understanding of the Muslim world,
what it believes, what it stands for, and what it seeks. This
work is offered as a slight contribution to that understanding.

J.B.H.

SOCIAL JUSTICE IN ISLAM

I. Religion and Society in Christianity and in Islam

In the world of economics an individual who has private
means does not resort to borrowing before he has examined
his means to see what resources he has there; nor does a
government resort to importing until it has scrutinized its
native resources, and examined its raw materials and their
potential. And so in the case of spiritual resources, intellectual capabilities, and moral and ethical traditions--are
not these things on the same level as goods or money in human
life? Apparently not; for here in Egypt and in the Muslim
world as a whole we pay little heed to our native spiritual
resources and our own intellectual heritage; instead we think
first of importing foreign principles and methods, or borrowing customs and laws from across the deserts and from beyond the seas.

We have only to look in order to see that our social situation is as bad as it can be; it is apparent that our social
conditions have no possible relation to justice; and so we turn
our eyes to Europe, to America, or to Russia, and we expect
to import from there solutions to our problems, just as from
them we import goods for our industrial livelihood. With this
difference--that in industrial importing we first examine the
goods which are already on our markets, and we estimate our
own ability to produce. But when it is a matter of importing
principles and customs and laws, we do no such thing; we
continually cast aside all our own spiritual heritage, all our
intellectual endowment, and all the solutions which might well
be revealed by a glance at these things; we cast aside our own
fundamental principles and doctrines, and we bring in those of
democracy, or socialism, or communism. It is to these that
we look for a solution of our social problem, although our circumstances, our history, and the very bases of our life,
material, intellectual, and spiritual alike, are quite out of
keeping with the circumstances of people across the deserts
and beyond the seas.

At this moment we profess Islam as a state religion; we claim in all sincerity to be true Muslims--if indeed we do not claim to be the guardians and missionaries of Islam. Yet we have divorced our faith from our practical life, condemning it to remain in ideal isolation, with no jurisdiction over life, no connection with its affairs, and no remedy for its problems. For, as the popular saying goes, "Religion concerns only a man and his God." But as for ordinary relationships, the bonds of society and the problems of life, political or economic theory--religion has nothing to do with these things, nor they with it; such is the view of those who are not actively hostile to religion. As for the others, their reaction is: Make no mention of religion here; it is nothing but an opiate employed by plutocrats and despots to drug the working classes and to paralyze the unfortunate masses.

How have we arrived at this strange view of the nature and the history of Islam? We have imported it, as we import everything, from across the deserts and beyond the seas. For certainly the fable of a divorce between faith and life did not grow up in the Muslim East, nor does Islam know of it; and the myth that religion is but a drug to the senses was not born of this faith at any time, nor does the nature of the faith even sanction it. We merely repeat these things parrot-wise, and accept them at second-hand like monkeys; we never think of looking for their origin and their sources, nor of learning their beginning or their results. Let us see first, then, whence and how these strange opinions came about.

* * * * * * *

Christianity grew up in the shadow of the Roman Empire, in a period when Judaism was suffering an eclipse, when it had become a system of rigid and lifeless ritual, an empty and unspiritual sham. The Roman Empire had its famous laws which still live as the origin of modern European legislation; the Roman public had its own customs and social institutions. Christianity had no need then--nor, indeed, had it the power-- to put before a powerful Roman Government and a united Roman public laws and rules and regulations for government or for society. Rather its need was to devote its power to moral and spiritual purification; and its concern was to correct the stereotyped ritual and the empty sham of ceremonial Judaism, and to restore spirit and life to the Israelite conscience.

Christ (upon whom be peace) came to preach only spiritual purity, mercy, kindness, tolerance, chastity, and abstinence. All His teachings were connected with social or economic or political customs; more, he showed by his behavior and by his opinions that he attached no importance to the narrow traditions of the priests and the scribes; they were concerned only with external acts, while his concern was with the moral and the spiritual realms. Thus he made the Jewish sabbath lawful to his disciples; and thus he allowed them to eat anything which entered the mouth, because it was not that which defiled, but rather that which came forth in the way of "Deceit, falsehood, and adultery." Thus he made it lawful for his disciples to break the fast on the Jewish fast-days; yet he would not stone the adulterous woman who was brought to him for questioning; for of those who should have been responsible for her stoning, according to the Mosaic Law, not one was free from guilt. He once said "You have heard that it has been said 'An eye for an eye, and a tooth for a tooth'; but I say to you 'Resist not evil; but whoever strikes you on the right cheek, turn the other to him also. And whoever wishes to quarrel with you and to take your undergarment, give him your overgarment also; and whoever forces you to go one mile, go with him two.'"[1]

The same spirit is apparent also in the words, "You have heard that it was said to those of old 'Do not kill; for whoever kills is liable to judgment.' But I say to you 'Indeed, everyone who is angry with his brother without cause is liable to judgment; whoever says to his brother "Raqa"[2] is liable to the Council; and whoever says "Imbecile," is liable to the fire of Gehenna. So if you bring your offering to the altar, and if you remember there that your brother has some cause of complaint against you, then leave your offering there in front of the altar, go first and settle your quarrel with your brother and then come and present your offering. Be reconciled with your opponent quickly while you are in the way... etc."

Or again: "You have heard that it was said to those of old 'Do not commit adultery.' But I say to you that whoever looks at a woman with desire has already committed adultery with her in his heart; if your right eye causes you to stumble, pluck it out and cast it from you, for it is better for you that one of your members should perish than that your whole body

should be thrown into hell-fire; or if your right hand causes
you to stumble, cut it off and cast it from you, for it is better
for you that one of your members should perish than that
your whole body should be thrown into hell-fire...etc."

Or: "Again ye have heard that it hath been said by them
of old, 'Thou shalt not forswear thyself, but shalt perform
unto the Lord thine oaths. But I say unto you, Swear not at
all. Not by Heaven, for it is God's throne; nor by the earth,
for it is His footstool; nor by Jerusalem, for it is the city
of the Great King. Nor shalt thou swear by thy head, for
thou canst make one hair white or black. But let your speech
be, Yea; nay, nay. Whatsoever is more than that cometh
of evil."[3]

Accordingly Christianity forgot about "Render unto Caesar
the things that are Caesar's, and unto God the things that are
God's," and it turned its full strength towards spiritual purity
and pious discipline. It took its stand upon the ground that
"Religion concerns only a man and his God," while the temporal law is concerned with the relationship between the individual and the state. And this was the more natural since
Christianity grew up in a corner of the Roman Empire, and
since it was a reaction against Judaism.

Accordingly the Christian faith pushed to the uttermost
limit its teachings of spiritual purity, material asceticism,
and unworldly forbearance. It fulfilled its task in this spiritual
sphere of human life, because it is the function of a religion
to elevate man by spiritual means so far as it can, to proclaim piety, to cleanse the heart and the conscience, to humble man's nature, to make him ignore worldly needs and
strive only for holy objectives in a world of shades and vani-
ties. But it left society to the State, to be governed by its
earthly laws, since to it society was connected with the outer
and temporal world, whereas the faith had its realm in the
soul and the conscience. In this,Christianity was logical on
three counts; first, because it grew up in a strictly limited
area; second, because of the particular needs of the Jewish
people to whom Jesus was sent in that they formed only a tiny
fragment of the totality of the great Roman Empire; and
thirdly, because of the limited time allotted to Christianity
before the appearance of the new worldreligion--the faith of
Islam.

Then God so willed it that Christianity should cross the

seas to Europe, taking with it all its forbearance and purity
and denial of the material world. There it met the Byzantines,
inheritors of the pagan and material culture of Greece, and
there it met also the peoples of the remoter parts of Europe,
its first contact with the barbarian world. They were peoples
of immense numbers, fighting bitterly over their narrow territories, ruthless and merciless in nature, mean and selfish
in outlook. Among them none could taste the savor of ease
for a moment, nor could put away his weapons for a minute,
nor could find time in the struggle of life for the speculations
of Christianity, this unselfish, excessively self-denying faith;
"Whoever smite thee on the right cheek, turn to him the other
also; and whoever wisheth to sue thee and take away thy undergarment, give him your overgarment also." Such peoples
early saw that religion was of no profit to life, and they concluded that "Religion concerns only a man and his God."
Accordingly they found it natural to seek the refuge of religion
while they were in the church, and to breathe its air in the
sanctuary, and after to return to the battle of life with all
their barbarian customs; so they settled their quarrels by
the judgment of the sword, or on occasion by that of the local
law. And religion was left in pious isolation, to deal only
with heart and conscience in the holy sanctuary and in the con-
fessional.

But the churchmen, the priests, the cardinals, and the
popes were unable thus to guarantee their own prosperity or
to preserve their influence, so long as the Church remained
isolated from the economic, social, and administrative life.
So it became inevitable that the Church should become a power
comparable to the power of kings and rulers--with an inevitable
weakening of its spiritual authority in the sphere of everyday
life. Then came the age when the Church had princes with
armies and authority not less than the most powerful of kings
with their troops and their sovereignty. Thus inevitably
there arose the dispute between the Church and temporal
power, between the popes and the emperors, with the common

Hence arose that division between religion and the world
in the life of Europe; for the actual truth inherent in the nature
of things is this, that Europe was never truly Christian. Hence
religion there has remained in isolation from the business and
the customs of life from the day of its entry to the present
day.

people largely on the side of the Church. But to this--again inevitably--there succeeded the alliance between these two powers, for each had a common interest in keeping the masses in subjection and in the exploitation of the common people. This alliance lasted as long as prosperity remained essentially economic and material, and as long as the dispute was basically concerned with temporal power. It was under these circumstances, and because of despots and religious tyrants that the saying arose that: Religion is the opiate of the masses. For it was thus that it happened in Europe.

So the Church remained the supreme spiritual power, with full authority over men, alike in this world and the next. It continued to sell its "plenary indulgences," and to preach its "eternal damnation"; it continued to hold sway over men's bodies and minds alike; further, it even had the power of inquisition to kill or burn anyone who raised his head in revolt, or who even inclined to doubt or heresy. Then came the age of the Renaissance, and the Church was quick to perceive the threat to its power which must result from the enfranchisement of mind and sense after the Dark Ages; there was no slight danger that it would be deprived of its power by the pride of the thought and knowledge now coming into being. So the Church set itself in opposition striving to muzzle liberty of thought and freedom of speech which contradicted its ancient and threadbare doctrines. And so from that time there has been bitter hostility between the Church and free thought. For the Church was unwilling to limit itself to spiritual affairs, which are the true sphere of Christianity; nor was it content to hold sway merely over the world to come, as is the claim of the Papacy. Therefore its doctrines have come into conflict with those of science on such matters as the world, the universe, and the nature of existence But the teachings of science are based on study and trial and experiment, and they are corroborated by experience and by proof, so that the discoveries of science leave no room for doubt concerning the strength of this new weapon; and so there have grown up generations of scientists and thinkers who dislike and even despise the Church, and who have in their hearts only hostility and loalthing for Church and churchmen. Hence has arisen the bitterness between religion and science, between the Church and the intellectual world in the life of Europe.

With the advance of time the new science bore its fruits, and there grew from it in the sphere of technology what is known as the great era of production. Capital increased and in the arena of industry there appeared two sharply divided camps, that of capital, and that of labor. The cleavage between the interests of these two soon became apparent, and the real authority passed from the hands of the state to those of the capitalists; and since the Church had no chance of sharing that authority, it joined itself to the capitalist camp.

I should not care to denigrate the whole body of European churchmen. There are some self-seekers who want only power and who devote themselves to its acquisition. To this end they draw from their religion an opiate for the masses of the workers, in order to restrain them from revolution in search of their rights; or they wean them from the pursuit of justice in this world by the promise of compensation in the next. But the majority must be sincere, by reason of their faith in the tenets of Christianity which is essentially ascetic. By its nature a denial of worldly life, it is a summons to avoid materialism, to despise the world, and to seek rather the Lord's kingdom in the Heavenly world.

But be that as it may, the laboring classes who contemplate a class struggle have concluded that religion will not serve their cause in that struggle. They affirm that the Church uses religion only as an opiate for the working classes, and they have turned completely against religion, saying of it that, "It is the opiate of the millions." Hence there has arisen the apparent Communist hostility to religion.

*　*　*　*　*　*　*

On the other hand, what of ourselves; what has all this to do with us? The conditions of our history, and the nature and circumstances of Islam have nothing in common with any of these things. Islam grew up in an independent country owing allegiance to no empire and to no king, in a form of society never again achieved. It had to embody this society in itself, had to order, encourage, and promote it. It had to order and regulate this society, adopting from the beginning its principles and its spirit along with its methods of life and work. It had to join together the world and the faith by its exhortations and laws. So Islam chose to unite earth and Heaven in one spiritual organization, and one which recognized no difference between worldly zeal and religious coercion. Essentially

Islam never infringes that unity even when its outward forms and customs change.

Such was the birth of Islam and such its task; so it was not liable to be isolated in human idealism far removed from practical worldly life; nor was it compelled to narrow the circle of its action out of fear for an Empire or a monarch. For the center of its being and the field of its action is human life in its entirety, spiritual and material, religious and worldly. Such a religion cannot continue to exist in isolation from society, nor can its adherents be true Muslims unless they practice their faith in their social, legal and economic relationships. And a society cannot be Islamic if it expels the civil and religious laws of Islam from its codes and customs, so that nothing of Islam is left except rites and ceremonials.

"No. by thy Lord, they do not believe until they make thee judge in their difficulties, and do not afterwards find difficulty in thy decisions, but assent to them heartily."[4] "What the Apostle gives you, receive it; and what he forbids you, refrain from it."[5] "And whoever does not judge by what Allah has sent down--is an unbeliever."[6]

One of the characteristic marks of this faith is the fact that it is essentially a unity. It is at once worship and work, religious law and exhortation. Its theological beliefs are not divorced in nature or in objective from secular life and customs. Thus its prayers, which are the highest expression of the theological side of religion, express the turning of the individual and of the congregation towards one single, mighty, and powerful God, and they entail submission to none save to Him. So too the direction of prayer[7] is uniform, nor can any deviate from it. Similarly Muslim prayers infer a kind of equality, since they express one faith to which all are obedient, and in view of which all are equal. Nay, more; "The credo is that there is no God save Allah," which is one of the most typical tenets of the faith, implying as it does for the worshippers a freedom of religion from any kind of servitude. Such a freedom is the fundamental basis of a healthy and worthy community, in which all men are equals.

However we approach the question there can be no shadow of doubt that the theory of society is obviously reflected in the beliefs and the customs of this religion, and that these latter represent the basic, powerful, and universal theory of all social life. So if in any age we find a desire to over-emphasize the pietistic aspect of this faith and to divorce it from the social aspect, or to divorce the social aspect from it, it will be the fault of that age rather than of Islam.

Now, these statements on Islam are not a new theory which is being propounded, nor is a reinterpretation of the faith here being made; this is Islam as it has manifested itself in history, and as it was understood by its first exponent, Muhammad (upon whom be the blessing and the peace of Allah). Thus it was understood also by all true believers as by its original adherents. There is a passage in the glorious Qur'an: "O ye who believe, when proclamation is made for prayer on the day of assembly, strive towards remembrance of Allah and leave off business. That is better for you if you are wise. But when the prayer is finished, scatter abroad in the land and seek the bounty of Allah."[8] Now all of us know how much time in the day is taken up by the statutory prayers, and how much remains for business and trade. The time given to prayer is but a small proportion of man's life, while for the needs of society and life there remains the whole length of day and night. So it is said in another place: "We have appointed the night for a cover, and we have appointed the day for a livelihood."[9] For the major factor in life is the making of a living, rather than any prescribed acts of worship.

So Islam does not prescribe worship as the only basis of its beliefs, but rather it reckons all the activities of life as comprehending worship in themselves--so long as they are within the bounds of conscience, goodness, and honesty. A man once passed by the Prophet, and the Companions of Muhammad noticed in him an eager intentness on his business which set them talking about him; they said, "O Messenger of Allah, would that this man had been in the path of Allah." Then said Muhammad, "If he has come to work for his young children, then he is in the path of Allah; or if he has come to work for his aged and infirm parents, then he is in the path of Allah; or if he has come to work for himself in all moderation, then he is in the path of Allah. But if he has come to work only for luxury or for self-glory, then he is in the path of Satan." Similarly the two following stories are authoratative indication of the spirit of Islam as understood by its founder, the Messenger of Allah. It is related on the authority of Anas[10] that he said: We were on a journey with the Prophet, some of us having fasted and some having eaten. We alighted somewhere in a day of scorching heat, and he who had a garment gave us its shade, but many of us had to shade ourselves from the sun with our hands. So those who had fasted lay helpless, but those who had eaten arose and went from door to door till they got water for the party. Then said the Messenger, "Those who did not fast have this day carried off the full prize." And again, a certain man, noted for his piety, was mentioned to the Prophet, who said, "Who lives with him?" "His brother." Then said he, "His brother is then more pious than he."[11]

Now all this does not mean that Muhammad, who surely knew his own religion better than any other, scorned the whole matter of fasting and prayer; it means rather that the essential spirit of this religion is found in this--that practical work is religious work, for religion is inextricably bound up with life and can never exist in the isolation of idealism in some world of the conscience alone. This is what Umar ibn al-Khattab had in mind when, seeing a man making a parade of asceticism and apathy, he struck him with his whip, crying, "Do not parody our faith to our face, may Allah destroy you."[12] Or on another occasion, when a certain man was giving evidence before him, Umar said to him, "Bring hither some one who knows you." So the man brought another who praised him highly. Then said Umar to the second man, "Are you this man's nearest neighbor, to know his comings and goings?" "No." "Have you, then, been his companion on a journey, whereon he gave evidence of nobility of character?" "No." "Have you perhaps had dealings with him in money matters, wherein he showed himself a man of self-control?" "No." "Then I suspect that you have only seen him in the mosque, mumbling the Qur'an, and now and then lowering and raising his head in prayer." "That is so." Then said Umar, "Away. You do not really know him." And turning to the man himself, "Go, and bring hither some one who really knows you."

In such stories Umar is at one with his Prophet, Muhammad. And such give a reliable indication of the nature of this faith, its opinion of worship and of asceticism, of faith which is hidden in the heart and of work which is apparent to the sight. "In the midst of what Allah hath given you seek the future world, but forget not your portion in this world."[13]

And "Work for this world as if you were going to live forever,
but work for the future world as if you were going to die tomorrow." "Whoever among you sees a stranger, let him
make provision for him." "And were it not that Allah sets
some men against others, the cloisters had been destroyed,
and the churches and the synagogues and mosques in which
the name of Allah is often repeated."[14] "And fight in the
way of Allah against those who fight against you, but do not
provoke hostility; verily Allah loveth not those that provoke
hostility."[15] "Piety lies not in turning your faces to East
or West; but piety is this, that a man believe in Allah and
the Day of Judgment, in the Angels, and the Book and the
Prophets; that he give generously and for love alone to
kindred and to orphans, to the poor and the wayfarer, to beg-
gars and to those under oppression; that he be constant in
prayer and that he give alms; that such men stand to their
word when they pledge their word, and that they have forti-
tude in poverty, in distress, and in time of evil."[16]

Such is the position of Islam in regard to works and faith;
and hence it is clear that there can be no separation between
the faith and the world, or between theology and social practice, as was the case in early Christianity.

Furthermore, in Islam there is no priesthood, and no intermediary between the creature and the Creator; but every
Muslim in the ends of the earth or in the paths of the sea,
has the ability of himself to approach his Lord, without either
priest or minister. Nor again can the Muslim administrator
derive his authority from any papacy, or from Heaven; but
he derives it solely from the Muslim community. Similarly
he derives his principles of administration from the religious
law, which is universal in its understanding and application,
and before which all men come everywhere as equals. So
there is no churchman who can have the right to oppress Muslims; nor has the administrator any power other than that of
transmitting the law, which derives its authority from the
faith. As for the world to come, all men are making their
way to Allah, "and all of them will come before Him singly
on the Day of Judgment."[17] Hence, too, there can be no
quarrel between the Church and the state concerning the control of the faithful or of their possessions. They cannot contend for economic or spiritual profits, for Islam has no knowledge of one ecclesiastical power and another temporal. So

there is no possibility of disagreement here, as was the case with the Emperors and the Popes.

Islam is not hostile to learning, nor in opposition to the learned; on the contrary it accepts learning as a divine and sacred possession which forms a part of religious duty. "He sought learning as being a God-like thing for every Muslim." "Seek learning even if it be found as far as China." "He who treads the path of the search for learning, Allah will facilitate his path to Paradise." So Islamic history has never known those strange, organized persecutions of thinking men or learned men, such as were known in the lands of the Inquisition; the short, scattered periods in which men have been victimized for their theories may be accounted as anomalous in Muslim history. In general such occurrences were the outcome of political necessity, the result of concealed party differences, and on the whole were not a normal feature of Islamic life. Also they arose among peoples who were converts to Islam, and who therefore could not be expected to understand it fully.

Such a tolerance was no more than natural in a religion which did not depend for its proof on wonders and miracles, which did not rely on strange events for the very heart of its message, but which relied rather on the examination and scrutiny of the evidence of life itself and its facts. "Surely in the creation of heaven and earth, in the division of night and day, in the ship which runs on the sea, carrying what is of profit to men, in the water which Allah has sent down from heaven to revive the earth after its death, spreading abroad in it every kind of cattle, in the changing of the winds and the clouds made to do service between heaven and earth--in all these are signs for a people who have intelligence."[18] "He bringeth forth the living from the dead, and He bringeth forth the dead from the living; as He quickeneth the earth after it is dead, so will you be brought forth. Among His signs is that He hath created you from dust, and lo. you are human beings, spreading abroad. And among His signs is that He hath created for you wives of your own kind that you may dwell with them, and hath set love and mercy between you; surely in that there are signs for a thoughtful people. Again, among His signs is the creation of the heavens and the earth, and the divergence of your tongues and complexions. Surely in that there are signs for those who know. Among

His signs is your sleeping by night and by day, and your
seeking a share of His bounty; surely in that there are signs
for a people who hearken. Among His signs is that He makes
you to see the lightning in fear and desire, and that He sends
down water from heaven, and thereby quickens the earth after it has been dead; surely in that there are signs for a
people who understand. "[19]

And again, this tolerance is but natural in a religion which
associates piety with learning, making the latter the pathway
to a knowledge and a reverence of Allah. "Only the learned
among His servants truly fear Allah"[20]; and so He exalts
the station of the learned above that of the unlearned. "Say:
Are they who have knowledge equal with them who have none?"[21]
"Surely the learned man surpasses the merely pious man in
excellence, as the moon on the night of its fulness surpasses
the remainder of the stars." So there is no gulf yawning between religion and learning, either in the nature or in the
history of Islam, comparable to that which existed between
the Christian Church and the liberal scholars in the age of
the revival of learning.

As for churchmen associating themselves with the power
of the state or with the power of wealth, and thus keeping the
workers and lower classes drugged by means of religion,
there is no denying that this did happen in some periods of
Islamic history. But the true spirit of the faith disavows
such persons; the faith indeed threatens them with dire punishments for having exchanged the signs of Allah for a trifling
price. And furthermore, history has preserved beside the
memory of such men the records of another type of churchman to whom no such blame could ever attach; such were
those who despised and rejected the power of poverty and the
demands of Allah. So they encouraged the under-privileged
to demand their rights, giving them leadership, and they attacked the oppressions of governors, they attacked the denial
of privileges, and they fought the persecutions.

* * * * * * *

We have, then, not a single reason to make any separation
between Islam and society, either from the point of view of
the essential nature of Islam, or from that of its historical
course; such reasons as there are attach only to European
Christianity. And yet the world has grown away from religion;
to it the world has left only the education of the conscience

and the perfecting of piety, while to the temporal and secular laws has been committed the ordering of society and the organizing of human life.

Similarly we have no good grounds for any hostility between Islam and the thought of social justice, such as the hostility which persists between Christianity and Communism. For Islam prescribes the basic principles of social justice, and establishes the claim of the poor to the wealth of the rich; it lays down a just principle for power and for money, and therefore has no need to drug the minds of men, and summon them to neglect their earthly rights in favor of their expectations in Heaven. On the contrary it warns those who abdicate their natural rights that they will be severely punished in the next world, and it calls them "self-oppressors." "Surely the angels said to those who died when they were oppressing themselves, 'In what circumstances were you?' They answered, 'We were poor in the earth.' The angels said, 'Was not Allah's earth wide enough for you to migrate?' "The abode of such is Hell--an evil place to go."[22] Thus Islam urges men to fight for their rights; "and he who fights without injustice, the same is a martyr." So while Europe is compelled to put religion apart from the common life, we are not compelled to tread the same path; and while Communism is compelled to oppose religion in order to safeguard the rights of the workers, we have no need of any such hostility to religion.

But can we be certain that this "two-in-one" social order which was established by Islam in one specific period of history will con nue to have the potential for growth and renewal? Can we be sure that it is suitable for application to other periods of history whose circumstances differ to a greater or lesser degree from those which obtained in the age which gave birth to Islam?

This is a fundamental question. It is not possible to give an exhaustive answer to it here, as it will be answered in detail in what is to follow; first we must examine this social order itself, define its sources and roots, and scrutinize its applications in every-day life. Suffice it here--for we are still in the stage of general discussion--to say that Islam has already experienced such an historical process, and the social, economic, and intellectual developments connected with it.

This process Islam has survived by laying down the general, universal rules and principles, and leaving their application in detail to be determined by the processes of time and by the emergence of individual problems. But Islam itself does not deal with the incidental related issues of the principle, except insofar as such are expressions of an unchanging principle whose impact is felt universally. This is the limit of the authority which can be claimed by any religion, in order that it may guarantee its flexibility and ensure the possibility of its own growth and expansion over a period of time.

For this reason the canon lawyers of Islam devoted themselves with a strong and praise-worthy effort to the science of application of the principle, to analogy, and to deduction; most of their work is, in our opinion, in agreement with the spirit of Islam. But in the case of a small proportion, a certain looseness appeared in some of their works, resulting in a greater or less divergence from the spirit of Islam. Still, in the majority of cases, it may safely be said that the principles of the faith have kept pace with the needs of the time. To this period of production of canon law there succeeded a long interval during which the growth of law came to a halt, until at the beginning of the present century new life began to pervade the subject as the Muslim world as a whole started to awake.

The conclusion from this is that we should not put away the social aspect of our faith on the shelf; we should not go to French legislation to derive our laws, or to Communist ideals to derive our social order, without first examining what can be supplied from our Islamic legislation which was the foundation of our first form of society. But there is a wide ignorance of the nature of our faith; there is a spiritual and intellectual laziness which is opposed to a return to our former resources; there is a ridiculous servility to the European fashion of divorcing religion from life--a separation necessitated by the nature of their religion, but not by the nature of Islam. For with them there still exists that gulf between religion on the one hand and learning and the State on the other, the product of historical reasons which have no parallel in the history of Islam.

This does not mean that our summons is to an intellectual,

spiritual, and social avoidance of the ways of the rest of the world; the spirit of Islam rejects such an avoidance, for Islam reckons itself to be a gospel for the whole world. Rather our summons is to return to our own stored-up resources, to become familiar with their ideas, and to proclaim their value and permanent worth, before we have recourse to an untimely servility which will deprive us of the historical background of our life, and through which our individuality will be lost to the point that we will become merely the hangers-on to the progress of mankind. Whereas our religion demands that we should be ever in the forefront. "You are the best nation which I have produced among men; you encourage what is approved of God, and you forbid what is disapproved."

It may well become apparent to us if we look back on our heritage that we have something to give to this unhappy, perplexed, and weary world, something which it has lost in the present material and unspiritual frame of mind which is the legacy of two world wars within a quarter of a century; something which the world is continually trampling under foot in its progress towards a third war, which all the present portents indicate will end in complete ruin.

Such is our position on this question. But we must not proceed to speak of the value of Muslim faith for the new society until first we have examined the nature of its relation to life and to all human problems; and particularly in the field of social justice, which is the main theme of this book.

II. The Nature of Social Justice in Islam

We cannot study the nature of social justice in Islam until
we have first examined the general lines of Islamic theory
on the subject of the universe, life, and mankind. For social
justice is only a branch of that great science to which all Islamic studies must run back.

Now the faith of Islam, which deals with the whole field
of human life, does not treat the different aspects of that
life in the mass, nor yet does it split up the field into a number of unrelated parts. That is to say Islam has one universal theory which covers the universe and life and humanity,
a theory in which are integrated all the different questions;
in this Islam sums up all its beliefs, its laws and statutes,
and its modes of worship and of work. The treatment of all
these matters emanates from this one universal and comprehensive theory, so that each question is not dealt with on an
individual basis, nor is every problem with its needs treated
in isolation from all other problems.

A knowledge of this universal theory is necessary to the
faith of Islam, because it enables the student to understand
its principles and beliefs and to relate the particular to the
general; it empowers him to study with pleasure and with
understanding its characteristics and its aims. While on the
other hand the fact that the basis is religious guarantees that
the theory will be both coherent and comprehensive, and not
departmentalized. For no theory of life can be of profit unless it comprehends all the departments and all the aims of
human life. So the best method of studying Islam is to start
by understanding its universal theory before going on to study
its views on politics or economics or the relationship between
communities and individuals. For such questions as these
are but issues arising out of that universal theory and they
cannot be truly or deeply understood except in the light of it.

Now the true Muslim philosophy is not to be sought in Ibn
Sina[1] or Ibn-Rushd,[2] or such men as these who alone are
known as the Muslim philosophers; for the philosophy which
they teach is no more than a shadow of the Greek philosophy,

17

and has no relation to the true Islamic philosophy. The faith
of Islam has a native universal philosophy which is to be
sought only in its own familiar authorities: the Qur'an and
the Traditions, the life of its Prophet and his every-day customs. These are the authorities in which the student must
delve deep to find the universal Islamic theory from which
come all the Muslim teachings and laws, its modes of worship and of work. Islam as a faith has laid down the nature
of the relation between the Creator and His creation, the
nature of man's relation to the universe and to the world, and
of man's relation to his own soul; it has laid down the relation
between the individual and society, between different societies
and mankind as a whole, and the relation between one nation
and another. All these teachings are the expression in different aspects of the one universal, comprehensive theory
which relates to one another all the separate aspects. All
of which together is Islamic philosophy.

The detailed study of this philosophy is no part of this
present work; here we shall confine ourselves to the examination of one specific subject, to the full completion of which
may Allah's help be vouchsafed. So here we shall merely
outline the main headings of the general scheme, in order
to facilitate our study of social justice in Islam.

* * * * * * *

Man lived for long ages without achieving a comprehensive
theory of his Creator and the universe, or of the universe,
life, and mankind. That is to say, man had never reached
the point of working out such a universal and comprehensive
theory until the birth of Islam.

The relation between the Creator and His creation is to be
found in the power of the Word, the Active Will from which
all creation came; "all that He needs to do when He wishes
anything is to say, BE; and it is."[3] There is no mediating
power of any kind between the Creator and His creation, but
from His universal and absolute Will proceed all existing
things in due and proper order; and by that universal, absolute, and active Will all things are sustained, ordered, and
energized. "He manages the affair, sets the signs in order."[4]
"He grasps the Heavens that they fall not upon the earth, save
by His permission."[5] "It is necessary for the sun not to overtake the moon, nor the night to outrun the day; but each in its
circle they revolve."[6] "Blessed be He in whose hand is the

kingship; and He over all things hath power. "[7]

So all creation, issuing as it does from one absolute, universal, and active Will, forms an all-embracing unity in
which each individual part is in harmonious order with the
remainder. And thus, too, every form of existence embodies
a principle which relates it to this perfect and comprehensive order. "He it is who hath created seven Heavens, one
above the other; thou canst not see any oversight in the
creation of the Merciful. Look again; canst thou see any
flaw? Look again and again; thy sight will turn back, dim
and wearied out. "[8] "And He set up upon it mountain peaks
above it, and blessed it, and arranged its various kinds of
food in it. "[9] "He it is who hath created death and life to try
you, to test which of you is the best in deeds. "[10] "Allah it
is who sends the winds to stir up the clouds, and He spreads
it in the Heavens as He wills, and breaks it up; so you see
the rain coming out of the midst of it; and when He causes
it to fall on which of His servants He wills, behold they re-
joice. "[11] Accordingly it is obvious that all creation must
have a fundamental connection with the creative purpose and
that the Will from which all creation finally proceeds, and
by which it is continually sustained and ordered, is related
to creation itself; thus only can that Will give to creation a
coherence and a completed meaning.

Thus, then, all creation is a unity comprising different
parts; it has a common origin, a common providence and
purpose, because it was deliberately produced by a single,
absolute, and comprehensive Will. Therefore it was suitable,
adapted, and ready for the appearance of life in the general
sense, and for the appearance of man, the highest form of
life, in particular. So the universe cannot be hostile to life,
or to man; nor can "Nature" in our modern phrase be held
to be antagonistic to man, opposed to him, or striving against
him. Rather she is a friend whose purposes are one with those
of life and of mankind. And the task of living beings is not to
contend with Nature, for they have grown up in her bosom,
and she and they together form a part of the single universe
which proceeds from the single will. Thus basically man
lives in a purely friendly environment, among the powers of
a friendly universe. So Allah, when He created the earth,
set up upon it mountain peaks above it, and blessed it, and
arranged its various kinds of food in it. "And He cast upon

the earth mountain peaks, lest it sway with you."[12] "And
the earth--He established it for mankind."[13] "He it is who
hath laid the earth low for you, so walk ye about in its regions, and eat of its provision."[14] "He hath created for you
what is in the earth, all of it."[15] So the Heavens with their
stars are a part of creation; they are connected with the other
parts, and everything that is in them and in the earth is
friendly, cooperative, and interrelated with all the remaining
parts. "And He decked out the lower Heavens with lamps."[16]
"Did we not make the earth a flat expanse, and the mountains
as tent-pegs? We created you in pairs, and We appointed
your sleep to be a rest. We made the night for a covering,
and We made the day for a livelihood. We built about you
seven firm Heavens, and We set a lamp ablazing. We sent
down from the rain-clouds copious waters to bring forth
grain, and vegetation, and luxurious gardens."[17]

And further, the Creator does not place living beings and
men in this world, without giving them also His kindly care
and constant attention, for His perfect Will is constant
throughout all the world, constant, too, over every individual
part of the universe at all times. "There is no beast in the
earth but its provision is a charge upon Allah; He knows its
lair and its resting-place."[18] "We have created man, and
We know what he whispers to himself; We are nearer to him
than his jugular vein."[19] "Your Lord said, 'Call upon Me,
and I shall answer you."[20] "And do not kill your children
because of poverty; We shall provide for you and for them."[21]
And so on.

Because, then, the Universe is a unity emanating from a
single Will; because man is himself a part of the world, dependent upon and related to all the other parts; and because
individuals are as atoms, dependent upon and related to the
world; therefore they must have the same dependence upon,
and relation to, one another. So the Islamic belief is that
humanity is an essential unity; its scattered elements must
be brought together, its diversity must give place to uniformit
its variety of creeds must in the end be brought into one.
For thus and only thus can man be made ready to be at one
with the essential unity of creation. "O ye people, We have
created you male and female, and We have made you races
and tribes, that you might know one another."[22]

There can be no permanent system in human life until this

integration and unification has taken place; this step is a prerequisite for true and complete human life, so that the rule of force may be done away once for all, and so that those who have wandered from the true path may be brought back to it. "The recompense of those who make war against Allah and His Messenger, exerting themselves to cause corruption in the earth, is that they be killed or crucified, or that their hands and feet on opposite sides be cut off, or that they be banished from the land."[23] "If two parties of the Believers fight, then make peace between them; if one of them oppresses the other, then fight the oppressing party until it returns to the affair of Allah; if it returns, then make a just peace between them, and act fairly."[24] "And if Allah had not resisted one party of the people by means of others, the land would have grown corrupt."[25] Accordingly the fundamental matter is this interdependence and solidarity of mankind, and whoever has lost sight of this principle must be brought back to it by any means. For the first great Divine law of existence is to identify the desires of individuals and of societies; and such mutual responsbility among all is in the end the sole aid of our unified world and of its Creator.

Now when we come to consider man as a race and as an individual, there is the same comprehensive unity to be observed; man's faculties which are so diverse in appearance are essentially one in purpose. Thus in this respect also man is comparable to the world in its entirety, since its power too is a unity, though diverse in appearance.

Man lived through long ages without arriving at any comprehensive theory of human and universal powers; he continued to differentiate between spiritual and material powers, he denied one of these in order to strengthen the other, or he admitted the existence of both in a state of opposition and antagonism. He organized his life on the basis that such an opposition between these two types of power was natural, and that the superiority of one was only to be gained at the expense of the other. He held that such superiority on the one side and inferiority on the other was inevitable, because, as he believed, such opposition was inherent in the nature of the world and of man.

Christianity is one of the clearest examples of this theory of opposition, because it was by such a theory that it was led to libertinism on the one hand and asceticism on the other,

according as these two alternated in its life. For Christianity
the salvation of the soul is to be gained by humiliating the
body, by punishing it, or even by destroying it, or at the
least by neglecting it and turning away from indulgence. In
Christianity and in other similar faiths this is the cardinal
principle on which are built up their systems of belief; to it
can be traced their doctrines on life and its purpose, on the
duties of the individual on the one hand and of society on the
other, and on man and the different powers and abilities which
attach to his existence.

Thus the struggle between the two types of power continued,
with men continually uncertain and perplexed, and without
any definite assurance as to the true solution. Then came
Islam, bringing with it a new, comprehensive, and coherent
theory in which there was neither this tension nor this opposition, neither hostility nor antagonism. Islam gave a
unity to all powers and abilities, it gave an identity of purpose
to all desires and inclinations and leanings, it gave a coherence
to all men's efforts. In all these Islam saw one embracing
unity which took in the universe, the soul, and all human life.
Its aim was to unite earth and Heaven in one world; to join
the present world and the world to come in one faith; to link
spirit and body in one humanity; to correlate worship and
work in one life. It sought to bring all these into one path--
the path which led to Allah.

In the same way the world is a unity, composed of things
which are seen and otherwise sensually perceived, and of
things which are unseen and imperceptible. Life is a unity,
made up of material abilities and spiritual powers, between
which no separation can ever be made without a resultant
disorder and confusion. And similarly human personality is
a unity of spiritual desires which rise toward Heaven, and
bodily appetites which cling on earth. No separation can be
made between these aspects of personality, because Heaven
and earth are one, because in the world there is a unity of
things seen and things unseen, and because in religion there
is a unity of this world and that to come, between daily life
and worship.

But beyond all this, there does exist one eternal and unchanging power, which has no beginning and no comprehen-
sible end. To it belongs the government of the world, of
mankind, and of life. It is the power of Allah. The human

individual in his transience seeks to attain to this power which eternally pervades life, and from it he seeks help in his misfortunes. He strives after it when he is in the mosque at prayer, lifting up his heart to Heaven, and he seeks it no less when he is abroad in the world, busily intent upon his livelihood. So he seeks to deserve the future life, not only when he fasts and denies himself all manner of pleasurable indulgence, but also when he breaks his fast and enjoys all the good things of life--so long as he does either of these two things with his heart firmly directed towards Allah. And thus the life of the present world, with all its prayer and its work, all its luxuries and its privations, is the only way to the future world, with its Heaven and its Hell, its punishment and its reward.

This surely is the true unity between the sundry parts of the universe and their powers, between all the diverse abilities of life, between man and his soul, between his experiences and his dreams. Such a unity it is which can set a lasting harmony between the world and human life, between life and living men, between society and the individual, and between man's spiritual desires and his appetites. In a word, it means a harmony between the world and the faith, between earth and Heaven.

This harmony is not established in favor of the physical side of man, nor yet in favor of the spiritual side; rather it imparts to both of them an equal freedom, thus bringing both to a healthy position of well-being and growth. Similarly this harmony is not established in the favor of the individual, or of society; nor in favor of one nation over another, nor in favor of one community over a people. But each of these is held to have its own rights and its own responsibilities. For the individual and society, the people and the community, the nation and all other nations--all are bound by one law which has but one aim: namely, that the freedom of the individual and of society should be equally recognized without any mutual opposition; and that the nations, one and all, should work together for the growth and progress of human life, and for its orientation towards the Creator of life.

Islam, then, is a faith of the unity of all the powers of the world; and beyond doubt it is a uniting faith. It stands for the unity of gods, and for the unity of all religions in the faith of Allah, and also for the unity of all the prophets in their testimony to this one faith since the dawn of time.[26] "Verily this community of yours is one, and I am your Lord; so worship Me."[27] So also Islam stands for the unity of worship and work, of faith and life, of spiritual and material realities, of economic and spiritual values, of the present world and the world to come, of earth and Heaven. From this pervasive unity there issue all the Islamic laws and ordinances, all its exhortations and rules, as well as its teachings on political and economic theory, on the balance of credits and debits, and on privileges and responsibilities. Thus in this fundamental principle of unity there are contained all the various rules of life.

While we are examining this universal theory which takes its rise from the nature of Islamic thought about the world and life and humanity, we may study also the fundamental outlines of social justice in Islam. Above all other things it is a comprehensive human justice, and not merely an economic justice; that is to say, it embraces all sides of life and all aspects of freedom. It is concerned alike with the mind and the body, with the heart and the conscience. The values with which this justice deals are not only economic values, nor are they merely material values in general; rather they are a mixture of moral and spiritual values together. Christianity looks at man only from the stand-point of his spiritual desires and seeks to crush down the human instincts in order to encourage those desires. On the other hand Communism looks at man only from the stand-point of his material needs; it looks not only at human nature, but also at the world and at life from a purely material point of view. But Islam looks at man as forming a unity whose spiritual desires cannot be separated from his bodily appetites, and whose moral needs cannot be divorced from his material needs. It looks at the world and at life with this all-embracing view which permits of no separation or division. In this fact lies the main divergence between Communism, Christianity, and Islam.

Thus, in the Islamic view, life consists of mercy, love, help, and a mutual responsibility between Muslims in particular and between all human beings in general. Whereas in the Communist view, life is a continual strife and struggle between the classes, a struggle which must end in one class overcoming the other; at which point the Communist dream is realized.

Hence it is patent that Islam is the undying goodness of humanity, embodied in a living faith, working in the world; while Communism is the evil of human nature, limited to a single nation.

* * * * * * *

There are , then, these two great facts: the absolute, just, and coherent unity of existence, and the general, mutual responsibility of individuals and societies. On these two facts Islam bases its definition of social justice, having regard to the basic elements of the nature of man, yet not unmindful of human abilities.

The glorious Qur'an says of man that "verily, for the love of gain he is violent"[28]; the "love of gain" belongs to his nature and to his native endowment. It says also, describing that greed which is of the nature and constitution of man, that "souls are close to avarice"[29]; it is always near to them. So also there occurs in the Qur'an a wonderfully skillful description of this human trait; "Say: If it were you who had in your power the treasures of the mercy of my Lord, then you would keep a tight hold for fear of spending; for man is niggardly."[30] But He is certainly liberal with His mercy in every way; and so, from this liberality of Divine mercy and from that human meanness, it is apparent how great is the extent of avarice in the nature of man if he is left without discipline or exhortation.

Accordingly, when Islam comes to lay down its rules and laws, its counsels and controls, that natural "love of gain" is not overlooked, nor is that deep natural avarice forgotten; selfishness is rebuked, avarice is dealt with by regulations and laws, and the duty laid on man is that of liberality. At the same time Islam does not overlook the needs and the welfare of society, nor does it forget the great achievements of individuals in life and society in every age and among different nations.

There may sometimes occur that type of social oppression which is inconsistent with justice, when the greed and cupidity of the individual prey upon society; or that same oppression may also take the form of society preying upon the nature and ability of the individual. Such oppression is a sin, not against one individual alone, but against the whole principle of the community. It is an encroachment upon the freedom of the

individual whose natural rights are infringed; but its evil
effects do not touch merely the welfare and rights of that
one individual; they go beyond him to touch the welfare of
the whole community, because it cannot profit to the full
from his abilities. So the regulations lay down the rights
of the community over the powers and abilities of the individual; they also establish limiting boundaries to the freedom, the desires, and the wants of the individual but they
must also be ever mindful of the rights of the individual, to
give him freedom in his desires and inclinations; and over
all there must be the limits which the community must not
overstep, and which the individual on his side must not
transgress. Nor must there be interference with great individual achievements; for life is a matter of mutual help
and mutual responsibility according to Islam, and not a
constant warfare, to be lived in a spirit of struggle and hostility. Thus there must be freedom for individual and general abilities, rather than repression and a restrictive constraint. Everything that is not legally forbidden is perfectly
permissible; and everything that is not useless is of value.
So the individual is to be encouraged by having every freedom in a life which reflects the Divine nature and which gives
promise of the highest achievement.

    This breadth of vision in the Islamic view of life, together
with the fact that it goes beyond merely economic values to
those other values on which life depends--these things make
the Islamic faith the more powerful to provide equity and justice in society, and to establish justice in the whole of the
human sphere. It also frees Islam from the narrow interpretation of justice as understood by Communism. For justice
to the Communist is an equality of wages, in order to prevent
economic discrimination; but within recent days when theory
has come into opposition with practice, Communism has found
itself unable to achieve this equality. Justice in Islam is a
human equality, envisaging the adjustment of all values, of
which the economic is but one.

    In the Islamic view values are so very composite that jus-
tice must include all of them; therefore Islam does not demand a compulsory economic equality in the narrow literal
sense of the term. This is against nature, and conflicts with
the essential fact, which is that of the differing native endowments of individuals. It arrests the development of outstandin

ability, and makes it equal to lesser ability; it prevents
those who have great gifts from using their gifts to their own
advantage and to that of the community, and it discourages
the community and the individual from producing such gifts.
There can be no profit in disputing the fact that the natural
endowments of individuals are not equal. And while we may
not be able to see this in the case of mental and spiritual
endowments as we can in the sphere of practical life--yet
we cannot deny that some individuals are born with endowments of disposition, such as goodness, or perfection, or
patience; while others are born with endowments of body,
such as sickness, or debility, or weakness. Nor can we
deny that others can earn their living by the pleasantness of
their conversation, by their pleasing appearance, or by their
agreeable nature; thus the gates of undertaking and accomplishment open before them, the same gates which remain
closed in the face of others not similarly endowed.

Accordingly, to deny the existence of outstanding endowments of personality, intellect, and spirit, is a piece of
nonsense which cannot explain the existing differences between
individuals. So we must reckon with all these endowments,
and to all of them we must give the opportunity to produce
their greatest results; then from these results we may take
that which appears to be of permanent profit to society. On
no account must we close off the outlet for such endowments,
or discourage them by making them equal in reward with lesser
abilities; we must avoid shackling such gifts and stifling them,
and thereby depriving of their fruits the community and the
human race alike.

Islam does, of course, acknowledge a fundamental equality
of all men, and a fundamental justice among all, but over and
above that it leaves the door open for achievement of preeminence through hard work, just as it lays in the balance values'
other than the economic. "Verily the noblest among you in
Allah's eyes is the most pious."[31] "Allah will raise up in
degrees of honor those of you who believe, and to whom knowledge has been brought."[32] "Wealth and children are an ornament to life in the world, but the things which endure, the
works of righteousness are better in thy Lord's eyes--better
for reward, and better for hope."[33] From this it is apparent
that there are values other than the merely economic; with these
values Islam reckons, and these it brings into relation with

the idea of justice in society, since different individuals have
different methods of gaining their livelihood. Islam admits
the reasonable causes of these differences, as being difference
in strength and in endowment. It does not admit differences
which depend on rank and station; such it absolutely denies,
as will be seen further in Chapter VI on economic theory.

Islam, then, does not demand a literal equality of wealth,
because the distribution of wealth depends on men's endowments, which are not uniform. Hence absolute justice demands that men's rewards be similarly different, and that
some have more than others--so long as human justice is upheld by the provision of equal opportunity for all. Thus rank
or upbringing, origin or class should not stand in the way of
any individual, nor should any one be fettered by the chains
which shackle enterprise. Justice must be upheld also by
the inclusion of all kinds of values in the reckoning, and by
the freeing of the human mind completely from the tyranny
of the purely economic values, and by the relegation of these
to their true and reasonable place. Economic values must
not be given an intrinsically high standing, such as they enjoy in those human societies which lack a certainty of true
values, or which give to them too slight an importance; in
such conditions money alone becomes the supreme and fundamental value.

In Islam money is not given this value; Islam refuses to
admit that life can be reckoned in terms of a mouthful of
bread, the appetites of the body, or a handful of money. Yet
at the same time it demands a competence for every individual
and at times more than a competence, in order to remove the
fear of destitution. On the other side it forbids that unbridled
luxury in possessions and desires, which produces social
divisions and classes. It prescribes the claims of the poor
upon the wealth of the rich, according to their needs, and
according to the best interests of society, so that social life
may be full, just, and productive. Thus it is not unmindful
of any one of the various aspects of life, material, intellectual
religious and wordly; but it organizes them all, that they may
be related together and thus furnish an all-embracing unity
in which it will be difficult to neglect any one of their various
integral parts. So these departments of life become an organized unity, similar to the great oneness of the universe,
and to that of life, of the nation, and of all mankind.

III. The Foundations of Social Justice in Islam

Islam establishes this social justice, whose nature we
have now analyzed, on solid foundations; for the accomplishment of its aims it lays down certain definite methods. It
does not treat the matter as a question of pure theory, nor
as a counsel of perfection. For by its own nature Islam is
a faith of achievement, of work in the sphere of practical
life; it is not a religion of mere words, or idle theory
existing only in a world of shadows.

As we have already seen, Islam has a basic theory of the
universe, of life, and of man. We have seen also that the
thought of "social justice" has its roots in that basic theory,
and enters into its general scheme. We have discovered that
the nature of Islamic belief about human life makes social
justice essentially an all-embracing justice which does not
take account merely of material and economic factors; for
Islam does not divide the individual into body and soul, into
differing intellectual and spiritual sides. It holds that the
values of this life are material and spiritual at one and the
same time, and that no division is possible in such a unity.
It holds also that mankind is essentially one body, its members mutually responsible and inter-dependent, a body in
which there are no isolated and outcast societies.

Many times it has seemed that the reality of history falsi-
fies this fundamental Islamic theory. So first we must discover what is this reality of history. The reality which Islam
regards as ultimately true is not the state of affairs of any one
individual, or in any one group or nation; rather it is that
limited, definite, and fixed reality on which the faculties of
frail human individuals are set, when they turn away from
the pursuit of eminence and fix their thoughts on the larger
and more comprehensive things in human life, the things
which endure from eternity to eternity. For Islam scans all
standards, and reckons with all kinds of interests; its aim is
the achievement of a purpose which includes all humanity from
beginning to end. So, while there may appear to be an incon-
sistency when we take the comprehensive view, which embraces

29

all men, rather than merely one individual, one group, or one nation.

This comprehensive view of social justice with its far-reaching aims will serve later on to explain the regulations which Islam lays down. These cannot be correctly understood when they are taken individually; nor when they are understood only of the individual in relation to society, or of society only in relation to the group; nor when they are understood only of the group in relation to the nation, or of the nation only in relation to other nations. This comprehensive view will serve to explain the regulations on individual possession; on the poor-tax; on the law of inheritance; on the rules for estates; on politics; on commercial transactions; in a word, it will explain all the regulations prescribed by Islam for individuals, societies, nations, and races.

At this point we have no intention of dealing with all this; we shall, then, content ourselves to deal with the general foundations on which Islam establishes its regulations for social justice, within the limits of its universal theory. And from the nature of these we will see that Islam believes in the unity of body and soul in the individual, and in the unity of the spiritual and the material in life. Similarly it believes in an identity of aim in the individual and in society, in the identity of interests of the various societies within a race, and in an identity of purpose among all the races of mankind. And this despite the apparent divergences of their more immediate and limited interests.

The following are the foundations on which Islam establishes justice:

1. Absolute freedom of conscience.
2. The complete equality of all men.
3. The permanent mutual responsibility of society.

With each of these foundations we shall deal in turn, explaining its nature and its objective.

Freedom of Conscience

Complete social justice cannot be assured, nor can its efficiency and permanence be guaranteed, unless it arises from an inner conviction of the spirit; it must be claimed by the individual, it must be needed by society; there must be a belief that it will serve the highest purposes of mankind. It must arise also from some material circumstances which prompts the individual to demand justice, as being required by the situation, yet unobtainable. No man will claim justice by law unless he has first claimed it by instinct and by the practical methods which accompany instinct. Similarly society will not proceed with such legislation, even when it is started, unless there is a belief which demands it from within, and practical threats which demand it from without. It is these facts which Islam has in mind in all its ordinances and laws.

It is the Christian view that freedom of conscience is one of the luxuries of life; and that to turn towards the Lord's Kingdom of Heaven and to spurn the life of this world is the true way of guaranteeing to man his freedom and to the soul its happiness. Now this is true; but it is not the whole truth. The needs of life are not paramount under all circumstances, nor do material necessities always outweigh man's final destiny; but at most times man must submit to their demands. So to ignore the material needs of life, or to refuse them, is not always the better way. It was Allah who created life, and He did not create it for no purpose; nor did He create it for man to neglect it and to check its growth. Certainly it is desirable that man should rise superior to material needs and above his bodily appetites. But it is not desirable that because of these aims he should neglect life altogether.

That is one way to achieve the realization of the powers latent in human nature together with the elevation of that nature above submission to the demands of material necessity; it is even the soundest and the safest way. But what Islam aims to do is this--to integrate the needs of the body and the desires of the spirit in one unity, and to satisfy by a freedom of conscience the inner instinct which is born of practical reality. So it is not unmindful of either side of the question.

On the other hand, the Communist view is that economic freedom alone satisfies the need for freedom of conscience, and that it is purely economic pressure on the individual which prompts him to overstep his legal rights of justice and equality. This too is true; but it is not the whole truth. For economic freedom of itself has no guarantee of permanence in society, unless there is also freedom of conscience within the mind. For alone it produces only another from of tyranny--the re-

pression of individual gifts and abilities and inclinations; and
these are things which cannot be satisfactorily dealt with by
legal methods alone. It produces also a repression of the
individual, inasmuch as his natural abilities are unable to
find an outlet and have no opportunity of growing in competition with others. Thus inevitably the individual is cheated
in his desire for that equity which the law has promised him,
because he has the inner conviction that he is getting less
than he deserves. And similarly on the other hand, laziness
and pride are encouraged. The man who has the greatest
abilities and who can produce the most will always overcome
the law of absolute equality. Or if he cannot do that, he will
hate and resent it; in which case, either he will rebel, or the
divine spark will be extinguished, his abilities will atrophy,
and his power of production will be lessened.

But where equality has its roots in a profound freedom of
the conscience as well as in civil and religious law, and if
the instinct for it is powerful among the strong and the weak
alike, then it will be accepted as a rise in status for the weak,
and for the strong a fall. It will answer the need of the soul
for a belief in Allah, and in the unity and mutual responsibility
of the community; more, it will inculcate a belief in the unity
of human nature and its attributes. Such is the aim of Islam
when it grants complete and absolute freedom to the human
conscience; but at the same time it stipulates that first the
needs of the body and the material necessities of life must be
guaranteed, alike by the authority of the law and by the
authority of the conscience.

* * * * * * *

Islam began by freeing the human conscience from servitude to any one except Allah and from submission to any
save Him. There is no supreme authority anywhere except
in Allah, nor can any other have power for evil or good. None
save He can supply provision of anything in earth or Heaven,
nor can there be any mediator or intermediary between man
and Him. Allah is the only possessor of power, and all others
are but underlings, without control either over themselves
or over others. "Say: He is Allah the One, Allah the Undivided. He brought not forth, nor was He brought forth;
there has never been any equal to Him."[1]

Since Allah is One, His worship is also one, and to Him
alone must all men turn. There is no object of worship ex-

cept Allah, nor can men take one another as Lords apart from Him. No man among them can excel any other, except by Allah's doing and through His grace. "Say: O people of the Book, come to a word which is fair between us and you; namely that we worship none but Allah, that we associate nothing with Him, and that we do not take one another as Lords apart from Allah."[2]

Islam has an intense interest in this belief, and the Qur'an emphasizes it in various passages. The prophets in their day imagined that their people would turn to them with some sort of worship, or with a reverence of some kind or another; but Islam strove to free the human conscience completely from this belief. So Allah says of His Messenger, Muhammad, "And Muhammad is only a messenger; messengers have passed away before him. So if he dies or if he is killed, will you then turn back upon your heels?"[3] And He addresses the Prophet himself with a great sincerity, saying: "Thou hast nothing to do with this matter; either He may relent towards them, or He may punish them."[4] In the same way He addresses to Muhammad in another place something like a threat: "If We had not made thee stand firm, thou hadst almost leaned towards them a little. In that case We would have made thee taste the double of life and the double of death; then thou couldst not have found a helper against Us."[5] So too He commands him to proclaim openly his true position: "Say: I call only upon my Lord, and with Him I associate nothing. Say: Verily I wield no power over you, either to harm you or to set you right. Say: No one can protect me from Allah, nor can I find a shelter from Him."[6]

And He speaks of those who deify Jesus the son of Mary, charging them with unbelief and folly: "They are unbelievers who say that Allah is the Messiah, the son of Mary. Say: Who, then, will control Allah in the least if He wishes to destroy the Messiah, the son of Mary, together with his mother and all those who are in the earth."[7] Or in another passage He says of the Messiah: "He is only a servant whom We have favored, and whom We have made a parable for the Children of Israel."[8] He takes him as one of the witnesses of the Resurrection, and in the Qur'an Jesus the son of Mary himself answers the assertion which some people make about his divine nature; he establishes his own innocence of this assertion in which he had no part, anwering it in a strong,

foreceful, and impressive manner. "When Allah said: O
Jesus, son of Mary, was it thou who didst say to the people,
'Take me and my mother as gods apart from Allah'? he replied:
Glory be to Thee, it is not for me to say what to me is not
the truth. If I did say it, then Thou knowest it. Thou knowest
what is within me, but I know not what is within Thee. Verily
Thou art He who knoweth secret things. I said nothing to
them save what Thou didst command me: 'Serve Allah, my
Lord and your Lord.' I was a witness to them as long as
I was among them; but when Thou didst take me away, then
Thou Thyself wast a watcher over them. Thou art a witness
over all things. If Thou dost punish them--they are Thy servants; if Thou dost forgive them--Thou art the Glorious, the
Wise."[9]

And other passages are similar. The Qur'an places insistent emphasis on this belief, on its proof and on its clarity,
in order to ensure freedom of the human conscience from
any form of association with Allah as regards His divinity
and His holiness. For such association would oppress the
conscience, and would make it worship some created thing
among the servants of Allah. If Jesus was a prophet or a
messenger, he was still only one of His servants. And if it
is held that he was not a servant in his nature--even one more
distinguished with Allah than others--then all mediation between Allah and His servants is denied; there can be no
priesthood and no mediator. So every individual can make
his own practical relationship with his Creator, and can
strengthen his own weak and frail nature with the Power which
is from eternity to eternity. So he can draw from that power
strength and glory and courage, can know Its mercy and care
and sympathy, can strengthen his faith and empower his
spirit.

Islam insists most strongly upon the reality of this experience, and upon the individual realizing that he has the
ability to call upon that great Power day and night. "Allah
is gentle with His servants."[10] "And when My servants ask
thee about Me, verily I am near to answer the prayer of him
who prays, when he prays to Me. So let them ask an answer
from Me, let them believe in Me, and perhaps they may be
guided aright."[11] "And despair not of the comfort of Allah;
verily none despair of the comfort of Allah except the un-
believing people."[12] "Say: O My servants who have squandere

your own resources, do not despair of the mercy of Allah;
verily Allah forgives all faults."[13]

Islam has prescribed five times of prayer, in which every
day the worshipper stands before his Lord, in which the
creature draws near to his Creator. These are at stated times,
and not merely when it occurs to anyone to stand before his
God, and to draw near in adoration and prayer. The purpose
of these prayers is not only words or movements; rather
their aim is to direct the whole man, heart, mind, and body
at the same time, towards Allah. This is in line with the
general theory of Islam on the unity of human nature in its
creatureliness, and of the unity of the Creator in His divinity.
"So woe to those who pray, and of their prayers are careless."[14]

* * * * * * *

When the conscience is freed from the instinct of servitude to and worship of any of the servants of Allah; when it
is filled with the knowledge that it can of itself gain complete
access to Allah; then it cannot be disturbed by any feeling of
fear of life, or fear of its livelihood, or fear for its station.
This fear is an ignoble instinct which lowers the individual's
estimation of himself, which often makes him accept submission, or abdicate much of his natural honor or many of
his rights. But Islam insists strongly that glory and honor
are the rights of man, and that to be proud of his rights and
to persevere in the search for justice is deep-seated in the
human soul. By reason of all this--over and above its religious laws--it insists on the guarantee of an absolute social
justice , under which man shall not suffer from neglect.
Therefore it is particularly anxious to oppose the instinct of
fear, whether of life or of livelihood, or of station. For life
is in the hand of Allah, and no creature has the power to shorten
that life by one hour or by one minute. More; no creature
has the right to cut off from life one single soul, nor has any
creature the right to inflict the slightest mark or the least
injury on any single living being. "But it is not given to any
soul to die, except by the permission of Allah, a permission
written and dated."[15] "Say: Nothing will come upon us save
what Allah has prescribed for us; He is our Master."[16]
"Each community has its appointed time, and when their time
comes they will not be an hour behind, nor will they go before
their time."[17]

In which case there can be no cowardice and no cowards; for life and destiny, good and evil are in the hand of Allah, and of no other. "Say: Shall I choose as a patron any other than Allah, the Maker of heaven and earth? He it is who giveth food, and who needeth not to be fed."[18] "Allah maketh wide provision for whom He will, or He is sparing."[19] "And how many beasts do not carry their own provision. Allah maketh provision for them and for you."[20] "Say: Who giveth you your provision from heaven and earth? Or who hath power over hearing and sight? Who bringeth forth the living from the dead, and bringeth forth the dead from the living? And who setteth the affair in order? They will say: Allah."[21] "O ye people, remember the favor of Allah towards you. Is there any Creator save Allah, who giveth you from heaven and earth your provision? There is no god save He. How, then, are ye kept from him?"[22] "And do not kill your children because of poverty; We shall provide for you and for them."[23] "And if you fear poverty, Allah will enrich you from His bounty if He wills."[24] The Qur'an lays it down that the fear of poverty is inspired only by the Evil One, in order to weaken and impede the soul in its trust in Allah and in its own nature. "The Evil One promises you only poverty, and bids you to indecency; but Allah promises you pardon from Himself, and bounty; Allah is bountiful, wise."[25]

In that case there is no reason for any man to be oppressed by anxiety about his livelihood, for his provision is in the hand of Allah, and in His hand alone; and not one of His created servants has the power to cut off any man's provision, or to withhold from him any part of that provision. This belief certainly does not rule out trade and commerce, but it does strengthen the human heart and empower the human conscience; it sets the poor man who is anxious over his livelihood on a level with the man who thinks that his provision is in his own hand, to be won with all his own strength and resource. The instinct of fear does not then keep the poor man from seeking what is his due, or from taking pride in himself; it means that he does not have to give up any of his rights or compromise his honor in order to ensure his provision. This is the meaning of the Qur'anic teaching, as it is the objective of Islam; this is the true application of the general Islamic philosophy in hortatory and legal form.

Fear for one's position or station in life often runs back to

the fear of death or injury, or to the fear of poverty or destitution; and Islam is insistent that the individual be freed from
this fear also, for no creature can have any power over another
creature in this matter, "Say: O Allah, wielder of the kingly
power, Thou givest that power to whom Thou willest; and Thou
takest the power from whom Thou willest. Thou dost exalt
whom Thou wilt, and Thou dost abase whom Thou wilt; in Thy
hand is the good. Verily Thou over all things art powerful."[26]
"Say: In whose hand is the rule over all things? Who giveth
protection and seeketh none? If you have any knowledge, you
will say: In the hand of Allah. Say: Then why are you be-
witched?"[27] "If Allah help you, then none can defeat you;
but if He abandon you, then who will help you after Him?"[28]
"Whosoever there be who desires honor, to Allah belongs all
honor."[29] "To Allah belongs all honor, and to His Messenger,
and to the Believers."[30]

So here again there can be no fear, for all power belongs
to Allah alone, and all honor is Allah's, "And He is supreme
above His servants; He is the Wise, the Informed."[31]

* * * * * * *

But sometimes the human spirit is freed from servitude
to priestly things, and from subservience to a fear for its
life or its livelihood or its station, only to fall a prey to social
values. Even though it derives from them neither profit nor
loss, it still may be under the influence of such values as
money, power, rank, or lineage. When the conscience recognizes its practical allegiance to any of these values, its very
observance of them renders it incapable of true freedom, so
that it cannot feel any real equality with its fellows. So here
Islam applies itself to all these values, and puts them in their
proper place; it pays them neither too little attention nor too
much, and thus it restores the true values to their proper
and essential status, the true values which are either latent
in a man's spirit or given expression in his acts. Thus it
minimizes the effect of the material values, and checks their
impact on the human spirit. So it makes this matter also--
so far as Islam can undertake to give practical and legal
guarantees--a means towards the complete freedom of the
conscience.

"Verily the noblest of you in Allah's eyes is the most pious
of you."[32] And the noble man in Allah's eyes is he who is
really and truly noble. "The Arab has no eminence over the

foreigner except his piety."[33] "And they said: We are the greater in wealth and in children, so we shall not be punished. Say: Verily my Lord maketh wide provision for whom He will, or He is sparing. But the majority of people will not understand. Neither your wealth nor your children are things which bring you near to Us; but only he who believes and who acts righteously will be near to Us. For such men there is a double recompense for what they have done, and they shall be safe in upper chambers."[34] So let them have their greatness in wealth and children; this is no value which will bring them any discrimination or any fame, but "only he who believes and acts righteously." For faith is the permanent value apparent in life; these are the two real values which can command respect.

At the same time Islam does not depreciate the value of wealth or of family; "wealth and sons are an ornament for life in this world." An ornament. But it does emphasize that such things are not such as to elevate or lower a man's true status. "The things which endure, the works of righteousness, are better in thy Lord's sight--better for reward, and better for hope."[35]

The Qur'an deals with material values and spiritual values by coining a parable about them in the souls of two men; it lays down no formal preference for one of them over the other, but at the same time it paints a clear and appealing picture of the believing soul, and of the reality of its values.

"Coin for them a parable. There were two men, to one of whom We gave two gardens of vines which We surrounded with palm trees. And between them We set a patch of arable land. Each of the gardens produced its fruit without failing in any way, and between the two of them We caused a stream to flow. So this man had his fruit, and in dispute with his neighbor he said to him: 'I have more wealth than you, and my family is mightier.' So he went into his garden, sinning against his own soul, and saying: 'I do not think that this will ever pass away, nor do I believe that "The Hour" will come. But even if I am taken back to my Lord, I will surely find something better than this in exchange.' But his neighbor said to him in dispute: 'Have you no belief in Him who created you out of dust, then out of semen, and then formed you as a man? Nay, Allah is my Lord, and I will not associate any other with my Lord. Why did you not say when you entered

your garden: "As Allah will; there is no power save in
Allah."[36] if you thought me inferior to yourself in wealth
and children? It may be that my Lord will give me something better than your garden; and that He will send down on
this a thunderbolt from Heaven, so that next morning it will
be only smooth, bare soil. Or the next morning the water
may have sunk so deep in the ground that you cannot find it."
Then his fruit was encompassed, and the next morning he
was turning down the palms of his hands in dismay at what
he had spent on it, for it had fallen down upon the trellisses;
and he was saying: 'Would that I had not associated another
with my Lord.' He had no party to help him except Allah,
and so he was helpless."[37]

In this there is apparent both the pride of the believer in
his faith, and his contempt for those values of which his
neighbor boasted, when he disputed with him. What confuses
the issue is that his neighbor, who is so proud of his garden,
does not appear to associate any other with Allah. But the
Qur'an accounts him as one who does so, and makes him
finally admit such an act of association. That is to say, he
associated with Allah a purely material value, and gave to it
a high mental regard; while by contrast the true believer
would not associate anything with Allah.

So too in the story of Korah the Qur'an portrays two
characters in face of the temptation of wealth and property.
There is a portrait of that character which is made conceited
by such values, the character which is weakened and made
mean, and which is seen to be small in contrast with the
great. And on the other hand there is the portrait of believing souls which are mighty and strong, and which never stoop
to smallness or weakness. "Now Korah was one of the people
of Moses, and had authority over them. We gave him so much
of the treasures that the keys of it weighed down a band, strong
though they were.[38] Then his people said to him: 'Do not exult;
for Allah loveth not those who exult. But rather, through what
Allah has given you, seek the future abode, without forgetting
your part in this world. Do good, as Allah has done good for
you, and do not seek to cause corruption in the earth; for
Allah loveth not those who cause corruption.' He said: 'This
has been given to me solely on account of the knowledge which
I possess.' Did he not, then, know that before his time
Allah had already destroyed generations which were stronger

than him in power, and which had gathered more wealth?
The sinners will not be asked about their crimes.

"So Korah went out among his people in his pomp, and
those who were eager for the life of this world said: "Would
that we had something the same as has been given to Korah.
Indeed he is a very fortunate man.' But those who had been
given knowledge said: "Woe to you. The reward of Allah
is better for him who believes and acts righteously; but
only those attain to it who have had endurance.' Then We
cleft the earth for him and for his house, and he had no party
to help him except Allah, nor was he one of those who could
help themselves. So in the morning those who the previous
day had envied his station were saying: 'Ah. How wide a
provision does Allah make for His servants as He wills, or
how sparing He is. If Allah had not been gracious to us,
He would have cleft the earth for us. Ah, how the unbelievers
fail to prosper."39

Islam is organized around its view of these teachings;
and so Allah forbids His Prophet, Muhammad, to attach any
value to those things in which some men find a deceitful enjoyment. "Do not cast your eyes longingly at those things
which We have given for the enjoyment of some classes of
men, things which are the flower of the life of the world. For
We gave them in order to test these men; the provision of
your Lord is better and more enduring."40 Some authorities
interpret this verse and its implications as meaning merely
that the rich should be left to enjoy their riches, while the
poor should be content with their poverty. But this is a false
exegesis which is inconsistent with the general spirit of
Islam. It is the explanation which is typical of those crafty
churchmen of despotic ages who use it to quiet the public
conscience and to divert it from the quest for social justice.
Such men must bear the responsibility themselves, for Islam
cannot countenance such an exegesis. In point of fact, this
verse and others similar to it refer rather to the rehabilitation
of the true human values, and to the necessity of rescuing
the poor from their state of weakness and helplessness under
the purely material values of wealth and possessions.

Corroboration of this exegesis is to be found in the fact
that Allah commands His Prophet not to attach importance
to these values, and not to encourage the people to respect
them. "Content yourself with those who pray to their Lord

in the morning and in the evening, as they seek His presence. Do not let your eyes wander from them, seeking the adornment of the life of this world. Do not obey anyone whose heart We have made careless of Our remembrance, who follows his own desires, and who lives in excess."[41] "Do not let their wealth astonish you, nor their children; Allah intends only to punish them in the life of this world, intends that they may themselves perish while they are yet unbelievers."[42]

In this connection we must also remember the story of Muhammad with the blind beggar, Ibn-Umm Maktum, and with Al-Walid ibn al-Mughira, the chief of his people. It is a story in which Allah delivers a sharp rebuke to His Prophet. "He frowned and turned away because the blind man came to him. What will teach you whether perhaps he will purify himself?[43] Or whether he might let himself be reminded, and the reminder profit him? The man who is rich--to him you give your attention, caring nothing that he has not purified himself. But the man who comes to you earnestly inquiring and in fear--him you neglect."[44]

A moment of human weakness had assailed Muhammad in his desire that Allah might bring Al-Walid over to Islam, and he was intent upon this matter when Ibn-Umm Maktum came to him, seeking some knowledge of the Qur'an, calling to him again and again while he was still occupied with Al-Walid. The Prophet was annoyed with the beggar, and frowned upon him; but his Lord rebuked him sharply for it in these words which are almost the strongest possible rebuke. Therein He endorses the values for which Islam stands, and points out what must be its true path and its constant endeavor--namely, to free the conscience.

* * * * * * *

So finally the human soul is freed from its bondage to holy things, is freed from its fear of death and injury, of death and humiliation--save for what Allah ordains; it is freed from all regard for outward appearances, and for the values of society; yet after all this it still remains in subjection to its own nature, swayed by its pleasures and its appetites, by its desires and its longings. Thus an inner tyranny replaces the outer which the soul has escaped, and the complete freedom of conscience which Islam desires is not achieved; nor can there be any realization of that supreme human aim, social justice.

Islam is not unaware of this hidden weakness in the freedom of the conscience, and it bestows upon it a profound attention. This is evidenced by its care for the innermost depths of the soul, and again by its preoccupation with all the abilities and endowments of the individual. And here Islam comes to the same point as Christianity, and takes as one of its aims that which Christianity makes its supreme objective. "Say: There are your fathers and your sons, your brothers and your wives; there are your tribes, and the money you have earned, the commerce which you fear may suffer, and the dwellings in which you take pleasure. If these things are dearer to you than Allah and His Messenger, if they are dearer than a holy war in His Cause, then wait in idleness till Allah starts on His work. Verily Allah does not guide people who are impious."[45] Here in one verse are gathered up all the attractions, the longings, and the desires --all the weak points of the human soul; and they are placed on one side of the balance. On the other side are placed the love of Allah and of His Messenger, and the love for holy war in His cause. It is a striking contrast, and it provides a complete escape from strangling desires. The soul which is thus completely freed is the soul which Islam seeks, and which it summons to its true destiny Thus man can rise superior to humiliating necessities, can control the direction of his own course, and can seek after things which are greater and further-reaching than his own little ephemeral pleasures.

Again He says: "The love of desires is made to appeal to men in their wives and their children, in hoarded hoards of gold and silver, in excellent horses, and cattle, and land; these things are the treasures of the life of this world. But with Allah is the best place of resort. Say: Shall I tell you of a better thing than these? For those who are pious there are Gardens in the presence of their Lord, through which rivers flow; and long shall they dwell there. There are pure wives for them, and there is favor from Allah; Allah is observant of His servants."[46] This is not an attempt to drug the mind, nor yet is it a summons to austerity or to a neglect of the good things of life, although in this way some have seen fit to interpret the Qur'an, and in this way others have

understood Islam. This is simply a summons to freedom,
and to an independence of the weakness of desires and passions. Accordingly there can be no harm in the enjoyment
of the good things of life, so long as a man can control them,
rather than they him. "Say: Who has forbidden the adornments of life which Allah has made for His servants; or who
has forbidden the good things of His provision?"[47] "And do
not forget your part in this world."[48]

To this same line of thought belongs the ordinance of fasting; for its purpose is to raise the soul for a space of time
above the necessities of all-powerful human nature. By fasting the will is strengthened and elevated, making man superior
to his nature, because he has risen above his necessities.

To this end the Qur'an recommends various methods,
among them being the inspired warning about the temptation
of wealth and children, which occurs in the phrase, "Your
wealth and your children are only a temptation."[49] In this
there is a stern warning which is sorely needed by human
weakness in the face of wealth and children. This is particularly shown in the covetousness which assails a man
where his possessions or his family are concerned; he accepts what he would not otherwise accept, submits to what
he would otherwise not submit to, and commits sins that he
would not otherwise commit. So that "a child is an induce-
ment to avarice, a cause of cowardice," as said the Messenger of Allah.

* * * * * * *

Yet even after this, when a man is freed from all the things
which would deprive him of his full spiritual status, he may
still be in need. He is in need of food, and so he is humiliated;
for there is no need which is more humiliating. The empty
belly cannot appreciate high-sounding phrases. Or else he
is compelled to ask for charity, and all his self-esteem leaves
him, lost forever. This is met in Islam by the religious law
which aims at preventing the causes of such need, and at
putting an end to them where they can be found. Accordingly
it makes the claim of the individual to a competence a responsibility of the state, and of the rich members of the community;
it is a responsibility whose neglect will be punished in the
world to come, as it is punishable by death in the present
world. A full discussion of this will follow when we come to

treat of economic theory in Islam. For this reason Islam
forbids begging, and envisages a community of Muslims who
have suffered loss by fighting in the cause of Allah, and who
cannot travel the earth for wealth; it describes their nobility
on the grounds that "they do not beg importunately from the
people."[50] So too the Prophet gives a coin to a beggar, and
then says: "Verily it is better that one of you should get a
rope and collect a bundle of firewood on his back and sell it,
even if Allah does not give prosperity; better this than that
you should beg from the people that they may give to you or
refuse you." Or again he says: "A generous hand is better
than a stingy hand." And he exhorts men to avoid all shameful means of getting money other than begging; for begging
is regarded by Islam as a necessary evil. As for the proceeds of the poor-tax,[51] this is the law: It is to be taken as
a right, and is not to be given as a charity. "And of their
wealth there was a settled share for the beggar and the outcast."[52] This share is taken by the state, and is spent on
the welfare of Muslims, to supply their bodily needs, to preserve their self-esteem, and to retain to them their power of
conscience. It this is not sufficient, provision is made to
take sufficient from wages and salaries from the wealth of men
of means and the richer classes to meet the needs of the poor
and the humble.

* * * * * * *

Thus Islam approaches the question of freedom from every
angle and from all points of view; it undertakes a complete
emancipation of the conscience. It does not deal only with
spiritual values, or only with economic values, but with both
together. It recognizes the practical reality of life, and
equally the spiritual power of the soul; it attempts to awaken
in human nature the highest desires, and to evoke the loftiest
abilities, thus bringing that nature to complete freedom of
conscience. Without such complete freedom human nature
cannot prevail against the force of humiliation and submis-
siveness and servility, nor can it lay claim to its rightful
share in social justice; nor can it sustain the responsibilities
of such a justice when it has attained to it.

This freedom is therefore one of the corner-stones for the
building of social justice in Islam. More: it is the principal
corner-stone on which all the others must rest.

Human Equality

Suppose, then, that the human mind has come to know all this freedom of conscience; it is free from the least shadow of servility, be it to death or injury, to poverty or weakness, unless what comes by Allah's permission. It is released from the tyranny of the values of social standing and wealth; it is saved from the humiliation of need and beggary, and it can rise superior to its desires and its bodily appetites. It can turn towards its One Sole Creator, to whom all things must turn without exception and without fail; and so it can find a complete independence of the material necessities of life.

When the human conscience has come to know all this, it will have no need of anyone to preach equality to it in words, for it will already have experienced the full meaning of equality. More: it will not endure the distinctions which arise from worldly values at all. It will seek equality as its right, and will strive to ensure that right; it will guard it carefully when it is gained, and it will accept no substitute for it. It will bear the responsibility of guarding and defending its equality, cost what it may in effort and labor.

When the establishment of equality is rooted in the conscience, when it is safeguarded by religious law, and when it is guaranteed by its own adequacy, the poor and the humble will not be the only persons to desire it. Even the rich and the powerful will support it, because their conscience acknowledges those values which Islam is intent on establishing and confirming, as we have already outlined them. This is what actually happened in Islamic society fourteen centuries ago, as will be shown in the course of this book.

But despite this, Islam is not content with the acknowledged, assured, and profitable results of freedom of conscience; rather it emphasizes the principle of equality in word and precept, so that everything may be clear and firm and definite. There was an age when some men asserted their claim to be of the progeny of the gods, while others asserted that the blood which flowed in their veins was not of the nature of common blood, but was blue blood, royal or noble blood. It was an age when there were faiths and religions which divided the nations into classes; some were created by the head of a god, and hence they were holy, while others, having been created by the feet of a god, were despised. A dispute centered around woman; had woman a soul, or had she not? It

was an age in which a master was permitted to kill his slave,
or to punish him in any way, because slaves belonged to a
different class of humanity from that of their masters. In
this age Islam was born; it taught the unity of the human
race in origin and in history, in life and in death, in privileges and in responsibilities, before the law and before Allah,
in this world and in the world to come; it proclaimed that
there was no virtue except in good deeds, and no nobility except in piety. That formed a revolution in human thinking,
and it has continued to this day; it was an achievement to
which humanity had not till then aspired. That is to say,
what was theoretically established by human laws during and
after the French Revolution was established as a matter of
practice by Islam more than fourteen centuries previously.

No god can possibly have progeny: "Say: He is Allah the
One, Allah the Undivided. He brought not forth, nor was He
brought forth; there has never been any equal to Him."[53]
"And they said, 'The Merciful has taken a son.' You have
committed a terrible thing, at which the very heavens almost
are torn apart, and the earth cleft asunder, and the mountains
fallen down in pieces. For they attribute a son to the Merciful, but the Merciful has no need to take a son. There is
nothing in heaven or in earth which does not approach the
Merciful as a servant; He has counted them and given to them
an exact number, and all of them must come before Him
singly on the Day of Resurrection."[54]

Or again, there can be no such thing as blue blood or noble
blood; and as for one being created by the head and another
by the foot of a god--"Did We not create you out of mere
water which We stored in a secure place until a decreed time?
We set the time, and good was Our setting."[55] "So let man
consider: from what was he created? He was created from
dripping water, from water issuing from between the loins
and the ribs."[56] "It was Allah who created you from dust,
then from a seed, and who then set you in pairs. No female
conceives or gives birth without His knowing it; none is given
long life and none is given short life, unless it be in a Book.
Verily that is easy for Allah."[57] "We have created man out
of an extract of clay; when We made him a seed lodged in a
secure place; We made the seed a clot of blood, and We create
the clot a morsel. We created the morsel bones, and We
clothed the bones with flesh. We made him grow as a new
creation; blessed be Allah, the best of creators."[58]

The Qur'an goes on to repeat this teaching in many passages, to impress on the mind of man the oneness of his
origin and his growth. The human race as a whole is made
from dust, and the individual--every individual--from mere
water. And the Prophet repeats this truth in the Traditions:
"Each of you is man; and man is of dust." Thus he increases
man's reliance on his senses and his intelligence.

When it is thus denied that one individual can be intrinsically superior to another, it follows that there can be no
race and no class which is superior by reason of its origin
or its nature. Yet there are some races which to the present
day insist that there does exist such a superiority. There
cannot be: "O ye people, reverence your Lord who created
you from one soul, creating from it its mate; and He spread
abroad from these two many men and women."[59] There was
originally only one soul; from it came its mate; and from the
two of them there spread abroad both men and women. So
all are of one origin, all are brothers in descent, all are
equal in origin and nature. "O ye people, We created you
male and female, and We made you races and tribes, that
you might know one another. Verily the noblest among you
is the most pious."[60] These races and tribes were not made
for the purpose of rivalry or enmity, but for that of mutual
knowledge and friendliness; all of them in the eyes of Allah
are equal, and there can be no superiority except in piety.
But this is another question, unconnected with origin and
nature; in these respects, "People are all equal as the teeth
of a comb," as says the noble Prophet of Islam.

This equality extends its compass over all mankind, and
transcends both patriotism and religion; for, since the Messenger said, "All Muslims are of one blood," Islam grants
to men of other faiths rights of blood equivalent to those enjoyed by Believers--so long as there is a compact between
them and the Muslims. "Whoever kills a Believer by mistake, the penalty is to set free one Believing slave, and to
deliver the blood-money to the dead man's family--unless
they give it as alms. If the killer is of a people who are at
enmity with you, but is himself a Believer, then he must set
free a Believing slave. If he is of a people with whom you have
a compact, then he must deliver the blood-money, and set
free a Believing slave."[61] Thus, the atonement to be made
by a non-Muslim killer whose people have a compact with the

Muslims is exactly the same as that to be made by a Muslim killer. The same tendency to equality is shown by the fact that Islam fixes the atonement for an accidental killing as the liberation of a slave; this indicates that it regards freeing a slave as a means of giving life to a soul. Thus this new life is given in exchange for the life which has been taken by the accidental killing; for in the eyes of Islam slavery is akin to death, while freedom is akin to life.

As for deliberate murder, in vengeance or in hatred, the principle is "A life for a life"; and there is no difference between a prince and a pauper, a seigneur and a slave. The Messenger said: "Him who killed his slave We have killed; him who mutilated his slave We have mutilated; him who gelded his slave We have gelded."

Thus Islam was freed from the conflict of tribal and racial and religious loyalties, and thus it achieved an equality which civilization in the West has not gained to this day. It is a civilization which permits the American conscience to acquiesce in the disappearance of the Red Indian race, a disappearance which is being organized in the sight and hearing of the government. It permits also Field-Marshal Smuts in South Africa to introduce racial laws which discriminate against Indians.

Islam follows up any suspicion of discrimination between men, or of superiority of one over another; no matter what its form or guise, no matter what its cause, Islam condemns it. Even in the case of the Prophet Muhammad, the Qur'an constantly reminds his people that he is human like the remainder of mankind; and Muhammad himself reiterates the same fact; he was a prophet, loved and respected by his people, yet always afraid that that love and respect might be led to make him preëminent or superior to others. So here he is, telling his people: "Do not venerate me, as the Christians venerate Jesus son of Mary; I am only a servant of Allah, and His Messenger." Or again, when he comes into a meeting in which all present rise to their feet out of respect for him, he says: "Whoever wishes that men may stand to greet him, let him take his seat in Hell-fire." And when Muhammad's family thought that as a Messenger he would raise their status or their rank, and would confer on them a form of aristocracy above the ordinary, Muhammad refused them everything of that kind, save the nobility of good works;

and he said to them plainly: "If my people cannot approach me through their good works, shall you, then, approach me through your genealogies? Verily the noblest of you in the sight of Allah is the most pious." So if Muhammad's family enjoyed no superiority except that of good works to raise them above the level of the people, no one ever can enjoy such a superiority. And again, when Muhammad was accosted by the blind man, when he turned away from the poor man, Ibn Umm Maktum, to pay attention to Al-Walid ibn al-Mughira, who was the chief of his people, there came swiftly upon him a stern reproof which was almost a condemnation; thus he was brought back to recognize the absolute equality and complete parity of all men. Or when some of the rich nobles looked with contempt on marriage for themselves or for their families with poor men or women, there came the command of Allah: "Settle the unwed among you in marriage, and those who are upright among your male and female slaves. If they are poor, Allah will enrich them of His bounty; Allah is generous and wise."[62]

* * * * * * *

As for the relation between the sexes, Islam has guaranteed to women a complete equality with men with regard to their sex; it has permitted no discrimination except in some incidental matters connected with physical nature, with customary procedure, or with responsibility, in all of which the privileges of the two sexes are not in question. Wherever the physical endowments, the customs, and the responsibilities are identical, the sexes are equal; and wherever there is some difference in these respects, the discrimination follows that difference.

In the spiritual and religious sphere men and women are equal. "Whoever does good works, man or woman, and is a Believer--such shall enter into Paradise and shall not be wronged one jot."[63] "Whoever does good works, man or woman, and is a Believer--We shall make them live a good life, and We shall give them their reward for the best that they have done."[64] "Then their Lord answered them: I shall not waste the work of any one of you who works, male or female; you belong to one another."[65]

Or again in the sphere of possessing and administering money they are equal. "Men shall have a portion of what

their parents and their near relatives leave; and women
shall have a portion of what their parents and their near
relatives leave."[66] "Men shall have a portion of what they
have gained; and women shall have a portion of what they
have gained."[67]

In the case of the law about a man getting double the share
of a woman in an inheritance, the reason is to be found in
the responsibility which a man carries in life. He marries
a woman, and he undertakes to maintain her and their children; he has to bear the responsibility of the whole structure
of the family. So it is no more than his right that for this
reason, if for no other, he should have the share of two
women. The woman, on the other hand, if she is married,
has the responsibility of providing for herself from what
her husband gives her; if she remains unmarried or if she
is widowed, she must provide for herself out of what she inherits. So the question here is one of difference in responsbility, which involves a similar difference in the law of inheritance.

Or there is the case of men being overseers over women.
"Men are overseers over women because of what Allah has
bestowed of His bounty on one more than another, and because
of what they have contributed in the way of wealth."[68] The
reason for this discrimination lies in physical endowment,
and in use and wont in the matter of oversight. Because a
man is free from the cares of the family, he can attend to
the affairs of society over considerable periods, and can apply to these affairs all his intellectual powers. On the other
hand a woman is restricted for most of her life to these family
cares. The result is that these responsibilities promote in
women a growth in the direction of the emotions and the passions, while in men growth is promoted in the direction of
reflection and thought. So when man is made to oversee
woman, it is by reason of physical nature and custom that
this ordinance stands. Besides which, the man has the financial responsibility, and the economic sphere is closely linked
with that of oversight, which is essentially the acceptance of
responsibility. Ultimately the fundamental point here is one
of the balance of privileges and responsibilities in the sphere
of the sexes, and in that of life as a whole. "The same is due
to women as is due from them; but men have a precedence
over them."[69] This "precedence" is the oversight, the reaso
for which we have demonstrated.

Again there appears to be an instance of discrimination in the question of the giving of evidence. "Call two of your men as witnesses; or if there are not two men, then call one man and two women from those on whom you agree among the people who are present. So if one of the women goes astray, the other may remind her."[70] In this verse itself the explanation is made clear; by the nature of her family duties the growth of the woman's spirit is towards emotions and passions, just as in man it is towards contemplation and thought, as we have already said. So when she is forgetful, or when she is carried away by her feelings, the other will be there to remind her. Thus the question in this case is one of the practical considerations of life rather than one of the inherent superiority of one sex to the other, or of a lack of equality.

But the strongest point in Islam is the equality which it guarantees to women in religion, as well as in their possessions and their gains. Also it gives them the assurance of marriage only with their own consent and at their own pleasure; they need not marry either through compulsion or through negligence; and they must get a dowry. "And give them their stipulated price."[71] They must also have the remainder of their married rights, whether they be married or divorced: "Retain them honorably, or send them away honorably. Do not retain them by compulsion in order to transgress."[72] "Associate honorably with them."[73]

We must notice that Islam guarantees these rights to women, and gives them full enjoyment of these privileges, in a sincerely humane spirit which is not influenced by the pressure of economic or material interests. Islam opposed the idea that a girl child was a disaster, and that she was better put away while she was still an infant; it was implacably opposed to the custom of burying daughters alive, which was current in the life of some of the Arabian tribes. It fought this custom in the sincerely humane spirit in which it looks at mankind, and it stringently prohibited such murder altogether and without exception. "Do not kill the person whom Allah has forbidden, except with justification."[74] It specifically forbids the killing of children, though the only children who were killed were the girls: "Do not kill your children out of fear of poverty; We will provide for them and for you."[75] In this verse providing for the children is mentioned first because they are the cause of the fear of poverty; thus it fills the heart of the father with trust in the provision of Allah, and in His care for the children even more than for the father. Then as the instincts of justice and mercy gain force He says concerning the Day of Resurrection "And when the girl child buried alive shall be asked for what fault she was killed."[76] So He poses in this passage a clear and decisive question for that terrible Day.

Thus Islam, in granting to women their full spiritual and material privileges, had regard to their human nature, and was acting in conformity with its own belief in the unity of mankind. "He created you from one soul, and He created from it its mate to dwell with it."[77] Islam's aim was to raise women in status to the point where they would be of necessity the half of the one single "soul." For this reason it grants to women, besides the right of spiritual faith and that of material independence, the right of intellectual achievement; more--it makes it obligatory for them. "The search for knowledge is incumbent upon all Muslims, men and women."[78] Similarly it grants to women the right to pay the poor-tax; more--it lays it down as their duty; for payment of the tax is obligatory for them as it is for men. In the giving of alms also they have the same part as men; "Verily men and women who give alms, and who have lent to Allah a fair loan--they will be recompensed double."[79]

We must also remember this about Islam--and in its favor--that the freedom which the material West grants to women does not flow from this noble and humane source; nor are its objectives the innocent objectives of Islam. It is well not to forget history, and not to be led astray by the misleading appearances of this present age. It is well to remember that the West brought women out of the home to work, only because their menfolk shrank from the responsibility of keeping them and caring for them; and that too, although the price was the chastity and honor of woman. Thus and only thus were women compelled to work.

It is to be remembered also that when women did emerge to work, the material West seized upon the opportunity offered by this event, and paid them lower wages; thus employers wer able to dispense with men in favor of women, who were cheape to pay, because the men were beginning to raise their heads and demand their true value. So when women in the West cam

to demand equality with men, it was first and most essentially
an equality of wages that they wanted, so that they might be
able to eat and to support life. When they could not gain this
form of equality they demanded the right of the franchise, so
that they might have a voice to speak for them. And finally
they demanded access to Parliament, so that they might have
the necessary representation when their equality was being
established.

It is well to bear in mind also that to this day France does
not grant to women the right of administering their property--
a right which Islam does allow--except by the consent of a
guardian. Yet at the same time France grants to women the
right of every kind of unchastity, public or private. This
"privilege" is the only one which Islam denies to its women-
folk, just as it also denies it to men; thus it guards the honor
and the instincts of man, and thus it makes the relationship
between the sexes a mutual affair, in the belief that there is
a physical bond over and above the ties of home and family.

And while today we watch the material West preferring
women to men in some professions, particularly in commerce,
in embassies, in consulates, and in information services such
as newspapers and the like, we must not forget the regrettable
and unsavory significance of this advancement. It is a form
of slavery and servitude in an atmosphere of the smoke of
incense and opium. It is the employment of the sex instinct
by the tycoons and potentates of the merchant world; and
similarly the government sends women into embassies and
consulates, and newspaper editors send women to glean
news and information. All of them are merely attempting
to make use of women; and they know what success a woman
can have in these fields. They know, too, what she must give
to achieve her success. And even if she gives nothing--which
is an absurd supposition--they know what hungrypassions and
eager eyes are on the watch about her body and about her
reputation. But they take advantage of women's hunger for
material gain, and for some slight success; for humane and
noble feelings are far, far from them.

As for Communism, it has a wide claim to uphold the
equality of women with men; its equality is that of work and
that of pay. But when there is equality of work and pay,
women become free, and they gain also the right of license,
just the same as men. Because in Communism generally the

question does not go beyond the sphere of money; whereas
in reality all the desires of man and all the instincts of human
nature are involved in this one aspect of life. The essential
fact is that men refused to support women, and that hence
women were compelled to work like men and in masculine
circles, in order to live. Thus it is that Communism is the
natural and logical outcome of the spirit of the material West
--at least in this respect; for the spirit of the West lacks
the generous and humane aspects of true human life.

All these things must be borne in mind before the false
flame blinds our eyes; Islam has for fourteen centuries
granted to women privileges which France does not yet grant
them. It has always granted them the right to work and the
right to earn which Communism now grants them. But it
retains for them the primary duty of upholding the family
circle; and that for several reasons. In the Islamic view
life is more than merely economic or physical, and in itself
can offer higher objectives than food and drink. Again Islam
looks at life from many sides, and envisages for individuals
duties which differ one from the other, but which are all
mutually connected and ordered; within this scheme is envisaged the respective duties of men and women, and it lays
on each of them the charge of fulfilling a duty primarily
towards the growth and the advancement of life as a whole;
and it ordains for each of them his guaranteed privileges, in
order to ensure this universal and humane aim.

* * * * * * *

And finally the whole human race has a nobility which
cannot allowably be lessened. "And We have ennobled the
sons of Adam; We have carried them by land and sea, and
have given them their provision of good things. We have
given them preference over much of that which We have
created."[80] We have ennobled them, that is, by their nature,
and not by their persons or their races or their tribes. And
that nobility attaches to all men, producing absolute equality,
for all alike are Man. It was Man who came of dust; it was
Man who was ennobled; therefore all the sons of Man are
equal in every respect.

Thus all alike have a nobility which must not be degraded,
and at which none may scoff. "O ye who have believed, let
not one people mock another, who are possibly better than

themselves. And let not women mock other women, who are
possibly better than themselves. Do not scoff at one another,
or shame one another with nicknames; it is bad to get the
name of evil conduct when you are a Believer; and those who
do not repent are evil-doers."[81] The complete and far-reaching point of the verse is: "Do not scoff at one another." For
when a man scoffs at his neighbor he scoffs at himself, for
all men come of one soul.

So there are some things which are prohibited for all men.
"O ye who have believed, do not go into houses other than your
own, until you are received as friends and have greeted the
inmates. That is better for you; perhaps you will remember.
If you find no one at home, do not go in until you receive permission; and if you are told to go away, then go away; that
is more innocent for you, and Allah knows what you do."[82]
"Do not spy into one another's affairs, and do not indulge in
backbiting against one another."[83] The value of these regulations is to make every individual aware that he has a certain sanctity which must not be violated by others; the sanctity
of one man is no less than that of another. In this respect
also they are equal, and all are trusted.

* * * * * * *

Thus Islam deals with every aspect of human life, spiritual
and social alike, in order firmly to establish the concept of
equality. There was in fact no need for it so to do; for it
treats of equality verbally and legally only after it has established in fact and in spirit, through the complete freedom of
the conscience from all artificial values, from all outward
appearances, and from all material necessities. It has an
intense passion for equality; it demands that it be universal
and complete, not limited to one race or one nation, to one
house or one city. Similarly it demands that equality embrace a wider sphere than merely the economic, to which the
teachings of the material West have confined it.

Mutual Responsibility in Society

No form of life can be satisfactory in which every individual
is bent on the enjoyment of his absolute freedom, without
bounds or limits. Such freedom he might be led to expect by
his belief in the absolute equality which exists between himself
and all other individuals, in respect of all his privileges; but
such an expectation is responsible for the destruction not only

of society, but also of the individual himself. For there is
the important matter of the welfare of society, short of which
the freedom of the individual must stop; there is also the
private welfare of the individual himself, which entails his
giving up his freedom at certain specific limits. Thus on the
one hand he may not allow himself to be carried to extemes
by his passions and appetites and pleasures; and on the other
hand his freedom may not conflict with that of others. For
when this latter takes place it produces unending disputes,
and makes liberty an unendurable burden; through it the
growth and improvement of community life are checked by
the claims of individual welfare, which is a much narrower
interest.

Islam grants individual freedom in the most perfect form,
and human equality in the most exacting sense, but it does
not leave these two things uncontrolled; society has its interests, human nature has its claims, but a value attaches
also to the lofty aims of religion. So Islam sets the principle of individual responsibility over against that of individual
freedom; and beside them both it sets the principle of social
responsibility, which makes demands alike on the individual
and on society. This is what we call mutual responsibility in
society.

Islam lays down the principle of mutual responsibility in
all its various shapes and forms. In it we find the responsibilities which exist between a man and his soul, between
a man and his immediate family, between the individual and
society, between one community and other communities, and
between one nation and the various other nations.

We have the responsibilities which a man has to himself.
He must restrain himself from being carried away by his
appetites, and he must cleanse and purify these appetites;
he must make them follow the path of righteousness and salvation, and must not let them go down in degradation. "As
for him who has been presumptuous and has sought the life
of the world, verily Hell will be his place. But as for him
who has feared the greatness of his Lord and has restrained
himself from desire, verily Paradise will be his place."[84]
"By a soul and what formed it, implanted in it its wickedness
and its piety, he who purifies it prospers, while he who corrupts it fails."[85] "Do not hand yourselves over to destruction.
But at the same time man is charged to enjoy himself within

those boundaries which will not admit the corruption of his nature; he must give himself his due, both of work and of rest, and he may not exhaust or weaken himself. "Through what Allah has given you seek the future abode, without forgetting your part in this world."[87] "O ye sons of Adam, take your adornment in every mosque; eat and drink, but be not immoderate; verily He does not love those who are immoderate."[88] "Verily you have a duty to your body."[89]

Thus individual responsibility is complete; every man has his own works, every man is responsible for what he does to his soul, good or evil, benefit or harm; and in his place no other can ever stand, either in this world or in the next. "Each soul is held in pledge by what it has gained."[90] "Or has he not been told of what is in the pages of Moses, and of Abraham, who fulfilled his task? That no burden-bearer can bear the burden of another; that man gets no more that he has striven for; that the result of his striving will be seen; and that then he will be fully recompensed."[91] "What it (i.e., the soul) has gained stands to its credit, and what it has piled up stands against it."[92] "Whoever is rightly guided, that is of profit to himself; and whoever goes astray, he does so to his own loss; you are not in charge of them."[93] "And he who acquires guilt acquires it only against himself."[94]

According to all this man is ever a watcher over his own soul, to guide it if it goes astray, and to ensure for it its legal rights, to call it to account if it sins, and to bear the responsibility of neglecting it. In all this Islam postulates two personalities in each individual, keeping watch on one another and observing one another, responsible, the one to the other, for the good or the evil which they share. This fact lies over against the other fact that Islam gives complete freedom of conscience to this individual, and complete equality with others; but freedom and responsibility are mutually compatible and mutually necessary.

We have also a mutual responsibility between the individual and his immediate family. "And use kindness with parents; whether one or both of them attain to old age with you, do not say to them, 'Bah.' do not rebuke them, but speak them fair. Lower the wing of humility to them in mercy, and say: 'O my Lord, have mercy upon them, as they brought me up when I was little.'"[95] "And We have laid a charge on man concerning his parents; his mother bore him in weakness upon weakness, and he was weaned in two years. Show gratitude to Me and to your parents."[96] "But blood relations are nearer to each other in the Book of Allah."[97] "Mothers shall suckle their children two full years, where it is desired that the period of suckling be complete; and the man to whom the child was born must feed and clothe them both suitably."[98]

The value of this responsibility within the family circle is that it is the basis on which the family stands; and the family is the basic unit on which society is built; hence there must be a regard for its value. It rests on the permanent characteristics of human nature, on the emotions of pity and love, and on the necessity of material needs and welfare. Thus it is the nest in which and around which are produced all the morals and the manners which are peculiar to the human race; these are essentially the morals of society, which is raised by them above the license of the animals, and above the anarchy of a rabble.

Communism has sought to condemn the family, on the plea that it fosters ideas which are essentially selfish and produces the love of private possession; whereas Communism itself forbids wealth, being the control of private individuals by the state. But so far as may be seen, Communism has failed completely in this matter; for the Russian people is a domestically inclined people, in whose life and in whose history the family has a large place. Further, the family is a biological and a spiritual institution, as well as a social institution; and the idea that a woman should belong exclusively to one man is biologically sound, and is conducive to the reproduction of healthy children. It has been noted that a woman who is shared by a number of men soon becomes barren or produces unhealthy children. From the personal point of view the feelings of love and compassion grow better in the atmosphere of the family than under any other form of institution; and the growth of personality is more complete in the family circle than under any other form of institution. Tests carried out during the last war among children in nurseries proved that the child whose upbringing is in the hands of a succession of nurses lacks personality, and has no self-control; nor has he the normal growth of the feelings of love and affection. So, too, the child who has no father has to struggle against a feeling of inferiority; from this hard reality he escapes by inventing a father who does not exist, a father

to whom he can go in imagination, and whom he invents in
various shapes and forms. [99]

But biological and personal factors are not the only ones;
we have here also the questions of material needs and welfare which bind a man and a woman together to set up a home
and to rear children. There are also the ties which unite the
individuals of one family and make them a social unit; this
unit relies upon its own members in good or in ill, and its
members are mutually responsible in work and in reward,
for one generation after another.

Another of the aspects of family responsibility in Islam
is the law of material inheritance of property which is analyzed in the following two verses: "With regard to your
children Allah commands you thus: The males shall have the
portion of two females; if the children are all female, and
more than two in number, then they shall have two thirds of
what their father has left; if there is only one, then she shall
have a half. Each of a man's parents shall have one sixth of what
he has left, if he had any children; but if he had no children
and his parents are his heirs, then his mother shall have a
third. If he had brothers, then his mother shall have a sixth
--after any bequests have been made and any debts paid.
Whether your fathers or your sons bring you more advantage
you do not know. This is an ordinance from Allah; verily
Allah is understanding, wise. You shall have half of what
your wives leave, if they had no children; but if they had
children, then a quarter of what they left shall be yours, after any bequests have been made and any debts paid. Your
wives shall have a quarter of what you leave, if you have no
children; if you have children, your wives shall have an eighth
of what you leave, after any bequests have been made and any
debts paid." [100] "They ask you for a decision; say: Allah
gives you a decision about distant relations. If a man dies,
leaving no children, and if he has a sister, then she shall
have half of what he leaves; and he shall be her heir if she
has no children. If there are two sisters, then they shall
have two thirds of what he leaves. If there is a family, both
male and female, then the male shall have the portion of two
females. Allah makes it clear for you, lest you fall into
error; Allah has knowledge of all things." [101] Concerning
the bequest which is the subject of the first passage, He has
explained it by saying: "A command is prescribed for you

when one of you is near to death and has property to leave;
he must make a declaration, leaving a suitable amount to his
parents and his near kin. This is a duty upon all who are
pious."[102] This bequest cannot exceed one third of the estate
after the payment of debts, and it does not apply to the principal heir; "there can be no bequest for the heir."[103] This
legislation is aimed only at obviating conditions under which
the proper person may not inherit the kinship gift which the
testator wished to give and bequeath to him. It is aimed also
at making available from the legacy some money for spending
for good and proper purposes. Thus this ordinance enacted
by Islam is one of the aspects of the mutual responsibility
which connects the individual members of the same family.
It is also one of the means of distributing property, so that
it may not become too great and prove injurious to society.
A discussion of this will follow in the chapter on economic
theory. As far as we are concerned here, we need only say
that the Islamic law of inheritance is an equitable balance between effort and reward, between credits and debits, within
the family circle. The parent who works knows that the fruit
of his labors will not be realized in the short and limited
span of his own life, but will stretch forward to be enjoyed
by his sons and his grandsons, who are his natural successors in life. Such a parent mustgive of his very best, and
must produce as much as he can; by which the welfare of the
state and of the human race as a whole is served. And besides, there is here an equal balance between the effort which
he puts forth and the reward which he receives. For as his
sons are a part of himself, he knows that in them his life is
perpetuated.

On the children's side it is but right that they should profit
from the efforts of their fathers and their mothers; for the
connection between parents and children would not be broken
even if the connection in property inheritance were broken.
Parents bequeath to their children traits and endowments in
their physical and mental composition; and these qualities remain with them all their lives, and to a great extent deter-
mine the course of their future, either for good or for evil.
And children have no power either to refuse or to nullify this
legacy. Sometimes the state or society steps in and refuses
a fair chance to a child to whom his parents have bequeathed
an evil legacy; he cannot be given physical health or strength

of constitution, because his parents may have given him only weakness and trouble; he cannot be given long life or ample health, because his parents have bequeathed to him only a tendency to swift decay or chronic illness. Therefore, if he must of necessity inherit all this evil, then it is only his right in society to inherit also the material possessions of his parents; thus there may be some fair balance between credits and debits in his case.

The Qur'an coins a parable of the mutual responsibility of fathers and children, when it tells the story of Moses and "one of Our servants upon whom We had bestowed mercy from Us, and whom We had taught knowledge from Us.... And the two of them set out and travelled until they came to the people of a town. From these people they asked food, but they refused to entertain them. In the town they found a wall which was ready to fall down, and Moses' companion set it up." Moses said to him, "If you had wished, you could have claimed a wage for that." But the people of the town still would not give them food.... Then his companion explained to Moses his secret reason for setting up the wall, saying, "As for the wall, it belonged to two orphan youths in the town, and under it was a treasure belonging to them. Their father was a worthy man, and your Lord wished that they might reach full age before finding out their treasure as a mercy from your Lord."[104] Thus the two sons profited from the virtue of their father, and inherited what he left to them, both in the way of property and in the way of virtue. That this is just there can be no doubt.

But when there is a fear that property may be kept in a narrow circle, then the remedy is at hand for the state to set things right. This rectification Islam provides for in its own particular way, as we shall see in the chapter on economic theory.

* * * * * * *

We must think also of the responsibility which the individual has to society, and of that which society has to the individual. On each of these two Islam lays responsibilities, and for each of them it defines the limits to which he may go. In dealing with these responsibilities Islam tries as far as possible to harmonize their interests, and to remedy or to punish any loss which either of them may suffer in undertaking the duties which attach to the various fields of life, spiritual and material alike.

Every individual is charged in the first place conscientiously to perform his own work; for the results of individual
work are in the long run advantageous and beneficial to the
community. "Verily Allah is glad when one of you does work
which He can be sure of."[105] "Say: Work and Allah will see
your work, as will His Messenger and the Believers."[106]

Again every individual is charged with the care of society,
as if he were a watchman over it, responsible for its safety:
"Yours is the care of one of the frontiers of Islam, so let
none overcome you."[107] Life is like a ship at sea whose
crew are all concerned for her safety; none of them may make
a hole even in his own part of her in the name of his individual
freedom. "Verily some people travelled in a ship, and they
were partners, of whom each one had his own place. One
man among them struck his place with an axe, and the remainder said to him, 'What are you doing?' He said, 'This
is my place, and I can do what I wish in it.' Then if they restrain him, he and they are safe; but if they let him be, he
and they all perish."[108] This is a striking picture of the way
in which the various interests are inextricably bound up together; over against it stands the selfish outlook which takes
account only of the outward appearance of actions, without
reckoning their results in practical terms. So here we have
an exact indication of what the individual must do and what
the community must do in cases such as this.

No individual, then, can be exempt from this care for the
general interest, but every one must have a constant care for
the community. "Everyone of you is a watchman, and everyone of you will be held responsible for his ward."[109]

Similarly the welfare of the community must be promoted
by mutual help between individuals--always within the limits
of honesty and uprightness. "Help one another in innocence
and piety, but do not help one another in crime and hostility."
"Let there be a community of you exhorting to good, urging
to virtue, and restraining from evil-doing."[111] Each individu
will be held personally responsible for having urged to virtue;
and if he has not done so, then he is a criminal and will be
punished for his crime. "Take him and chain him; then roast
him in Hell; then thrust him into a chain of seventy cubits'
length. Verily he would not believe in Allah the Great; he
would not urge the feeding of the poor. So he has no friend
here today, nor any food save foul corruption which only

sinners eat."[112] Not having urged to feed the poor will be
accounted one of the signs of unbelief and of repudiation of
the faith. "Have you seen him who repudiates the faith? He
it is who repulses the orphan and does not urge the feeding
of the poor."[113]

Every individual, again, is charged with the duty of putting
an end to any evil-doing which he sees. "Whoever among
you sees any evil-doing, let him change it with his hand; if
he cannot do that, let him change it with his tongue; and if
he cannot do that, let him change it with his heart; and that
shows the weakest faith." Thus every individual will be held
responsible for every evil-doing in the community, even if
he has had no part in it. For society is a unity which is
harmed by any evil-doing, and the duty of every individual
is to guard and to protect it.

The whole community is to blame and merits injury and
punishment in this world and in the world to come if it passively accepts evil-doing in its midst by some of its members.
Thus it is charged with the duty of watching over every one
of its members. "When We wish to destroy a town We command its luxury-loving citizens, and they deal corruptly in
it; thus the sentence upon it is justified, and We destroy it
utterly."[114] Even if the majority of the people in it were
not corrupt, but merely accepted the corruption passively,
He would still have counted their destruction justifiable.
"And fear a trial which will not fall only upon those of you
who have done wrong."[115] There is no injustice in this, for
the community in which there is an immoral element, and in
which evil-doing flourishes unchecked is a community which
is exhausted and decayed, on the way to its end. The ruin
which will overtake it is a natural fate, brought on by its own
condition.

So the Hebrew people merited the curse which their prophets
laid upon them; the nature of their kingdom changed, and their
spirit left them because they would not change the wrong-
doing in their midst, nor did they restrain one another from
it. "Those of the Children of Israel who became unbelievers
were cursed by the tongue of David and of Jesus son of Mary.
That was because they rebelled and transgressed; they did
not restrain one another from evil-doing, but practiced it.
Bad indeed is what they were doing."[116] Or again in the
Traditions: "When the Children of Israel fell away into re-

bellion, their wise men rebuked them, but they would not
desist. They sat in company with the evil-doers in their as-
semblies, and they ate and drank with them. So Allah
struck the hearts of some of them with others. He cursed
them in the words of David and of Jesus son of Mary, because they rebelled and were hostile." As for the Believers
on the other hand, they are of the number of those of whom
the Qur'an says: "And the believing men and women are
friends one of the other; they urge to virtue, and they restrain from evil-doing."[117]

Now concerning the verse: "O you who believe, look after yourselves; he who goes astray will not harm you, so
long as you let yourselves be guided."[118] Some have argued
that this verse justifies an abstention from combatting wrong-
doing and from changing it. But Abu Bakr[119] (Allah be pleased
with him) reminds them that this is a mistaken interpretation.
He said: "O people, you read this verse, and you put a wrong
construction on it. I myself have heard the Messenger of
Allah say: 'Verily people who see wrong-doing and do not
change it--Allah will speedily bring punishment upon all of
them.'" This is the true interpretation, which is in conformit
with the aims of Islam. For what this verse actually contains
is a statement of individual responsibility. Wickedness which
is negative, which has no compulsive force on others is a
matter which concerns only him who indulges in it; the duty
of others is to seek guidance; if the sinner does not seek
guidance, the responsibility is on himself and his own possessions.

The community is also responsible for the care of its weak
members; it must watch their welfare and guard them; it has
also the duty of fighting in defense of those whom it guards.
"It is not for you to refuse to fight in the cause of Allah and in
defense of the weak, men, women, and children."[120] It must
also guard the property of the young until they attain to years
of discretion. "Make trial of the orphans until they reach the
age of marriage; then if you perceive discretion in them,
hand over their property to them. Do not eat it up in extravagance before they grow up. Let him who is rich restrain himself from touching any of it, and let him who is poor use a
reasonable amount of it. When you hand over their property
to them have witnesses present for them. Allah is sufficient
as a reckoner."[121] Or in the Traditions: "He who strives

on behalf of the destitute or the poor is like one who wages
hold war in the cause of Allah, or like one who rises to pray
by night and fasts by day."[122]

The community is responsible for the provisions of a
competence for its poor and destitute members; it has the
care of the money from the poor-tax and of its expenditure
on various objects. If this is not enough, the rich are obliged to contribute as much as will meet the wants of the
needy; there is no restriction and no condition, except that
there shall be sufficient. If any individual pass the night
hungry, the blame attaches to the community because it did
not bestir itself to feed him. "Nay, but you do not honor the
orphan, nor do you urge the feeding of the poor; you eat up
the inheritance altogether, and you love wealth with an excessive love. Nay, but when the earth is ground down, down,
when your Lord comes with the angels rank upon rank, when
Hell is brought forth--then indeed man would let himself be
reminded; but whence shall he find the Reminder? He will
say: 'Would that I had sent forward good works during my
life.' On that day no one will punish as He punishes, and
none will bind as He binds."[123] Or again in the Traditions:
"Whatever people suffer knowingly that a man remain hungry
among them, the protection of Allah is taken from them--
Blessed and Great is He." And: "He who has an abundance
of profit, let him use it on behalf of him who has none." And:
"He who has food for two, let him take a third man with him;
and he who has food for three, let him take a fourth." And:
"He has no faith in Me, who sleeps replete, while his neighbor
beside him is hungry, and he is aware of the fact." Where
neighborliness is concerned, prosperity obliges a man even
to give away one garment out of two. So the story goes that
a man came to the Prophet, and said to him, "Give me clothing, O Messenger of Allah." He turned away from him, not
having the means to comply, and the man said again, "Give
me clothing, O Messenger of Allah." Muhammad replied:
"Have you no neighbor who has more garments than he needs?"
"Certainly I have. More than one." Then said Muhammad:
"Then let Allah not put both you and him in Paradise."

The whole Islamic community is one body, and it feels all
things in common; whatever happens to one of its members,
the remainder of the members are also affected. This is the
perfect, descriptive simile which the noble Messenger uses

of it when he says: "The likeness of the Believers in their mutual love and mercy and relationship is that of the body; when one member is afflicted, all the rest of the body joins with it to suffer feverish sleeplessness." In the same way he portrays the mutual help and responsibility between one Believer and another in a second finely expressed description: "One Believer strengthens another as one building strengthens another." And this is the best possible description of the power of mutual help and responsibility in life.

On this foundation the laws against social crimes are built up; they are very severe, because mutual help cannot exist except on the basis of the safety of a man's life, property, and rights. "Every Muslim is sacrosant to a fellow-Muslim --his blood, his honor, and his property." Thus the penalty for killing or wounding is laid down as an exact equivalent: "Free man for free man, slave for slave, female for female."[1] The crime of murder is reckoned as equal in punishment to that of unbelief; "Whoever kills a Believer intentionally, his punishment is Hell, and there shall he continue."[125] "Do not kill the person whom Allah has made inviolate, except for some justifiable cause; if anyone is unjustly killed, We have given authority to his kinsman."[126] "We have prescribed a law for them in this matter; a life for a life, an eye for an eye, a nose for a nose, an ear for an ear, a tooth for a tooth, and for wounds the equivalent."[127] He emphasizes the retaliation, seeing in it the life of the community: "In this retaliation there is life for you, O ye who have understanding; perhaps you may be pious."[128] And in fact it does mean life; for it safeguards life by discouraging murder, and because it preserves the vitality and the power of the life of society.

The punishment for immorality, again, is severe, because it involves an attack on honor and a contempt for sanctity and an encouragement of profligacy in society. From it by a gradual process there come license, the obscurity of family ties, and the loss of those essential feelings of fatherhood and sonship. The penalty for this must be severe; for married men and women it is stoning to death; for unmarried men and women it is flogging, a hundred lashes, which in most cases is fatal. "The man or woman guilty of fornication shall be flogged with a hundred lashes; and let no pity for them effect you in the faith of Allah."[129]

A punishment of eighty lashes is fixed for those who stone

chaste women, Believers, who have been innocently careless; such men are cowardly and falsely inpugn the women's honor. In this case the crime of falsehood is closely akin to that of immorality, for it is an attack on reputation and honor, an incitement to hatred and bitterness, and an evidence of corruption of thought. "As for those who cast imputations on chaste women and then cannot bring four witnesses, flog them with eighty lashes, and never again accept evidence from them."[130]

The punishment for theft is likewise severe, because it is an offense against property; it is fixed at the cutting off of a hand; for a second offense the other hand is cut off, for a third offense a foot, and then the other foot. "As for the thief, man or woman, cut off their hands as a recompense for what they have piled up--a chastisement from Allah."[131]

There are some today who profess to find this a shocking punishment for the theft of property from an individual; but Islam looks at the matter only from the point of view of the safety, the security, and the stability of society. So too it has regard to the nature of the circumstances of a crime. This is a crime which is committed secretly; such secret crimes have need of stern punishments, firstly to recompense the criminal adequately, and secondly to make him an example through his suffering and his fear of the punishment. And in addition, this stern penalty is not exacted in full if the theft was committed under compulsion, such as the need to ward off the evil of hunger from oneself or from one's children. The general rule is that no guilt attaches to things done under compulsion. "He who is under compulsion, who acts against his will and not of malice, has committed no crime." Thus Umar enacted during his Caliphate, as we shall see.

As for those who threaten the general security of society, their punishment is to be put to death, or to be crucified, or to have their hands and feet cut off, or to be banished from the country. "The punishment of those who war on Allah and His Messenger and who strive to cause revolt in the land is to be put to death, to be crucified, to have their hands and feet cut off on opposite sides, or to be banished from the land."[132] For the concensus of public opinion holds that revolt and civil war are a greater crime than individual crimes, and that they justly merit being followed by a rigorous punishment.

* * * * * * *

Thus Islam legislates for mutual responsibility in society in all shapes and forms; these forms take their rise from the basic principle that there is an all-embracing identity of purpose between the individual and society, and that life in its fullness is all interrelated. So Islam lays down a complete liberty for the individual, within limits which will not injure him and will not favor society at his expense. It safeguards the rights of society, and at the same time specifies its responsibilities on the other side of the balance. Thus it enables life to progress on a level and even path, and to attain to the highest ends which can be served by the individual and by society alike.

On these three foundations, then--an absolute freedom of conscience, a complete equality of all mankind, and a permanent mutual responsibility in society--social justice is built up, and human justice is ensured.

IV. The Methods of Social Justice in Islam

Islam operates on the inner, spiritual side of human nature, rather than on the external; it is from the depths of
the conscience rather than on the surface that it seeks to
improve man. But at the same time it is never unmindful
of the practical situation in the realm of wordly life; it does
not forget the true nature of the human spirit, nor the things
which influence it for good or evil, for better or worse; it
has a care both for the aspirations which soar aloft and for
the material necessities which are chained to earth, for
human strength which is ever limited and for the perfection
which is always absolute. Thus because it has a profound
knowledge of the depths of the human spirit, Islam makes
use both of laws and of exhortations, it formulates command-
ments and prohibitions, it lays down limitations and enforces
them. But it also encourages the human spirit to rise above
such legalistic responsibilities as far as it can.
   Life becomes possible and profitable only as we observe
the lowest limit of the legal responsibilities of this faith;
but even then it still lacks the perfection at which Islam aims,
so long as it is not inspired by the prompting of conscience
towards self-control, loftiness, and nobility. So in Islam this
prompting of the conscience is complementary to all legal
duties; conscience must reinforce these duties, making their
performance a pleasure, and thus imparting to human life a
value and a nobility which are above the range of compulsion.
   When Islam seeks to establish a complete social justice,
it sets it on a higher level than a mere economic justice, and
on a more elevated plane than can be attained merely by legis-
lative measures; thus it establishes a comprehensive human
justice, established on two strong foundations: first, the
human conscience, working within the spirit of man; and
second, a system of religious law, working in the social
sphere. These two powers it unites by an appeal to the depths
of feeling in the human consciousness. "Verily in that there
is a reminder for every one who has a heart, or who will lend
an ear; he is a witness of it."[1] Islam does not overlook the

weakness of man, or his need for external compulsion. "Allah guides by his power more than by the Qur'an."[2]

Anyone who bestows even a passing and casual glance on this religion must perceive the immense effort which it devotes to the reformation of the human spirit in all its aspects and from every side. And it is not without our subject to take a brief and summary look at this effort. It is designed for the good of society only to the point at which there can be a permanent control by human conscience; it works to guarantee all human society only until the individual becomes aware of his own practical obligations. "Do not play the spy, and do not backbite one another. Would one of you care to eat his dead brother's flesh? You would abhor it."[13] Spying is the worst crime against personal freedom and against the sanctities of the individual, just as backbiting is the worst characteristic which can find a lodgment in the weakness of personality; not only does it render a character incapable of praise, but it robs it eventually of all vital and practical courage. "O you who believe, do not go into houses other than your own, until you are received as friends and have greeted the inmates."[4] Individual sanctities must be respected, because individual honor is the first requisite of social justice. "O you who have believed, let not one people mock another who are possibly better than themselves. And let not women mock other women who are possibly better than themselves. Do not scoff at one another, nor shame one another with nicknames; it is bad to get the name of evil conduct when you are a Believer; and those who do not repent are evil-doers."[5] Mocking one another and scoffing at one another and calling one another by unpleasant nicknames are things which are forbidden alike by the essential values of personality, by human equality, and by social justice. "And do not walk the earth in pride; verily you cannot split the earth, nor can you reach the mountains in height."[6] Vanity and arrogance are characteristics which are unpopular in personality; similarly they are in opposition to the instinct for equality and justice and brotherhood. In a word Islam has the highest regard for the saying of its Prophet that "Verily you are of a great character."[7] Character is the most essential foundation for the building of a firmly based society, for the joining of earth to Heaven, the temporal to the eternal in the human consciousness with all its finitude and its frailty.

Islam places a great deal of reliance on the human conscience when it is educated; it sets it up as the guardian of
the legal processes, to see that they are observed and maintained, and for the observance of the major part of the laws
conscience alone is accountable. The giving of evidence, for
example, is a fundamental matter which must be governed
by laws, yet which, at the same time, must ensure the rights
of men; and the giving of evidence is a question which runs
back to the individual conscience and to the dependence of
society on that conscience. "As for those who cast imputations upon innocent women, and then do not bring four witnesses in corroboration, flog them with eighty lashes and
never again accept evidence from them; they are those who
deal corruptly."[8] "And as for those who cast imputations
upon their wives, and who have no witness but themselves--
let the evidence of one of them be a fourfold testimony in
the name of Allah that he is of those who speak the truth.
And let the fifth testimony be to invoke the curse of Allah
upon himself if he is of those who lie. And punishment may
be averted from the woman if she testify four times in the
name of Allah that the man is of those who lie; and the fifth
testimony shall be to invoke the curse of Allah upon herself
if he is of those who speak the truth."[9] So too even where a
written agreement is demanded, it must necessarily be wit-
nessed. "O you who believe, when one of you contracts a
debt to another for a stated time, write it down; let a scribe
write it down between you justly; let not the scribe refuse to
write as Allah has taught him, but let him write, and let the
debtor dictate. Let him fear Allah his Lord, and let him not
lessen the amount in any way. If the debtor is a fool, or if he
is in weak health, or if he is unable to dictate, then let his
kinsman dictate for him, justly. Then have the writing wit-
nessed by two of your men; or if there are not two men, then by
one man and two women out of those on whom you agree as
witnesses; so if one of the women should err, the other may
remind her."[10] The duty of witnessing is statutory and a
matter of principle: "Let not witnesses refuse when they are
called."[11] Similarly the giving of evidence is a statutory responsibility in cases of legal dispute: "And do not conceal evidence; for whoever does so, his heart is guilty."[12] Thus
Islam places reliance on the human conscience in matters
which go as far as flogging, or stoning, and in matters touch-

ing the rights of property. Such a reliance must necessarily
ennoble human nature and raise it towards the equality for
which it longs and searches.

Islam does not leave the human conscience to its own resources; it allots to it these noble duties, making it the
guardian of the observance of the law and of the carrying out
of human responsibilities, and at the same time challenging
it to rise above what law and responsibility prescribe for it.
It has set the fear of Allah as a sanction on the conscience,
and has placed over it the thought of Allah's omniscience,
with the aim of ensuring and inspiring its activity. "There
is no private talk between three, but He makes a fourth, nor
between five, but He makes a sixth; and whether there be
less than that or more, He is always with them, wherever
they are. Then on the Day of Resurrection He will tell them
what they have done. Verily Allah is aware of all things."[13]
"We have created man, and We know that his soul whispers
within him; We are nearer to him than his jugular vein. When
the two meet and sit, one on the right hand and one on the
left, he cannot utter a word without a watcher being beside
him, ready."[14] "Verily he knows what is secret and what
is hidden."[15]

Thus Islam preached to men in warning, taking into account not only in this world but also in the next every single
human action, for which there is no escaping punishment
and no avoiding recompense. "We shall set up the balances
of justice on the Day of Resurrection, and no soul will be
wronged in the slightest degree; even if it is only the weight
of a grain of mustard seed, We shall produce it; for We are
sufficient as a reckoner."[16] "When the earth quakes with a
great quaking; when the earth brings forth what has been
buried in it; when man says 'What is the matter with it?';
on that day the earth shall tell her tidings, because your Lord
has inspired her. On that day men shall come forward
separately to see their works; whoever has done the weight
of an atom of good shall see it; and whoever has done the
weight of an atom of evil shall see it."[17] Thus runs the
constant teaching of Islam, making reverence and piety a
sanction upon the conscience; and thus it makes the human
conscience the means of advancement by making it responsible for the observance of all that the faith lays down in
the way of laws and duties.

* * * * * * *

In this twofold way Islam proceeded to set the foundations of a social justice, and by this means it succeeded in producing a balanced and interrelated human justice. We shall examine some aspects of this justice in a future chapter; for the moment it will be sufficient to consider one example of this system of law and custom. We shall choose the subject of the poor-tax and the alms, because it has an intimate connection with the subject of this book.

Islam makes the poor-tax an obligatory claim on the property of the wealthy in favor of the poor. It is a due which the government can exact by the authority of the law and by the power of its administration; but the public conscience has progressively taken over the enforcement of the payment of this due, until such payment has become a natural part of the will of the wealthy.

The poor-tax is one of the pillars of Islam, one of the essentials of the faith. "Prosperous are the Believers who are humble in their prayers, who turn away from idle talk, and who are active in paying the poor-tax."[18] "These are the signs of the Qur'an, which is a Book which makes clear, a guidance and a gospel for the Believers, who observe the prayers, who pay the poor-tax, and who are certain of the world to come."[19] On the other hand the act of withholding the poor-tax is a form of heresy and of unbelief in the world to come: "And woe to the heretics who do not pay the poor-tax and do not believe in the world to come."[20] But payment of the poor-tax is a method of gaining the mercy of Allah: "Observe the prayers, pay the poor-tax, and obey the Messenger; it may be that you will receive mercy."[21] Help from Allah comes to those who pay this due and who discharge their obligations to society, thus meriting their place in the earth. "Allah will surely help the man who helps Him; verily Allah is Powerful, Mighty. Such, if We establish them in the earth, will observe the prayers, will pay the poor-tax, will urge to good and will restrain from evil."[22]

The poor-tax is a human institution of long standing, advocated by the commands of the prophets before Islam; thus there is no religion devoid of this important social responsibility. "And make mention in the Book of Ishmael; he was true to this promise, and was a messenger, a prophet; he bade his people pray and pay the poor-tax, and he was ac-

ceptable in the eyes of his Lord."[23] So too the Qur'an says
of Abraham: "We gave to him Isaac and Jacob as an extra
gift; We made them upright men and We made them patterns
to guide men by Our bidding. We inspired them to good works,
to observe the prayers,and to pay the poor-tax; so they
served Us."[24]

And woe to him who does not discharge this legal obligation. Said the Messenger of Allah: "The man to whom Allah has given wealth, and who yet will not pay his poor-tax
shall be thus recompensed on the Day of Resurrection; a
huge snake with glowing eyes will encircle his neck on the
Day of Resurrection, will grasp him by the maxillaries--
that is to say, by the jaws--and will say, 'I am your wealth;
I am your treasure.'" Which is a fearful, terrible, and awe-
some picture.

* * * * * * *

This poor-tax is a due imposed by the force of the law,
an amount of money at a specified proportion. But in addition to this there is the institution of almsgiving which is
imposed on the individual conscience without any fixed rate;
it is at the discretion of the will and the conscience. It is
the outward sign of charity and brotherly feeling, to both of
which Islam attaches a supreme importance; it is an attempt
to establish the mutual ties of mankind and the responsibilities
of society along the line of an individual perception of what is
necessary, and along the line of a personal conception of
charity. It serves two purposes: first, to establish an inner
control of the conscience; and second, to foster a belief in
the inherent solidarity of mankind. Islam makes this charity
a pure and humane thing, not limited by the bounds of a
religious fellowship; so the Qur'an says: "Allah does not
forbid you to act righteously and justly towards those who have
not fought against you in the matter of religion, and who have
not expelled you from your homes."[25] And the Messenger
says: "You will never be Believers until you show charity."
They said to him, "O Messenger of Allah, all of us are charitable." He replied: "It is not a question of your charity to
your neighbor, but of your charity to men in general." And
thus he sets a lofty pattern of charity which is pure and universal, to the point of making it a feature of the faith.

He even takes the final step and includes in the scope of

charity all living things. Thus the noble Prophet of Islam said: "Once while a man was travelling he became violently thirsty, so he found a well, went down to the water, and drank. When he came up again he noticed a dog panting and licking the dust in an agony of thirst. He said to himself, 'This dog has the same violent thirst which I had'; whereupon he went down again to the water and filled his boot with liquid. Grasping it in his mouth, he climbed out of the well and gave the dog to drink. And Allah the Exalted gave him praise and pardon." His hearers asked him: "O Messenger of Allah, is there such a reward for us in the case of animals?" He replied: "There is such a reward in the case of every living creature." Or again he said: "There was a woman who went to Hell only on account of a cat; she had tied it up, and had not fed it, nor had she even given it to eat of the herbage of the earth."

Such charity is a fundamental part of Islam, as it is one of its characteristic signs; it indicates the religious sincerity and depth of the conscience, and it testified to the existence of that humane spirit without which, in the Islamic view, there can be no religion.

It is on this basis that Islam establishes the custom of almsgiving and charity; it makes one fond of spending voluntarily and freely, in anticipation of the approval of Allah, of a return from Him in this world, and of a reward for Him in the world to come. Thus too one may escape His anger, His vengeance, and His punishment.

So the good news is for the humble, those who are obedient to Allah, and who spend of their wealth according to His will. "And give good news to the humble whose hearts are afraid when Allah is mentioned, who are patient in their afflictions, who observe the prayers, and who expend freely of what We have given them."[26] This is a picture to inspire the heart of man, and the same idea appears in another connection, where it is written: "Only those believe in Our signs who, when they are reminded of them, fall down in adoration and celebrate the praises of their Lord, and are not puffed up. As they leave their beds they call upon their Lord in fear and in hope; and of what We have given them they expend in alms. No one knows what pleasure is reserved for such, as a reward for what they have been doing."[27]

And the same inspiration is to be found in the beautiful and

touching picture of the character of the people of Medina
when they received the Emigrants and gave them shelter,
sharing with them their property and their houses in cheerfulness and gladness of spirit. "As for those who occupied
the houses and the faith before them, they loved those who
emigrated to them, and they found no desire in their hearts
for the share which had fallen to the others; they preferred
them before themselves, though there was poverty among
them. Those who are preserved from niggardliness of soul
shall be prosperous."28

This is a picture of human nature in its highest and best
aspects; and here is another description which is not inferior
to the first, of the kindness, the compassion, and the sympathy of a community of Allah's servants; some authorities
hold that the people in question here are Ali and his wife,
Fatima, the daughter of the Messenger, and their house-
hold.28 "They fulfill their vows, and they fear a Day the
evil of which will fly broadcast. For love of God they give
food to the poor, the orphan, and the prisoner, saying, 'It
is only for the sake of Allah that we give you food; we want
from you neither reward nor gratitude. We fear from our
Lord a day which will be grim and forbidding.' So Allah
has preserved them from the evil of that Day, and has given
them cheerfulness and joy; He has rewarded them for their
endurance with Paradise and silk clothing. There they recline on couches, and there they see neither sun nor bitter
cold; near over them is the shade of the garden of Paradise,
and hanging low around them are its clusters of fruit. They
shall be served round with vessels of silver and goblets of
glass, with glasses of silver whose measure they have themselves determined; in these they shall quaff a drink tempered
with ginger, drawn from a spring named Salsabil. There
pass round among them boys of eternal youth, whom to see
is to imagine that they are unstrung pearls, and whom to see
is to envisage delight and a great kingdom. They are clothed
with garments of green satin and brocade, and they are
adorned with bracelets of silver; their Lord has given them
to drink a pure draught. Verily this has come to you as a
reward, and thus your life's striving has been recompensed."30

So the giving of alms is to make a loan to Allah, a loan
which is certain to be repaid: "Who is he who will make a fair
loan to Allah, and He will double it for him. For such a one

there is a noble reward."[31] "Verily men and women who
give alms and thus make a loan to Allah, He will double it
for them. For such there is a noble reward."[32] Or it may
be regarded as a profitable and remunerative business:
"Verily those who recite the Book of Allah, who observe the
prayers, and who expend in alms of what We have given them,
both secretly and openly--such hope for a business that will
not fail. So He may pay them their rewards in full, and
may give them increase of His bounty; verily He is forgiving,
grateful."[33] In either case almsgiving is profitable, and
does not involve loss or injury. "That which you expend in
alms of your possessions is to your own advantage, even
though you expend it only for the love of Allah; what you expend in alms of your possessions will be repaid you in full
measure, and you will suffer no injury."[34]

So in the next world Paradise is the worthy recompense
of those who expend freely in alms. "And hasten to forgiveness from your Lord, and to a Paradise whose width is as
that of the heavens and the earth, a Paradise prepared for
those who are pious; they it is who expend in alms both in
prosperity and in adversity, who curb their wrath, and who
deal leniently with others. Allah loves those who act well."[35]

Again almsgiving is a means of purification for one's
character and for one's property; the Messenger of Allah commanded that a portion of their property should be taken from
people who have sinned and have acknowledged their sins, and
that this should be spent on good causes; thus such people might
be purified and cleansed. "Others have acknowledged their
sins; they have done both deeds that are good and deeds that
are evil; it may be that Allah will relent towards them, for
Allah is forgiving and compassionate. Take of their property
an alms which will purify and cleanse them, and pray over
them; verily your prayers will mean a repose for them, for
Allah hears and knows. Have they not learned that is is
Allah who receives repentance from His servants, and who
accepts the alms? Have they not learned that it is Allah who
is relenting and compassionate?"[36]

Thus expenditure on alms is encouraged by repayment according to the compact of Allah, by reverence for Him, and
by fear of an evil record; to give alms indicates wisdom and
understanding. But to refrain from almsgiving is to nullify
what Allah has commanded to be accomplished; it is a form

of violating the compact and of dealing corruptly in the earth. "Only those who have insight are reminded, those who fulfill the compact of Allah and who do not violate the agreement. They accomplish what Allah has commanded to be accomplished they reverence their Lord, and they fear an evil record. They endure with patience out of regard for the love of Allah, they observe the prayers, and they expend in alms out of what We have given them, both secretly and openly; they drive away the evil by means of the good. Such shall have the recompense of the Abode, gardens of pleasure into which they shall enter, they and those of their fathers and their wives and their descendants who have been upright; angels shall come in to them by every gate, saying, 'Peace be upon you for your patient endurance; good is the recompense of the Abode.' But as for those who violate the compact of Allah after coming to an agreement with Him, who nullify what Allah has commanded to be accomplished, and who deal corruptly in the earth--for them is the curse, and for them there is an evil abode."[37]

To refrain from expenditure in the way of Allah is destruction: "Expend freely in the way of Allah, and do not hand yourselves over to destruction."[38] The "destruction" of the individual is to lay oneself open to the punishment of Allah in the world to come, and to the vengeance of others in this world. The "destruction" of society is the discrimination and the oppression which come in the train of the absence of free expenditure in alms, together with the accompanying discords and hatreds, debility and weakness.

To hinder good works is a form of hostility: "Cast into Hell every obstinate unbeliever who hinders good works, who is hostile and contentious."[39] "And do not obey any contemptible swearer, any slanderer who goes about maligning, who hinders good works, who is hostile and guilty."[40] He is hostile to the claims of Allah, to the claims of his own soul as a member of that society.

Charity leads to Paradise, and the charitable man will pass over the hard path which leads thither; the path consists in the setting free of slaves, and in the provision of food in a case of hunger and destitution. "And what has taught you the nature of the 'hard path'? It is to set free slaves, to give food in a day of famine to an orphan who is of your kin, or to a poor man in destitution."[41] But to refrain from charity leads to the Fire, and he who merits it will go thither along with the unbelievers. "What made you go into Hell-fire? They replied: 'We were not among those who prayed, nor were we among those who fed the poor; we plunged into discussion with others, and we scoffed at the Day of Judgment, until the final account came upon us."[42] "As for those who have been niggardly with what Allah has given them of His bounty, let them not think that it will be well with them; nay, it will go ill with them, for on the Day of Resurrection that which they have stingily withheld will be hung about their necks."[43] "As for those who have heaped up for themselves treasures of gold and silver, and who do not expend them in the way of Allah, announce for them a painful punishment. On that day their treasures will be heated in the fire of Hell, and they will be branded with them on their foreheads, their sides, and their backs. 'These are the treasures which you heaped up for yourselves, so taste now of what you have heaped up."[44] The treasures which are referred to in this verse are explained in a tradition: "Whoever collects dinars or dirhams, gold in the nugget or silver, and does not pay it over to a creditor or expend it freely in the way of Allah-- that is a treasure, and he will be branded with it on the Day of Resurrection." Treasure, properly understood, is not merely money on which no poor-tax is paid, as some have maintained; all money which is hoarded and which is not paid out for these specified purposes is treasure, even if poor-tax has been paid on it. And the other tradition which indicates that money on which poor-tax has been paid is not treasure, is not in opposition to this tradition; for the latter tradition merely makes the former specific.

Indeed, in the case of men who hoard, punishment sometimes overtakes them in this world as a reward for their niggardliness, and for their hindering of good works. The noble Qur'an tells a parable of such in a short story concerning a community which had a walled garden, from the produce of which they used to feed the poor. Then it occurred to them to be niggardly and to keep the fruit for themselves; but a change of fortune fell upon their garden, and Allah took away their produce, so that the next morning they were regretful. "We have tested them as We tested the owners of the garden when they resolved that they would reap it in the morning, and made no qualification of their resolve. So while they slept a disaster from your Lord encircled it, and in the morning it lay like a garden already reaped. That morning they called to one another, 'Come early to your field, if you intend to reap,' and they went their way, whispering to one another, 'Let no poor man come upon you in the garden today.' So they went out early with this settled purpose, but when they saw it they said, 'Verily we have erred, and we are cheated of our fruits.' The most fair-minded of them said, 'Did I not say to you, Will you not give praise to Allah?' They said, 'Praise to our Lord. Verily we have been evildoers.' So they turned upon one another, blaming one another, and saying, 'Alas for us. Indeed we have been presumptuous; it may be that our Lord will give us something better than this in exchange. Verily our desire is towards our Lord.' Such was the punishment; and the punishment of the world to come is yet greater, if only they knew."[46]

So the Qur'an summons men to be generous before the opportunity is lost to them. "Say to My servants who have believed that they must observe the prayers and expend freely of what We have given them, both secretly and openly, before there comes a Day on which there will be neither bargain nor friendship."[47] "And expend freely of what We have given you, before death comes upon one of you, and he says: 'O my Lord, Would that my death might be deferred for a short space, so that I might give alms and thus become one of the righteous.' But Allah will not defer the death of any soul when its time is come."[48] Similarly the Qur'an cautions men against avarice, that they may guard themselves from it, and that they may not be betrayed into it by their desire for wealth and children; for these things are only a trial and a temptation for men. "Your wealth and your children are only a temptation but Allah has a great reward. So be pious towards Allah as far as you are able, attend and obey. Expend freely in alms; that is better for yourselves. It is those who are protected from avarice of soul who prosper."[49]

The Prophet makes almsgiving a duty for every Muslim, even though he may have nothing. The explanation of that is this saying of his: "The giving of alms is a duty for every Muslim. They asked him: 'O Prophet of Allah, what of him who has nothing?' He replied: 'Let him turn his hand to labor, and thus profit himself, and then let him give his alms.' They said: 'And what if he can find nothing to do?'

He answered: 'Let him find some unfortunate soul who is in
need.' They said: 'Suppose he cannot find such a one?' He
replied: 'Then let him do some one a service, or let him
restrain some one from evil, and that shall be his alms.'"
Thus all men have an equal opportunity for generosity, each
according to his means, and each according to his ability.

* * * * * * *

The recipients of charitable expenditure must vary according to varying needs and circumstances; relatives have
the prior claim on a man's benefactions, but there are others
also who are joined with them, and who are mentioned side
by side with relatives in the passages of the Qur'an which
urge to charity. For charity is a universal emotion, and
must take precedence over family consciousness; and indeed the mention of charity in the Qur'an is generally linked
with that of faith. More than that--it is an indication of faith,
as we have shown. "Serve Allah, and do not associate any
other with Him. Show kindness to parents and relatives, to
orphans and to the poor, to the stranger under your protection,
whether or not he be a relative, to the companion at your
side and to the wayfarer, and to those who are your possession (i.e., such as slaves). Verily Allah does not love any
crafty boaster. Those who are niggardly and who urge others
to niggardliness, who conceal what Allah has given them of
His bounty--for such unbelievers We have prepared a shameful punishment."[50] "They will ask you how they should expend
money in alms. Say: What you expend is for the benefit of
parents, relatives, orphans, the poor and the wayfarer.
Whatever good you do, Allah is aware of it."[51]

Thus the stranger under a man's protection and the companion are placed alongside of parents and relatives, just as
the poor and the wayfarer are grouped with all of them. All
have an equal right to the alms. And this is so, even in the
case of those who have committed some evil deed, as in the
occurrence connected with Mistah, a relative of Abu Bakr,
who shared in the slanderous story about A'isha, the daughter
of Abu Bakr and wife of the Prophet. Islam ordains that
such persons be forgiven, and it forbids that they be punished
in this way. Abu Bakr swore that he would cut off the charity
which he had been extending to Mistah, for he was exceedingly
angry at the calumnies which the latter had been spreading
about the character of A'isha. But this verse was revealed to

Muhammad: "As for those of you who have abundance and ample means, let them not abstain from giving to relatives and the poor and to those who have emigrated in the way of Allah; rather let them pardon and forgive. Do you not wish that Allah should pardon you?"[52] Thus Islam seeks to raise human instincts to a high and noble level which does honor to human nature in all ages, which makes human nature a proud thing in the past, the present, and the future, as long as Allah wills.

Islam also elevates the conception of charity itself by making it charity for the sake of Allah the Glorious. It depicts charity in this striking picture which has come down through the Traditions. "On the Day of Resurrection Allah will say: 'O man, I was ill, and you did not visit Me.' Then man will reply: 'O my Lord, how could I visit You, since You are Lord of the Worlds?' Then Allah will say: 'Did you not know that such and such a servant of Mine was ill, and you did not visit him? If you had visited him, you would have found Me there.' 'O man, I gave you your food, but you have given Me no food.' He will answer: 'O my Lord, how could I give You food, seeing that You are the Lord of the Worlds?' And Allah will say: 'Did you not know that such and such a servant of Mine gave you food, yet you gave him none? Surely if you had given him food, you would have found it with Me.' 'O man, I gave you to drink, but you did not give to Me.' Man will say: 'O my Lord, how could I give You to drink, seeing that You are the Lord of the Worlds?' And Allah will reply: 'Such and such a servant of Mine gave you to drink, yet you did not give to him. Had you given him to drink, you would have found it with Me.'"

Islam also makes almsgiving a matter of the public conscience, thus raising it above the stage where it is merely a mark of the superiority and preëminence of the rich over the poor, and thus rasing it also above the stage where it may be only a form of hypocrisy arising from ignoble instincts. For if the impulses leading to almsgiving are allowed to deteriorate or if charity is followed by a sense of obligation on the part of those who receive it, then it becomes an ungracious business which can only injure the soul, the nature, and the conscience, and which can only injure society also by injuring its individual members. There is nothing like attaching a sense of obligation to an act of benevolence for paining people, for humbling them,

and rendering them unwilling to accept benevolence. Similarly
there is nothing like hypocrisy in almsgiving for corrupting
the conscience and sapping the moral fibre. Accordingly
Islam labors to elevate the nature both of those who give and
of those who receive, and it is this result which it seeks most
strenuously to achieve. "Those who expend their wealth freely
in the way of Allah are like a grain which produced seven ears
with a hundred grains in each ear; so Allah will give a double
return to whom He wills, and verily Allah is powerful and
aware. Such as expend their wealth in alms in the way of
Allah and do not follow this expenditure with obligations or
annoyances shall have their reward with their Lord; no fear
shall oppress them, nor any sadness rest upon them. Favorable speech and forgiveness are better than alms followed by
annoyance; Allah is rich and clement. O you who have believed, do not make your alms in vain by putting obligation
or annoyance upon the recipients, as he does who gives alms
for the sake of appearance before the people. He has no belief in Allah or in the Last Day, and he is like a smooth rock
with earth on it; if a heavy rain falls upon it, it is left bare.
Such men have no power over what they have amassed, and
Allah does not give guidance to people who are unbelievers.
But those who expend their wealth in alms out of a desire for
the approval of Allah and as a support from themselves are
like a garden on a hill; if a heavy rain falls upon it, it brings
forth its fruit in double measure; and even if no heavy rain
falls upon it, yet still there is the dew. Allah is aware of
what you do. Would any one of you like this to happen? Suppose he has a garden of palm trees and vines with perpetual
water flowing through it, so that he has all kinds of fruits in
it; old age comes upon him, and he has only a weak family;
then a fiery whirlwind strikes his garden, so that it is burnt
up. In such a way does Allah make the signs clear to you;
it may be that you will consider."[53]

For this reason it is desirable that alms be given in secret
and privately to the necessitous. Thus on the one hand the
self-esteem of the recipients is safeguarded, and on the other
hand a check is put upon conceit and pride. "If you give alms
in public, that is good; but if you do it secretly and give to
the poor, that is better for you."[54] And there is a tradition
of the Prophet in praise of the man who "gives his alms, but
conceals the fact to the point where his left hand does not know

what his right hand is giving." This is an outstandingly fine
picture of the way in which charity should be kept secret, and
should not be accounted a matter for pride or publicity.

* * * * * * *

Islam is aware of the power of the love of material gain,
and the power of the love of money. It is convinced that
avarice is always threatening the soul, and is never far away.
"Souls are ever liable to avarice."[55] So it treats all of this
as a personal matter, using the methods which we have seen;
it stimulates the will, it warns, it exhorts, it depicts; in
this way its aims may be achieved, and thus it can beseech
this naturally niggardly disposition of man to attain a standard
of nobility in dealing with that which he loves dearly and which
has a powerful hold upon him. "You will not attain to charity
until you expend in alms of that which you love."[56] In this
way man reaches the height of generosity, the limit of liberality, and the noblest form of beneficence which can possibly
arise from the human spirit. Thus man is raised above his
natural state, and thus the higher side of his nature over-
comes the lower, his spiritual nature conquers his animal
nature. By its very nature this is by itself a lofty and universal aim which must command all support. How much more
so, then, seeing that it is also an objective for society. The
purpose is to create a balance of wealth, to oppose destitution,
to establish the responsibilities which exist between rich and
poor, and thus to shape a society which has a sense of mutual
relationship and mutual help, and which is therefore a healthy
society.

* * * * * * *

Islam follows this method, with one example of which we
have now dealt in detail. Islam is concerned to persuade the
conscience in the case of every duty which it prescribes. It
imposes no more duties than are demanded by the safety of
society, and no more than can be accepted by the limited
ability of the general mass of mankind. Beyond that stage it
appeals to the conscience, persuading it of its responsibility,
and seeking to raise it above its normal scope; thus it attempts to elevate human life, and to draw it ever onward and
upward. It recognizes the wide interval which lies between
the lower level of duty which is prescribed by the law and
the higher level of conscience which is so desirable, and

towards which individuals and nations have striven in every age and century.

Thus, for example, Islam prescribes a principle of vengeance, awarding it as a legal right to the next of kin, and permitting him to exact it in full; yet at the same time it exhorts as strongly as possible that men should forgive, forbear, and pardon. "If any man is unjustly killed, We have given authority to his next of kin; but let him not be immoderate in killing; verily he has been helped."[57]

Or again it prescribes holy war in the way of Allah as a responsibility incumbent on every one who is able for it. But over and above that it kindles a love for holy wars by inciting the conscience to accept it, by depicting it in glowing terms, and by emphasizing its justice and the glories which it brings to a society. "Allah has purchased from the Believers their persons and their wealth, for the price of Paradise reserved for them; so they fight in the way of Allah, so they kill and are killed."[58] "And were it not that Allah sets some men against others, the cloisters had been destroyed, and the churches and synagogues and mosques in which the name of Allah is often repeated." "What is the matter with you that you do not fight in the way of Allah, and in defense of the oppressed, men, women and children."[60]

It forbids usury, and goes on to attack its evil character and the evil character of its results; thus it seeks to arouse the conscience to condemn usury and to reject it. "Those who eat up the fruits of usury will not arise on the Day of Resurrection, except in the same way as he whom Satan has sent mad by a touch. That is because they have said: 'A bargain is just the same as usury.' But Allah has allowed bargaining, though He has forbidden usury. If anyone receives a warning from his Lord and desists, then he shall keep what he has already gained, and his destiny shall be in the hand of Allah. But if anyone continues to practice usury, then he is one of those destined to Hell, there to abide. Allah will blot out usury, but He will mutiply money given in alms; Allah does not love any guilty unbeliever."[61] "O you who have believed, act piously towards Allah and abandon the usury which is still unpaid, if you are really Believers. And if you do not do this, then know that there will be war from Allah and from his Messenger."[62]

Islam forbids the drinking of wine and gambling, and it

links up these things with the custom of divining the future
by the casting of lots or sacred arrows; this occurs in one
verse which places all these things together as being outside
the bounds of common sense and logic. Then it goes on to
persuade the conscience of the reasons for this prohibition.
"O you who have believed, wine and gambling, sacred lots
and arrows are only an abomination, a work of Satan. Turn
away from them, then, and it may be that you will prosper.
Satan desires only to cause enmity and hatred among you by
means of wine and gambling, to keep you from the remembrance of Allah, and from the prayers; so will you refrain?"[6]

Thus Islam continues through all its commands and prohibitions; the same course is followed. It is the wisest and
the most profitable course for human nature, and its results
have already been proved in the early history of Islam and
throughout the long period of the past fourteen centuries.
This method can be repeated for the present and the future,
so long as its essential nature is understood, so long as this
direction is followed, and so long as men will follow this
straight path.

V. Political Theory in Islam

Any discussion of social justice in Islam must necessarily
include a discussion of political theory in Islam, according
to the principle which we have already laid down when we
were discussing the nature of Islamic social justice; namely,
that it must embrace all the aspects of life and all varieties
of endeavor; similarly that it must include both spiritual and
material values, since these are inextricably interwoven.
With all of this political theory is connected; and the more
so, because in the final resort it is concerned with observance
of the religious law, with the care of society in every respect,
with the establishment of justice and equity in society, and
with the allotment of wealth according to the principles
which are accepted by Islam.

Any full treatment of political theory in Islam would be
lengthy, and would require a separate treatise. But our purpose in this work is merely to point out the bearing of such
theory on social justice, and therefore we must as far as
possible consider only this aspect of the matter.   And this
despite the fact that the major difficulty of studying Islam is
that the enquirer finds that all its aspects are inter-connected,
so that one cannot possibly be separated from another. Because this religion is essentially a unity; worship and work,
political and economic theory, legal demands and spiritual
exhortations, faith and life, this world and the world to come,
all these are related parts of one comprehensive whole. It is
difficult to single out one part for treatment, without being
led to deal also with the remaining parts. Yet this is what
we shall attempt, as far as may be possible.

Some writers, discussing the Islamic political system,
labor to trace connections and similarities between it and
the other systems known to the ancient or the modern world,
in the ages before and after Islam. And some of them really
believe that they find a strong support for Islam when they can
trace such a connection between it and one of the other ancient
or modern systems. In reality this idea represents nothing
but an inner conviction that the Islamic system is inferior to

88

those of the Western world. But Islam has no need to take
in the fact that there are similarities between it and these
other systems, nor can this fact injure it in any way. For
Islam altogether presents to mankind an example of a political
system, the like of which has never been found in any of the
other systems known to the world either before or after the
seventh century. Islam does not seek, and never has sought,
to imitate any other system, or to find connections or similarities between itself and others. On the contrary it has
chosen its own characteristic path, and has concentrated its
attention on all the problems of human nature.

It is sometimes said in dealing with man-made political
systems that they agree with Islam in some respects, and
differ from it in others. But Islam is in itself a completely
independent system which has no connection with these others,
either when they agree with it, or when they differ from it.
Such divergence or agreement is purely accidental and occurs
in scattered points of detail; in such coincidence or in such
divergence there can be no significance. The truly significant
thing is the underlying theory, or the philosophy peculiar to
the system; Islam has both of these, and it is from these
that the details of the system take their rise. These details
may either agree with or differ from similar details in other
systems, but Islam continues on its own way, irrespective
of such agreement or divergence.

Thus it is not the task of the Islamic enquirer who embarks
on a study of the Muslim political system to look for similarities to, or agreements with, any other system, old or new.
Nor do such similarities and agreements add anything to the
strength of the Islamic position, as some Muslims believe--
especially since they are superficial and in matters of detail
only; they arise from chance in merely particular matters,
and not from any general philosophy or underlying theory.
The true method is to turn to the fundamentals of the religion
itself in the firm belief that in them lie the complete bases of
the system. It makes no difference whether all other political
systems agree or disagree entirely. The sole reason for
seeking to strengthen Islam through its similarities and agreements with other systems is the conviction of inferiority, as
we have said; no Muslim scholar should venture on such a
course, but rather should know his own faith with a true
knowledge and study it with a true zeal.

In the course of its growth and development the world has known a number of political systems, but the Islamic system is not one of these; it is not derived from them, nor does it depend on them. It is a system which stands by itself, independent in its theory and individual in its methods. We must necessarily regard it as independent, since it was in independence that it started, and since it is the path of independence which it follows.

For these reasons the suggestion of Doctor Haikal is unacceptable, that the Islamic world was "the Islamic empire"; similarly unacceptable is his dictum that "In fact Islam was an imperial power." Nothing can be further from a true understanding of the spirit of Islam than to call it imperial; and that is so, no matter what distinctions we may draw between the characteristics of an Islamic empire and those of the more familiar imperialism. Again nothing can be further from an understanding of the true nature of the bonds uniting the Islamic world than to call it the Islamic empire.

Thus it is strange to find Doctor Haikal in his treatment of Islamic administration in "The Life of Muhammad," or "Al-Sadiq Abu Bakr," or "Al-Faruq Umar" seeking some real and deep-seated difference between the nature of Islam and the nature of the other systems familiar to the world. But he is driven irresistibly to these two positions by his belief in the inspired force of foreign institutions. And indeed there are some institutions which are similar in Islam and in imperialism. Perhaps the most convenient instance is that of the Muslim world; this comprises a number of provinces of contrasting races and cultures, yet the matter of its government is handled from one capital. This is certainly an imperial custom. But this is only an isolated instance, and in any case the points of importance are the way in which the capital regards the provinces and the nature of the relation between it and them.

Anyone who studies the spirit of Islam and its method of administration must recognize clearly that it is as far from familiar imperialism as it can be. Islam holds that there is an equality for Muslims in all parts of the world, and it forbids any racial or local loyalty; rather, as we have seen, it encourages religious loyalty in many places. In accordance with this idea it does not make its provinces into mere colonies or storehouses, sources from which supplies may

be poured into the capital for its sole profit. Each province
is a member of the body of the Islamic world, and its people
have the same privileges as the people of the capital. When
one of the provinces is administered by a governor from the
Islamic capital, he can administer it only in virtue of his
character as a Muslim who is suitable for the position, and
not as a colonial governor. But many of these provinces which
were originally conquered were administered by one of their
own people, chosen, not because he was a native, but because
he was a Muslim suitable for the position. Again, it is required that what money is collected in any province shall be
spent there as a matter of priority. If there is a surplus, it
must be contributed to the Muslim public treasury, to be
spent on the Muslim world generally according to need. It
must not be appropriated to the use of the population of the
capital city, even at the cost of destitution in the province,
as is the imperial custom.

All this constitutes a great difference between the Islamic
world on the one hand, or the Islamic community in a narrower
instance, and imperialism on the other hand. So the statement that Islam is "an imperial power" is liable to correction
since it is foreign alike to the spirit and to the history of
Islam. This, rather, must be our primary statement: Islam
is universal in its aim, because of its strong belief in the
unity of human nature and because of the effort it makes to
sum up all this universality in a system of equality and
brotherhood.

Dr. Taha Hussein has been more circumspect in his definition; in the preface to "The Great Civil War; Othman" he
deals with the Islamic political system and compares it with
all the other systems. His conclusion is that it is by nature
fundamentally different from all others. This is undoubtedly
correct with regard to the spirit of Muslim administration,
though not with regard to its institutions and details.

Islam, as we have said, proposes independent solutions
to human problems; these solutions it derives from its theory
of unity, from its fundamental beliefs, and from its various
methods. So we must be careful when we describe Islam not
to relate it to other principles and theories in order to explain
it by means of them, or to relate it to them. Islam is a
comprehensive philosophy and an homogeneous unity, and to
introduce into it any foreign element would mean ruining it.

It is like a delicate and perfect piece of machinery which may be completely ruined by the presence of a foreign body.

And this is the consideration which I would urge in summing up here; there are many who have introduced into their thought and their reasoning foreign bodies taken from the machinery of alien systems of government. They believe that they are contributing a new access of strength to Islam when they connect it with these systems. But in reality all that they are doing is an error, spoiling Islam and ruining its spirit that it cannot operate. And at the same time this is the product of a hidden feeling of inferiority, even though such writers may not openly mention the word inferiority.

* * * * * * *

The Islamic political system is based on two fundamental conceptions, both of which originate in its universalist idea of the universe, of life, and of man. One is the idea of the equality of mankind in class, in nature, and in origin; the other is the belief that Islam represents the eternal system for the world throughout the future of the human race.

The first of these we have already discussed in the chapter on the foundations of social justice in Islam. There we indicated the rights which Islam extends to protected peoples,[1] and to infidel peoples who have a compact with the Muslims. These are rights which derive from the permanent and fundamental rights of humanity; no difference is made between one religion and another. And the same principle is extended to cover human relationships in general. When Islam commands war against infidel peoples, the command refers only to defensive war which is aimed at stopping aggression. "Permission is granted to those who fight because they have been wronged; verily Allah is able to help them."[2] "And fight in the way of Allah against those who fight against you; but do not open the hostilities, for Allah does not love those who open the hostilities."[3] This is war solely to defend the Muslim world against physical aggression, so that its members may not be seduced from their faith; it is war to remove all material obstructions from the path of the gospel, that it may reach out to all men.

Islam goes far to discharge its obligations to non-Muslims; indeed it goes the length of refraining from helping Muslims against non-Muslims with whom a compact exists. "And if

they ask help from you in a matter of religion, it is your
duty to render such help; except against a people with whom
you have an agreement."[4] This is a typical instance of Islam's care to discharge its obligations, and it rests on a
view of life which is universal and worldwide in scope. It
goes beyond local interests and limited aims in anything to
do with religion.

As to the second conception, namely that Islam represents
the eternal system for the world throughout the future of the
human race, this originates in the fact that Muhammad was
the Messenger of Allah to all men, that he was the Seal of
the prophets, and that his religion is the most permanent of
all religions. "And We have not sent you unless inclusively
to all people."[5] "And We have sent you only as a sign of merc
to the worlds."[6] "...the Messenger of Allah, and the Seal
of the prophets."[7] "Today I have perfected your religion
for you, have completed My favor towards you, and have approved Islam as your religion."[8] "Verily this Qur'an guides
you to what is more upright."[9] But in spite of this Islam
does not compel others to embrace it: "There is no compulsion in religion."[10] Rather Islam grants to men an extreme freedom and protection to continue in their own religious beliefs. It goes so far in its interpretation of this
freedom as to impose the duty of paying the poor-tax on Muslims alone, while it exacts from protected peoples only the
land-tax; this is demanded because they share in the protection afforded by the Muslim state, and all the proceeds of this
tax are spent on their welfare. But it does not impose the
poor-tax on protected peoples, because it is a religious ordinance of Islam, and a form of religious service applicable
only to Muslims; Islam has no desire to compel protected
peoples to perform the religious services proper only to Muslims. So it takes money from them on a purely monetary
basis which has no religious significance such as is contained
in the ordinance of the poor-tax. Surely this is the height of
a discriminating perception of justice in dealing with others.

In granting this extent of freedom to others Islam is
prompted by its general and universal spirit; it believes that
when they have the opportunity of examining Islam, their
examination will then be careful and assiduous, since it will
owe nothing to the intervention of material force or of intellectual ignorance. Islam holds that by their very nature men

will turn towards it because it insures a perfect balance of
all the aims for which previous religions have striven and
between all the passions and the desires of human nature.
Because under Islam all and sundry are guaranteed an absolute equality and a complete mutual responsibility, and because the aim of Islam is to secure a unity of all men alike
in the spiritual and in the political sphere.

The fact that the Islamic political system is based on these
two conceptions has had its effect on the nature and the methods
of that system. It has made it operate through laws and exhortations, through political and economic theory, and through
all the other systems which it includes. Thus it does not
legislate for one class or for one nation, but for all classes
and for all nations; it followed universal and comprehensive
principles when it laid down its laws and its systems of government; it laid down general principles and broad fundamentals only, leaving the application of these to the process of
time and to the emergence of specific problems. This reliance on general principle is most clearly perceptible in the
field of political theory, which is the specific concern of this
chapter.

* * * * * * *

Political theory in Islam rests on the basis of justice on the
part of the rulers, obedience on the part of the ruled, and
collaboration between ruler and ruled. These are the great
fundamental features from which all the other features take
their rise.

There must first be justice on the part of the rulers. "Verily Allah commands justice."[11] "And when you judge between
the people, you must do so with justice."[12] "And when you
speak, act justly, even though the matter concerns a relative."[13]
"And be not driven by hatred of any people to unjust action; to
act justly is closer to piety."[14] "Verily on the Day of Resurrection he who is dearest of all men to Allah, and he who is
nearest to Him will be the just leader; but he who is most
hated by Allah on that Day, and he who is most bitterly punished will be the tyrannical leader."[15]

This refers to that impartial justice which is absolute, and
which cannot be swayed by affection or by hatred; the bases
of this justice cannot be affected by love or by enmity. Such
justice is not.influenced by any relationship between individuals,
or by any hatred between peoples. It is enjoyed by all the

individual members of a Muslim community, without discrimination arising from descent or rank, wealth or influence.
In the same way, such a justice is enjoyed by other peoples,
even though there may be hatred between them and the Muslims. This is a high level of equity, to which no international
law has so far achieved, nor any domestic law either.

Those who reject this justice must necessarily return to
that form of justice which depends on the strength of the
weakness of communities, which is the mark of those who
are regularly at variance one with another. That is, they
must return to that form of justice which the white man administers to the red man in the United States, or which the
white man administers to the colored man in South Africa.
There are other similar instances from contemporary conditions with which everyone is familiar.

The principal care of Islamic justice is that it shall not
be purely theoretical, but that it shall be applied in the realm
of practical life. The historical development of Islam supplies a succession of illustrations of this, which we shall consider in their proper place; here we are concerned to consider only the theoretical aspect, as it is revealed to us in
the ordinances of Islam.

And secondly, there must be obedience on the part of those
who are ruled. "O you who have believed, obey Allah, and
obey the Messenger of Allah and those who hold authority
among you."[16] The fact that this verse groups together Allah, the Messenger, and those who hold authority means that
it clarifies the nature and the limits of this obedience. Obedience to one who holds authority is derived from obedience to
Allah and the Messenger. The ruler in Islamic law is not to
be obeyed because of his own person; he is to be obeyed only
by virtue of holding his position through the law of Allah and
His Messenger; his right to obedience is derived from his
observance of that law, and from no other thing. If he departs from the law, he is no longer entitled to obedience, and
his orders need no longer be obeyed. Thus one authority says
that, "There can be no obedience to any creature which involves disobedience to the Creator." Or again: "Hear and
obey--even if your ruler is an Abyssianian slave with a head
like a raisin, so long as he observes the Book of Allah the
Exalted." It is made very clear by this tradition that to hear
and obey is conditioned by the observance by the ruler of the

Book of Allah the Exalted. An absolute obedience such as this is not to be accorded to the will of the ruler himself, nor can it be a binding thing if he abandons the law of Allah and of His Messenger. "If anyone sees a tyrannical power which is contrary to the will of Allah, which violates the compact of Allah, and which produces evil or enmity among the servants of Allah, and if he does not try to change it by deed or by word, then it is Allah who must supply the initiative."[17] This tradition indicates the necessity of getting rid of a ruler who abandons the law by deed or by word, but with the minimum use of force. This is another necessary step beyond the mere withholding of obedience which is in itself a purely negative measure.

We must make a distinction between the fact that a ruler derives his authority from his observance of the religious law and the theory that a ruler draws his authority from the faith. No ruler has any religious authority direct from Heaven, as had some rulers in ancient times; he occupies his position only by the completely and absolutely free choice of all Muslims; and they are not bound to elect him by any compact with his predecessor, nor likewise is there any necessity for the position to be hereditary in the family. Further, in addition to this, he must derive his authority from his continual enforcement of the law. When the Muslim community is no longer satisfied with him his office must lapse; and even if they are satisfied with him, any dereliction of the law on his part means that he no longer has the right to obedience.

In this we see the wisdom of the Prophet, who did not specify anyone as his successor; had he done so, such a man might have laid claim to some religious authority, as having been appointed by the Messenger.

Thirdly, there must be collaboration between ruler and ruled. "Take counsel with them in the matter."[18] "And their affair is a matter for collaboration between them."[19] Collaboration is one of the fundamentals of Islamic politics, although no specific method of administering it has even been laid down; its application has been left to the exigencies of individual situations. The Messenger used to take the advice of the Muslim community in matters which did not pertain to the spiritual; thus he would ask their opinion in wordly affairs in which they had some skill, such as positions on a field of battle. Thus he listened to their opinion at the battle of Badr, and encamped at the well of Badr, though originally he had been some distance away from it;[20] similarly he listened to them in the matter of digging the trench,[21] and also, against the advice of Umar, in the matter of prisoners, though in this case there eventually came a revelation which supported Umar's point of view.[22] So far as spiritual matters were concerned, of course, in the very nature of the case there was no room for collaboration, since such matters were of the substance of the faith, and were therefore the private affair of the Messenger, the Trusty One.

In the same way the Caliphs continued to collaborate with the Muslims. Abu Bakr did so in the case of those who withheld the poor-tax; he held strongly that war should be declared on them, and though Umar at first opposed him, he finally came to agree with Abu Bakr must fully, Allah having opened his mind to understand that Abu Bakr was set on such a course.[23] Again Abu Bakr took counsel with the Meccans concerning the war in Syria, against the opposition of Umar.[24] And Umar himself took advice in the matter of going into a plague-stricken country; he came to his own conclusion, and subsequently found a precedent in the custom of the Prophet which confirmed him, and thus he kept to his course.[25] Such has been the method of collaboration; it has not followed any well-marked or definite system, because the needs of the moment have never demanded more than this type of informal counsel. And the wide variety of questions which arises leave ample room for a wide range of systems and methods; hence no system is specified by Islam, which is content rather to lay down only the general principle.

* * * * * * *

A ruler, then, has no rights other than those which belong to any individual of the Muslim community--except that he can claim obedience to his command, advice, and help in the enforcement of the law.

Although the Prophet was not strictly a ruler, but rather a religious lawgiver, he yet established the customary limitations which must be oberved by any ruler as governing the rights which Islam grants to him. And Muhammad's successors followed his example in this respect, as we shall see when we deal with the historical development of Islam. Thus he allowed every man to defend his rights, but added that a privileged individual ought to show forgiveness. So when a creditor of his came to him on one occasion and up- braided him, the Muslims were concerned about such a hap- pening; but Muhammad advised them to let the man be, be- cause a creditor had the right to speak his mind. Or again, one day as the camels carrying the alms passed him he stretched out his hand towards a woolen garment carried by one of the beasts, and said: "I have no more right to that garment than has any other Muslim." He once said to Ali and Fatima who were his nearest relatives, "I cannot give to you while leaving the poor members of the community with their bellies racked by hunger."[26] Or once he said to the members of his own clan, the Hashemites, "If my people cannot approach me through their good works, shall you, then, approach me through your genealogies?"

A ruler therefore has no extra privileges as regards the law, or as regards wealth; and his family have no such privileges either, beyond those of the generality of Muslims.

And that is essentially Islam.

No ruler dare oppress the souls or the bodies of Muslims, nor dare he infringe upon their sanctities, nor touch their wealth. If he upholds the law and sees that religious duties are observed, then he has reached the limit of his powers. At that point his power over his people has reached its end; Allah Himself protects them from his power, in soul and body, in their sanctities and their wealth. For the Muslim faith safeguards them in these respects by clear and unmis- takable commands. This it does in a way which leaves no room for doubt of the intensity of its desire to safeguard faith and peace and honor to all and sundry. "O you who have believed, do not enter houses other than your own without first being received as friends and giving a greeting to the inmates."[27] "It is not good to approach your houses from the back."[28] "But approach your houses by the doors."[29] "Do not play the spy."[30] "Every Muslim is sacrosanct to every other Mus- lim, his blood, his honor, and his property."[31] A life for a life, and retaliation for wounds.

* * * * * * *

But while Islam sets a strict limit to the power of a ruler so far as he is personally concerned, it gives him the broad- est possible powers in looking after matters of welfare which pertain to the community; such matters are those in which

there is no guiding precedent in existence, and which evolve
with the processes of time and with changing conditions. The
general principle is that "A ruler may make as many new
decrees as he finds new problems." This is the application
of the Qur'anic saying "And He has put no limitation on you
in the matter of religion."[32] and of the Messenger's phrase,
"There must be no hardship and no contention." It also con-
firms the general aims of this faith, namely, to improve the
status of the individual, as well as that of society and that
of man in general; this must be done in accordance with the
principles established by Islam, and must be conditioned by
the conception of universal justice.

It is the responsibility of the ruler to put an end to anything which occasions hardship in the community, no matter
what it may be; it is similarly his duty to encourage anything
which is of any kind of profit to the community. But at all
times he must be careful not to depart from the ordinances
of Islam.

These are wide powers which touch every aspect of life;
and the establishment of social justice in all its aspects is a
matter which is bound up with these powers. A ruler may,
for example, go beyond the legal requirements in the matter
of money; in addition to the poor-tax he may introduce other
taxes by which to encourage equality and justice; by these he
may check malice and ill-feeling, and by these he may remove from the community the evils of luxury and penury, as
well as that of artificially high prices, all of which evils are
the product of the growth of excessive wealth. And similarly
with all the other matters which are within the disposal of
the ruler.

The historical development of the life of the Islamic community has provided many examples of this care for the public welfare. Illustrations can be given from every period,
and a discussion of this will follow in due course. The important thing for the moment is to establish the fact that Islam is not a rigid system, and that its practical applications
are to be found not merely in one age of history, nor only
in one quarter of the world.

* * * * * * *

To continue: This discussion so far has been only of the
statutory aspect of political theory in Islam. But beyond this
there lies the voluntary aspect in which exhortation passes

beyond what the law dictates; this is the Islamic custom in
dealing with all its responsibilities and all its requirements.
It leaves the lower level of achievement to the law, while to
exhortation it prescribes the achievement of the higher level;
thus it leaves for man a wide space between these two, a
gap which he can overcome as best he may.

Political theory in Islam stands on the foundation of conscience rather than on that of law. It stands on the conviction
that Allah is present at every moment alike with the ruler
and with the ruled, watching over both. "Whatever servant
there may be to whom Allah gives the care of his subjects,
if he does not guard them carefully, he shall never see a
trace of Paradise." "And do not consume your wealth among
yourselves vainly; do not display it before rulers in order
guiltily to consume a part of the people's wealth, while you
are aware of it."[33]

The ruler and his subjects together must bow to the
authority of Allah in all things; reverence for Allah is the
final guarantee of the establishment of justice. We have already discovered that Islam lays upon the reformed human
conscience great responsibilities in the matters of politics
and economics. But when reverence for Allah is not in that
conscience, then there is no safeguard; for the law can always be deceived or evaded, and the ruler, the judge, or
the people be cheated.

We shall see later that this consciencewhich Islam fosters
and reforms has undertaken momentous things, and has produced results which appeared to be impossible and amazing
in Muslim life through the passage of the centuries.

VI. Economic Theory in Islam

A treatment of economic theory is perhaps the most essential part of any discussion of social justice, and it may
be that many readers have thought the promise of this book
slow of realization as they have read through the opening
chapters to this point. But this delay has been deliberate;
for social justice in Islam is a greater thing than mere economic theory, as we have already seen, and it seemed necessary first to discover the general teaching of Islam on
social justice. It was necessary also to discuss the nature,
the foundations, and the methods of this justice in the broadest
sense. And only now are we ready to turn to the matter of
money itself, though it is this matter that takes pride of
place in the materialistic philosophies which emphasize the
economic values at the expense of all others.

Islam enters the field of economic theory under the influence of its universal philosophy, and guided by its general
ideology. Its interests are the welfare of the individual and
the ensuring of the welfare of society. In these interests it
holds a position of doing injury neither to the individual nor
to society; it does not oppose human nature, nor on the other
hand does it seek to impede the fundamental customs and the
high and far-reaching objectives of life.

In order to implement this ideal Islam makes use of its
two fundamental methods: legislation and exhortation. By
the former it achieves the practical objective of being responsible for the maintenance of a healthy community, capable
of growth and improvement; by the latter it aims at raising
men above the level of instinct to achieve a more developed
form of life. Its objective is to improve life in general to
that ideal state which admittedly all men cannot achieve under
all conditions, but to the height and perfection of which Islam
ever keeps the way open.

First, then, we shall discuss one illustration, the matter
of property, and after that we shall proceed to treat of economic theory in detail.

Islam has always laid one duty upon property, and that is

the payment of the poor-tax; this is the one ground on which
a ruler may use force against his subjects, if they withhold
this tax, and similarly it is the one thing which he can impose
on them by legal right, because his powers cover such impo-
sition. Further, Islam has given to a ruler the right of
exacting in addition to the poor-tax as much as will prevent
hardship and do away with penury and preserve the well-
being of the Muslim community. This, when there is need
of it, is a right similar to that of the poor-tax, a right whose
use depends on the communal welfare and on the justice of
the ruler.

So far the law can go; thereafter exhortation has com-
mended to the people the practice of getting rid of all money,
expending it entirely in the way of Allah. This is the meaning of the tradition related by Abu-Dharr concerning Muhammad, as follows: The Messenger of Allah went out one day
in the direction of Uhud,[1] and I went with him. He said, "Abu-
Dharr," and I answered, "At your service, O Messenger of
Allah." He said, "The greatest shall be the least on the Day
of Resurrection, except for the man who spends thus and thus";
and he gestured to right and left, in front and behind; "And
little indeed shall they be." Afterwards he said, "Abu Dharr."
and I replied, "Yes, Messenger of Allah; you are dearer to
me than my father and mother." He said, "It gives me
pleasure to have something such as my possessions at Uhud,
which I can expend in the way of Allah, so that when I die I
shall leave only two pennies' worth of it." I said, "Nay, but
rather you should leave two thousand, O Messenger of Allah."
He replied, "No; it will be but two pennies' worth." Then
he added, "Abu Dharr, you desire the most, I the least."

So when Muhammad came to the last hour to which all men
must come, when he was acutely ill and near to death, he
remembered that he had six or seven pounds in his possession.
He commanded his household to give this away in alms; but
immediately a fainting fit overtook him, so that his household were too busy attending him to carry out his order. When
he recovered from his faint, the first thing he asked was,
"What has happened to that money?" Discovering that it had
not yet been given away, he fell into a fit of anger and commanded that A'isha be brought in; then he took the money in
his hand, saying, "How could Muhammad face his Lord if he
were to meet Allah with these in his possession?" And at
once all the money was given as alms.

Thus there are these two things, legislation and exhortation, which together are the groundwork of economic theory, as they are the groundwork of all Islamic theory.

And now we may start on our detailed explanatory study.

* * * * * * *

The Right of Individual Possession

Islam ratifies the right of individual possession--by legal means of acquisition which will shortly be explained--and to this ratification it adds the corollaries which will ensure this right to its possessor. It guards him from theft, from being plundered or robbed, and from being cheated by any means whatever. To accomplish all this, it lays down restrictive legislation; but in addition it provides reformatory exhortations to prevent men coveting what is not their own, but belongs to other people. Upon the same basis are laid the other corollaries, such as the right to dispose of personal property by sale or mortgage or contract, by presentation or bequest or legacy. And so on through all the legal methods of property disposal and all the customary means of relinquishing money.

There is nothing else similar to this clear and definite ratification of such rights, as it is made by Islam. "Men shall have a portion of what they have earned, and women shall have a portion of what they have earned."[2] "Give to orphans their money, and do not exchange the good for the evil."[3] "As for the wall, it belonged to two orphan youths in the town, and under it was a treasure belonging to them. Their father was a worthy man, and your Lord wishes that they might reach full age before finding out their treasure as a mercy from your Lord."[4]

The stern Islamic punishment for theft is an indication of the sanctity of this right of possession, of the way in which it is guarded, and of the necessity for preventing its being infringed. "As for the thief, man or woman, cut off their hands as a recompense for what they have piled up--a chastisement from Allah."[5] Or in the case of rape, the man who perpetrates such a crime is excommunicate and accursed; the Messenger of Allah said: "Whoever violates the marriage bond on the earth shall have seven earths hung about his neck." And the same with plundering: "He who plunders is not one of us." "Surely no man's property is lawful for you, save only with the good will of the owner." "Every Muslim is sacrosant to every other Muslim--his blood, his honor and his property."

Similar to the right of possession is that of receiving and giving an inheritance. "Men shall have a portion of what their parents and their near relatives leave; and women shall have a portion of what their parents and their near relatives leave." "Allah commands you concerning your children that a boy shall receive the same share as two girls." "They will ask you for a decision. Say: Allah gives you a decision about relationships. If a man dies without a son and if he has a sister, then she shall have half of what he leaves...etc."

This ratification of the right of individual possession and the guarding of it ensure an equality between effort and recompense. This is over and above the fact that it is in accordance with human nature and in agreement with the fundamental inclinations of man's soul; for it is with these inclinations that Islam reckons when it establishes its whole social system. But at the same time this conception is in accordance with the welfare of society, because it encourages the individual to give his utmost to the advancement of life.

Every man is created with a natural love of wealth for its own sake; "Verily the love of wealth is strong." He is naturally endowed with a love of possession, and with a niggardliness of what he possesses: "Say: If you had possessed the treasures of the mercy of my Lord, then you would have been gripped by the fear of spending." "And souls are near to avarice." There is no harm in the competition which arises from these natural inclinations; for it encourages every man to give of his best so that he is zealous to work and to earn; and such work he both wants and needs. He is not conscious of being forced to work, and hence he does not expend his labor grudgingly or hopelessly. But in the end it is society which profits from his labor and his toil; and so Islam lays down principles which will ensure that profit to society, and which will make it certain that no harm can arise from such complete freedom of the individual, or from the ratification of his right of personal possession.

Justice demands that the social system shall conform to the desires of the individual and satisfy his inclinations--at least so far as will not injure society--as a return for his contribution to it in the way of ability and labor; in the sweat of his brow, in the labor of his thought, and in the work of his hands. Justice is the greatest of the foundations of Islam; but justice is not always concerned to serve the interests of

the individual. Justice is for the individual, but it is for
society also, if we are willing to tread the middle way;
and so we must have in our life justice in all its shapes and
forms.

Over and above all this, it is undeniable that the breaking
down of natural and accepted barriers may bring some benefit to the individual and to society; but it is low estimate of
human nature which would make such reckless breaking of
all bounds the one and only method of achieving justice. On
the other hand, it is only fanciful theories, not rooted in
practical experience, which would suppose that such bounds
can be imposed from without through systems of government
or law, in one nation or in a number of nations. Islam has
no such low estimate of human nature; but at the same time
it has no intention of building all its social structure on such
fanciful theories which ignore all the depths of experience.

Similarly it is possible to say that the sanctity of human
nature claims the profoundest and greatest respect from us,
because of its intrinsic value, its exalted character, and its
noble origin; when we seek to exhort that nature or to legislate for it, we must do so with great wisdom, with passionate
honesty, and with penetrating insight. For it is unthinkable
that the experience of millions of years through which man
has lived should be spent in vain; or that we should construct
theories based on man's character and nature and ways, and
then suffer these theories to be submerged by violence and
force.

With the ratification of the right to receive or give an inheritance we have already dealt in the section on mutual
social responsibility. This right is inconformity with the
nature of man which we are discussing here, just as it is in
conformity with justice in the highest sense of equality; it is
equally in conformity with the welfare of the community,
using that term in the widest sense which knows no barriers
between one nation and another throughout the human race.
And not only so, but this right of inheritance is one of the
methods of putting an end to excessive wealth, as we shall
see.

The Right of the Disposal of Property

But Islam does not establish the right of personal possession absolutely, without bounds or limitations; it certainly

ratifies that right, but along with it are ratified other principles which almost make it theoretical rather than practical.
They almost strip a man bare of his right to possession by
the time that he has fulfilled all the necessary conditions.
Islam establishes such limitations and bounds as almost
render a man bound rather than free in his disposal of his
property, whether he increases, spends, or administers it.
But it is consideration for the welfare of society which lies
behind all this; it is also consideration for the welfare of
the individual himself with regard to the universal objectives
by which Islam orders its view of life.

The cardinal principle which Islam ratifies along with that
of the right of individual possession is that the individual is
in a way a steward of his property on behalf of society; his
tenure of property is a form of salary which is greater than
the actual right of possession. Property in the widest sense
is a right which can belong only to society, which in turn receives it as a trust from Allah who is the only true owner of
anything.

Thus the glorious Qur'an says: "Believe in Allah and in
His Messenger; and spend of that of which He has given you
the stewardship."[6] The text of this verse needs no explanation to bring out the meaning; for its meaning is apparent,
namely, that property which is in the hands of men belongs
to Allah, and that men are its stewards rather than its masters. Or in another verse which concerns those who give
certificates of manumission to slaves, "Give them of the
property of Allah, which He has given you."[7] They are not
giving to the slaves this property out of their own possessions, but out of the property of Allah of which they are the
guardians. Or clearest of all in a third verse, "Allah has
favored some of you more than others in the matter of a
competence. Yet those who have been thus favored will not
give back such provision to the slaves whom they possess;
in that respect they are equal. Will they thus deny the goodness
of Allah?"[8] Here we have the definite affirmation that when
those who have been favored in their competence give to their
slaves, it is not only an equitable division between some who
are rich and others who are poor. Not that in the least. This
share is nothing more than the basic right of the latter, who
have just as good a claim to it; and so they are equal in it.
There is only one solution: one party has exactly the same

right to receive as the other has to give. Then follows the
disapproving question, "Will they thus deny the goodness of
Allah?" Property is "the goodness of Allah"; it is not man's
own possession.

There can be no clearer indication of the true nature of
the possession of property than to describe it as the power
of disposal and of profit. The outcome of this definition is
that there can be no real place for personal possession unless it carries with it the rights of disposal and profit. The
condition on which this right must stand is that of wisdom in
the disposal; if the disposal of property is foolish, then the
law of society may withdraw this right of disposal. "Do not
give to fools the property which Allah has given you to manage,
but rather provide for them out of it, and clothe them."[9]
Thus the right of disposal depends on being of sound mind and
on complete fulfillment of one's duties; when the possessor
does not meet these requirements, then the natural fruits of
ownership come to an end; that is, the right of disposal is
annulled. This is also clearly shown in the fact that if a man
dies without an heir, his legal heir is the Imam (the head of
the religious community); thus it appears that the property
belongs to society and is merely administered by an individual,
so that when his stewardship is over the property reverts to
its original ownership, the community.

I have not emphasized this principle in order to teach any
communistic doctrine of property, for the right of personal
possession is firmly established in Islam. I have emphasized
it because it is significant in the creation of a true understanding of the nature of personal possession, and an understanding of how these two ideas are reconciled in the general
Islamic view of property. In other and clearer words: The
individual must realize that he is no more than the steward
of this property, which is fundamentally the possession of
society; this must make him accept the restrictions which
the system lays upon his liberty, and the bounds which limit
his rights of disposal. On the other side, society must realize
its fundamental right to such property, and must thus become
bolder in prescribing the regulations and in laying down the
laws which concern it. Thus only may we arrive at principles
which will ensure complete social justice in the profitable
use of property, which cannot be an end in itself, nor an object of any man's purely personal possession. The clearest

instance of this is the matter of the tenure of land; thought
cannot conceive that any man should be the owner of the land
itself; all that he can possess is its produce and its crops,
which means that the matter is one of the profitable use of a
possession rather than one of a purely personal possession.

Another principle which Islam ratifies is that of the profitable use of property, though of this the faith does not wholly
approve, because such property may be retained in the hands
of a small number of individuals who share it between them,
so that others can have no part in it. "In order that it may
not be passed around between the rich among you." A story
attaches to this text, which gives us the full meaning of this
general Islamic principle.

The Emigrants had gone with the Prophet of Allah from
Mecca to Medina; the poor had no money to take with them,
and the rich had left their property behind them, so that they
were as poor as the poor. But the Helpers were of generous
mind, and were above the natural avarice which lies in the
human soul; so they took the Emigrants as brothers in everything that they possessed. Out of the goodness of their hearts
and of the nobility of their minds this action extended as far
as their most intimate personal belongings. "They loved
those who had emigrated to them, and they found no desire
in their hearts for the share which had fallen to others; they
preferred them above themselves, though among themselves
there was poverty."[10] Thus they provided a pleasing example
of the effect of religious belief on individuals, and thus they
gave a perfect pattern for the attaining of freedom from
worldly desires and the achievement of freedom to seek
higher things.

Yet there continued to be a wide gap between the rich
Medinese and the poor Emigrants; the Prophet saw the generosity and liberality of the Helpers, but saw no need to
check it; for he wanted to give them back more than they had
given. Hence he saw no need to order them to take back any
of what they had given to the Emigrants, since they had
adopted them as brothers in everything they possessed. Then
came the affair of the Banu Nadir,[11] when there was no warfare, because the Prophet made a truce with these opponents.
Accordingly the booty in this case belonged rightfully to Allah and His Messenger in its entirety; it is not so in a case
of active war, where four-fifths of the booty belongs to those

who have done the fighting, and only the remaining fifth to
Allah and to the Messenger. In this case the Messenger decided to restore some form of equality to the Muslim community as regards the possession of wealth; accordingly he
presented the booty of the Banu Nadir to the Emigrants for
their personal use. With them he included two of the poorer
Helpers who were specifically mentioned when the decision
was revealed to him that the entire booty was to be given
over to the Emigrants.

Concerning this event the Qur'an says: "What Allah has
given to His Messenger as booty from the people of the villages belongs to Allah and the Messenger , to the relatives,
the orphans, the poor, and the wayfarer, in order that it may
not be passed around between the rich among you. Take what
the Messenger gives you, and refrain from what he forbids;
show piety towards Allah, for Allah can punish severely. The
booty shall be for the Emigrants who were expelled from their
dwellings and their property, seeking favor and approval from
Allah. They helped Allah and His Messenger; they are the
upright."[12]

This disposal of property by the Messenger and the emphasis on that disposal in the Qur'an provide a clear and self-
evident proof of the correctness of the Islamic principle that
it is undesirable to have wealth concentrated in the hands of
a few members of the community. It means also that there
must be a readjustment of the foundations underlying this
custom, so that here also there may be some form of equity.
"In order that it may not be passed around between the rich
among you."

That is to say, an excess of wealth on one side and a lack
of it on the other produces a profound corruption, greater
even than that produced by hatred and rancor. Wherever an
abundance of wealth is found, it is like an abundance of vital
strength in the body; it must find outlets, and there can be
no permanent guarantee that such outlets will be moral and
worthy. Thus wealth also must take its course, sometimes
in the form of a luxury which corrupts the soul and enervates
the body, sometimes in the form of desires which have to be
satisfied. The effect of these desires is to be found on the
other side of the community, which lacks wealth; here this
effect takes the form of the sale or barter of personal honor,
or the form of flattery, or falsehood, or the destruction of

personality--all simply to satisfy the desires of the wealthy
and to pander to their false vanity; for necessity easily over-
comes opposition. The over-wealthy man on the other hand
is concerned only to find an outlet for his excess of vitality
and for his excess of wealth. And thus moral degradation in
all its forms--drinking, gambling, slave-trading, and pro-
cury, the spoiling of manhood and the loss of honor--is only
the outcome of an excess of wealth on one side, and a lack
of it on the other. And the unequal balance of society is a
product of this discrimination.

All this takes no account of the personal hatreds and the
individual jealousies roused by those who have immoderate
wealth in the hearts of the poor who cannot find enough for
their needs. The reaction here is sometimes hatred, sometimes a feeling of degradation and debasement; such men
feel that their status is lowered in their own eyes and their
honor sullied in face of the power and influence of wealth.
Thus they are reduced to a small and humble manhood which
knows nothing but the desire to please the rich and the powerful.

Islam, despite the emphasis which it lays on the spiritual
values, is not unmindful of the importance of economic values;
and no matter how much it seeks to raise men above the
material considerations of this world, it never lays greater
obligations on them than their human nature is able to bear.
Therefore it disapproves of money being circulated only
among the rich, and so it makes the avoidance of this one of
the principles of its economic theory.

Thus we have here the concept of a communal wealth which
cannot be restricted to individuals, a wealth of which the Messenger enumerated three aspects, water, herbage, and fire.
"All men share in three things, water, herbage, and fire."
In these terms he described the essentials for the life of the
community in his native Arabia; and so the profitable use of
these things must be for the community as a whole. Now the
necessities of communal life vary from one country to another,
and from one age to another; but the analogy--for this is one
of the fundamental laws of Islam--is easily applied to all
other things which fall into the category of necessities. But
this is another subject which will be discussed in its proper
place in the course of this book.

There is, then, a proportion of all wealth which belongs

by right to the needy members of the community; this proportion is prescribed as the poor-tax. "And of their wealth
a portion belongs by right to the beggar and the destitute."
Nor is this concept restricted to personal possessions; it
covers communal possessions also, and the money arising
from it must be used in specified ways. "The alms money
is only for the poor and the destitute...etc."

A true statement of the Islamic view of individual possession would therefore be this: The fundamental principle is
that property belongs to the community in general; individual
possession is a stewardship which carries with it conditions
and limitations. Some property is held in common, and this
no individual has any right to possess. A proportion of all
property is a due which must be paid to the community, in
order that the latter may disburse it to specified individuals
of its own number; these constitute cases of need which may
thereby be remedied so that the community may preserve its
health.

The Methods of Individual Acquisition

On the basis of this theory of the nature of possessions
Islam organizes its logical results; it lays down the conditions
of acquisition and the limitations of disposal; it establishes
customary limits for profitable use, in cases where these
are not immediately derived from considerations of social
welfare and of individual welfare which forms a part of social
welfare.

Thus it emphasizes first of all that possession in the sense
of profitable use of property is impossible except by the authority of the law which is the guardian of social affairs. "It
is the law which really gives to men their possessions, because it gives them legal status." And the same thought occurs among the definitions: "Possession is a legal matter,
whether it be absolute possession or possession for usufruct;
and he who has the profitable use of anything or who accepts
an equivalent value for anything needs the ratification of the
law."

"This definition means that possession cannot be permanent
unless it is legally declared to be so and ratified; and this
finding is confirmed by all the canon law of Islam. For all
rights, that of possession among them, are lacking in permanence except by legal process and ratification of the trans-

action. Right of possession is not an intrinsic quality of things, but arises from the sanction of the law, which alone can give legal effect to the preceding transactions."113

This ruling must be borne in mind by anyone who tries to explain the Islamic theory of the right of possession; it represents the handing over by the law, acting for the community, to an individual of some particular thing to which the individual has no right except in virtue of this legal act. For the principle is that everything belongs to the community, and therefore all permission for personal possession must come from the law, virtually or actually.

The only method in Islam of gaining the right of acquisition is by work of any kind or variety. Here again we see the idea of equality between effort and reward. To explain this we may say that the methods of acquisition of wealth which are recognized by Islam are as follows:

First, hunting. This was the original desert method of livelihood in human history; and it still exists as a means of gaining a form of wealth by more advanced and modern methods; for fishing and pearl-diving, coral-fishing and sponge-diving are profitable pursuits both for governments and for individuals. There is still also the hunting of birds and animals, both for sport and for profit.

Second, irrigating waste lands which have no owner, by any method of irrigation. Here the individual must continue his irrigation of the ground for a space of three years after he has put his hand to it. If he does not, then his right of possession lapses, because the purpose of irrigating waste land is to ensure general prosperity through its full employment. Three years is a sufficient test of the ability of any man who puts his hand to the task; if such ability has not then shown itself, the land reverts to the community and no individual can sequestrate it. "The land belongs to Allah and His Messenger, and after that to you; if any man irrigates waste land, then it shall be his, and none shall have the right of sequestration after three years."

Islamic law here is wiser than common law which is derived from French law. For in common law, "setting the hand to it" must be followed by a period of fifteen years before the land can pass into the possession of him who sets his hand to it. And the result is the same whether he has irrigated the land or left it waste during that period and the en-

suing period. Such a result is of course incompatible with
the Islamic emphasis on the true nature of possession, for
what we find here is purely a theory of practical expediency.
So great is the difference between Islamic theory and that of
common law.

Third, the production of minerals hidden in the earth, or
mining. This occupation leaves four-fifths of the value of the
minerals produced as the possession of the worker; the other
fifth is poor-tax, since such mining is allowable, and the
individual earns by his own labor and toil. But here we must
reckon with this saying: All the mining which has been done
up to the time with which this statement deals has been of
metals which are little used, such as gold and silver; or it
has been of things which are not necessities for the whole of
the community, such as petroleum and coal. Can petroleum
and coal and similar things be compared with the common
necessities such as water and herbage and fire? Or can they
be compared with that mining which was profitable in the first
days of the Islamic era? We shall leave our discussion of
this to its proper place in this book.

Fourth, raiding. From this comes the possession of plunder, which consists of everything possessed by an unbeliever
who has been killed by a Muslim. "The plunder of an unbeliever who has been killed belongs to the man who killed him."
Again there comes under this head the possession of booty;
four-fifths of this go to those who have done the fighting, while
the other fifth goes to Allah and the Messenger. "And know
that whatever you take as booty, one fifth of it belongs to
Allah and the Messenger, to the relatives, the orphans, the
poor, and the wayfarer."[14]

Fifth, working for a wage for others. Islam gives regard
and honor to this type of work, and calls for the prompt payment of wages in full and without deductions. The Qur'an advocates such work, making it a source of honor in the eyes
of all who see it, and a matter for regard and esteem. "Say:
Work, and Allah will see your work, as will His Messenger
and the Believers."[15] In this there lies an incitement to true
and faithful work. There is also honor for work, because it
is worthy of regard and consideration and esteem. So in
another passage the Qur'an urges men to effort and exertion
in the earth for this same cause: "So walk about in the earth
in all its regions, and eat of what it provides."[16]

The Messenger also went far to give religious sanction to personal work, when he accepted a hand swollen with constant toil, saying: "This is a hand which is beloved of Allah and His Messenger." And many other traditions have come down to us, which reiterate this religious sanction. "He who in the evening is weary from manual labor shall receive pardon for his sins that very same evening." "Verily Allah loves the servant who practices a trade." "Whatever food any one of you eats, let it be nothing but the fruit of his hands." And we have already seen how Islam makes work a form of worship, and how indeed it rates it above all formal worship. Thus it estimates that the man who works and supports a brother renowned for his piety is actually the more pious of the two. [17]

On the basis of this theory which attaches a religious significance to work, Islam gives a religious sanction also to the claim of the worker to his wage. It demands first of all that he be paid in full; it warns any employer who acts unjustly towards his men that he is earning for himself the enmity and the hatred of Allah. The Messenger of Allah once said: "Thus saith Allah, the Great, the Glorious: Three there are whom I will hate on the Day of Resurrection--a man to whom I have been generous, and who has betrayed My generosity, a man who sells a free man into slavery and lives off the price, and a man who hires another at a stipulated wage, and then will not give him his due." The collocation of these three forms of disobedience and the identity of their punishment have a particular significance. The first is deceit because it is a betrayal of the protection of Allah, the second is an unavenged crime against the essential nature of a free man for motives of profit, and the third is living off the sweat of a hired man. This last is similar to living off the price of a free man sold into slavery, thus betraying his essential humanity; it is similar to breaking an oath which has been sworn in the name of Allah, thus betraying the protection of the Creator. All of these things merit the enmity and the hatred of Allah because of their infamy, and because of the disgraceful nature of such a betrayal.

In the second place Islam demands that the payment of wages be punctual. It is not enough that they should be paid in full; they must also be paid in time. The Messenger says: "Pay your hired man his wages before the sweat is dry on him." Islam here seeks to meet both a spiritual and material need in the life of the worker. The spiritual need is that he must know that he is an object of care and concern; speed in the payment of wages conveys this knowledge, and makes him realize that his labor is valuable and his place in society assured. The material need is that the worker is generally in need of his wage from day to day in order to provide the material necessities for himself, his wife, and his children. So late payment harms him by denying him the fruits of his labor and toil at the most necessary time, and it lessens his zeal and willingness to work. Whereas Islam is insistent that all should work who are able, and that they should do as much as they can; thus from work they may gain a spiritual satisfaction and a material sufficiency at the same time.

Again Islam prohibits any worker from allocating any part of his wages to anyone such as an overseer, as if there could be here any "workers' leader," who does not work himself but who demands a share of the wages of every worker. The Prophet said: "Beware of allocations." When we asked, "What are allocations?" he replied: "A man controls a party among the people, and he exacts a due from this one and a due from that one." This is contrary to one of the principles of Islam, that there must be no pay without work, no wealth without labor. And over and above this, such a system contains the possibility of oppression and ruin for the worker.

In return for this care for the rights of the worker, Islam requires of him that he on his side shall perform his work fully and faithfully; for every right carries a corresponding responsibility in Islam. "Verily Allah is pleased when one of your does a piece of work of which He can approve." This is but natural as a consequence of the equality between effort and reward; it is natural also from the point of view of the character on which Islam insists as the basis of true life. For dishonesty and careless work indicate a corruption of the spirit of man, and a deadness of his conscience. To indulge in such laziness and to become habituated to it tends to make the spirit of man idle and his conscience void. And beyond that, the welfare of society as a whole is disturbed and menaced by poor work.

Sixth, the assigning of ownership of a piece of land which does not belong to anyone. Such is land pertaining to the Muslim public treasury, taken from the unbelievers who can-

not have the right of inheritance; its custodian is the Imam.
Or it may be land which is waste; it again has no owner. The
Prophet assigned land to Abu Bakr and Umar, and the Caliphs
after him did the same, as a reward for meritorious effort
or service to Islam. But this was always done within narrow
limits, and always of land which had no owner or waste land.
When the Umayyads[18] came to power they assigned lands to
their relatives, but they were oppressive tyrants rather than
orthodox Muslim rulers, as we shall see.

Seventh, money necessary to sustain life. Islam prescribes
the use of money drawn from the poor-tax in specified ways.
"The alms money is only for the poor and the destitute, for
those employed in collecting it, for those who have to be won
over to Islam, for the ransom of slaves and the relief of
debtors, for spending in the way of Allah, and for the wayfarer."[19] Any man who comes into any one of these categories is eligible for a share of the poor-tax. There are
some who will not work and who draw the poor-tax as being
in need; but need is an unsatisfactory substitute for work. It
is work to which Islam gives religious significance, and which
thereby becomes the first and the best means of acquiring
the right of possession.

These are the methods which Islam recognizes as the
methods of legal acquisition; anything outside of these is rejected and condemned. Thus plundering, theft, robbery,
and misappropriation do not confer the right of possession.
Neither does gambling, which is forbidden: "Wine and gambling,
the use of lots and arrows are only an abomination, a work of
Satan. Turn away from them, then, and it may be that you
will prosper."[20] Money which comes by a forbidden method
is also forbidden, for gambling is not work but simply robbery. In addition it gives rise to enmity and hatred between
the gamblers themselves, because it is incompatible with the
original practice of Islam, which was to spread the spirit of
love and mutual help and fellowship. "Satan only wishes to
cause enmity and hatred among you by means of wine and
gambling."[21]

The reason for the acceptance of these seven methods of
acquisition is clearly the fact that they are all based on the
expending of effort; this effort must be rewarded, for it is
one of the valuable things in life; in it there lies power for
the cultivation of the earth, for the profit of society, for the

reformation of the spirit of man, and for the purification of his conscience. There is nothing like work for reforming the soul, strengthening the body, and guarding the whole nature of man from the diseases of flabbiness and weakness.

So long as there is work it will remain the prime cause of the right of acquisition; it will also be of itself the ratification of the right of individual possession--but always within limits already described, to ensure that no one is injured by it. Rather it must provide an incentive to the individual to give his utmost effort, so that his natural desire for possession may be satisfied. But he must always work in the legally accepted ways, and must injure no other by his work. When he departs from these ways, then in order to achieve justice he must be brought back to them without losing his zeal for work and becoming one of the idle and profitless weaklings.

Along with the Islamic theory of the possession of property we must enter into the method of passing on such possessions. Here no absolute freedom is granted, a fact which is clearly seen in the regulations governing inheritance and bequest. Gifts and presents alone are free of all restraint; in these matters the individual is given full liberty to give away or donate as much of his property as he wishes, while he is still alive. The reason for this freedom is that there is an inherent personal restriction on such giving, inasmuch as a man of property cannot continue to give money away, and will not donate more than a part of his wealth, so that his heir may not suffer as he well may in the case of bequests.

But when a man dies and his money passes to those who succeed him as heirs or as beneficiaries under his will, the passing on of such money is liable to regulations under a system which is laid down on certain bases. There can be no bequest to the heir, and there can be no bequeathing of more than one third of the total estate; this is the extreme limit. Bequests are controlled, as we have said, in order to avoid some of the emergencies which may arise; for examp it may happen that near relatives are unable to inherit, though their relationship entitles them to a share, because their degree of relationship lets other heirs take precedence of them in the estate. So bequests are controlled, as being more of the nature of inheritance than a form of generosity or almsgiving.

The passing on of property by inheritance is governed by the specific regulations contained in the two verses of the Qur'an dealing with this question; these we have already quoted in the section on mutual responsibility in society.[22]

The general principle of the division of an estate is this: a man shall have the same share as two women, the reason for which we have already explained. An heir from the paternal side of the family takes precedence over one from the mother's side, even though there may be circumstances under which the latter should have the larger share; this is the result of a balancing of responsibilities against rights. For the inheritor on the paternal side was charged with greater responsibilities to the testator. In the same way the son in a family inherits everything after the grandparents have received their portion; for it was he who was primarily responsible for maintaining his father during the lifetime of the latter, if need arose. A full brother takes precedence over a half-brother, because it was on him that the responsibility fell of maintaining his brother if he was unable to earn his own living. Thus by a just system of division a balance is struck between obligations and rewards, between responsibilities and privileges.

The reason for this principle of inheritance has already been sufficiently discussed in the section on mutual responsibility in society; there we showed its connection with the basic principles of Islam as they apply to this mutual responsibility, and as they apply to the ties of relationship and nationality. We also showed the interest which Islam has in this regard for the nature, the inclination, and the needs of the individual and of society alike.

Here we must only discuss the reason for the inheritance regulations as touching society. As we have already seen, Islam is opposed to the heaping up of wealth, and to its being confined within a limited circle. The inheritance regulations are a means towards decreasing the swollen fortunes of the whole world. For the one property passes at the death of its owner to a multitude of children and relatives, and so becomes a number of fortunes of medium or small dimensions. It is seldom that such a fortune retains its original unity under this system, except under rare and anomalous conditions; for example, a man may die leaving only one son to inherit the whole estate, because he has neither father nor mother,

wife nor daughter. But in the majority of cases the fortune
is divided up between a number of individuals.

When we compare this with the English system, under
which the whole estate goes to the eldest son, the wisdom
of Islam is apparent in dividing up the one single fortune; it
is equally clear that the system is just to the various heirs,
for it does not give them any ill-feeling for the eldest son.

Ways of Increasing Possessions

Along with the Islamic theory of the possession of property
we must consider the question of the way of increasing and
using it. The wealthy man is not allowed absolute freedom
to dispose of his money in this way as he may wish. For beyond his individual interests there are those of society, in
the service of which his property must be used.

Every individual has freedom to increase his wealth, but
only within legally prescribed limits. He is permitted to till
the ground, he is allowed to transform raw materials into
finished products, he may carry on retail trade; but he may
not hold a monopoly on any of the necessities of life, and he
may not put out his money at interest, thus to grow and increase. All these things are forbidden. These reputable
methods of increase are the only methods which Islam coun-
tenances for the growth of wealth, but these do not generally
produce that degree of capital which sets a wide gulf between
the social classes. Capital only reaches the disgracefully
swollen proportions which we see today when it is amassed
by swindling, by usury, by oppression of the workers, by
monopolies or exploitation of the needs of the community, by
robbing, plundering, despoiling and pillaging--and by all the
other semi-criminal methods of contemporary exploitation.
This is what Islam does not permit. We shall now consider
these in turn; and we start with an explanation of the wisdom
of Islamic law on the methods of increase.

* * * * * * *

Islam forbids dishonesty in business; "He who swindles is
not one of us." "When two make a bargain and are not at
variance, so long as they tell the truth and deal openly, bles-
sings shall attend their bargain; but if they deal covertly and
falsely, all blessing is denied to their bargain." So you must
buy and sell without dishonesty, both in commodities and in
labor. If your article has a blemish,. you must point it out;

if you do not do so, then you are being dishonest and your
profit is unlawful. Nor can you escape the punishment of
your dishonesty by giving away the unlawful profit as alms;
for alms cannot be reckoned to your credit unless they are
given from your lawful possessions. It is told on the authority of Ibn Mas'ud that the Messenger of Allah said: "No servant of Allah who makes unlawful wealth can give it away in
alms and expect it to be received; nor can he spend it and
expect to receive a blessing from it; nor even can he leave
it behind his back without its pushing him forward into Hell-
fire. Verily Allah does not blot out one evil by another;
rather He blots out evil with good. So wickedness cannot
blot out wickedness." Again he said: "Flesh fattened upon
unlawful profit shall not enter Paradise, but Hell shall have
possession of all such."

In this matter Islam is following its essential principles,
just as it does in preventing injury to men and in emphasizing
the need for mutual help between all men. For dishonesty in
business is a defiling of the conscience; it involves the injury of others and the destruction of the trusting nature of
men; and there can be no mutual help without trust. Besides
which, the proceeds of dishonesty represent an access of
wealth without effort in the legal sense, and the general Islamic
principle is that there can be no gain without effort, just as
conversely there must be no effort without reward.

* * * * * * *

Monopolies on the necessities of life are not recognized
by Islam as one of the legal methods of gain, or of the increase of wealth. "He who imports goods shall be given his
provision, but he who monopolizes goods shall be accursed."
"The monopolist is a sinner." That is to say, a monopoly
is an infringement of the right to trade and to manufacture,
and the monopolist permits no one but himself to import or
to manufacture his chosen goods. Thus he can control the
market, and can impose on the people what prices he wishes,
can inflict on them hardship and distress, and can injure them
through their livelihood and through their necessities. In
addition, he closes the door of opportunity against others who
desire to gain their living as he gains his, or to succeed as
he has succeeded. It sometimes happens even that the holder
of a monopoly will cut off the supplies or destroy a glut of

goods, so that he may be able to impose an exorbitant price. This represents stopping or lessening the flow of supplies which are for general use, and which Allah has ordained for the use of all men on the earth. Thus we have seen how loads of Brazilian coffee were burned, in order to prevent a drop in the market price of coffee; but at the same time millions of people could not buy coffee to meet their needs. Similarly we find the medicine markets monopolized by Jews and others such; so the sick undergo suffering or are left to die, while the monopolists make their disgraceful profits and thereby amass their unlawful wealth.

In its desire to check this method of increasing wealth Islam goes so far as to put outside the pale of the faith all who hold monopolies to excess. "He who holds a monopoly on food for forty days is clear of Allah and Allah of him." Such a man is no Muslim, who can thus injure society by engendering in it fear and lack of its necessities, solely in order to make an unlawful gain, and thus to increase his private wealth at the expense of the general welfare.

* * * * * * *

Usury is another method of increase which is unlawful; Islam is strongly opposed to this custom, and condemns it outright, warning those who practice it of the most terrible consequences. "O you who have believed, do not live on usury doubled and redoubled; but act piously towards Allah, and it may be that you will prosper."[23] This is not a case of prohibiting merely doubling and redoubling, while allowing smaller gains; the mention of doubling is no more than an emphasis on actual fact, a description of what takes place. This prohibition strikes rather at the very root and principle of usury, a fact which is made clear in other verses. "Those who live off usury will only arise at the Day of Judgment as those arise whom Satan has overthrown by a touch. This is because they have said, 'A bargain is just the same as usury.' But Allah has allowed bargaining, though He has forbidden usury. If anyone receives a warning from his Lord and desists, he shall keep what he has already gained, and his affair shall be in the hands of Allah; but anyone who continues on his way is destined for Hell-fire, long to stay there."[24] "O you who have believed, show piety towards Allah, and leave alone what remains unpaid of your usury, if you are true Believers. If you do not, then be warned of enmity from

Allah and from His Messenger. But if you repent, you may keep your capital, no wrong being done on either side."[25]

In its loathing of the practice of living on usury Islam goes so far as to make its shamefulness even greater than that of adultery; and this it holds to be something which destroys honor, violates true relationships, and is a disgrace to society. Thus the Messenger says: "A pennyworth of usury which a man uses knowingly is worse than thirty-six acts of adultery."

In all this Islam is true to its fundamental beliefs on wealth, human nature, and the welfare of society. Property is something granted for the use of its possessor, who is thereby obliged to use it for the general good of society; it must not be subverted and used as an instrument to oppress and plunder the people. No man of wealth may pounce on the hour of his fellow's need as an opportunity for taking advantage of his position, in order to demand a return of more than he has given. Sometimes such need is for necessary food, for medicine for the treatment of disease, for expenses on education or other things; then the alternative is, either that all these things be left unattended to, or that the wealthy man have his way with the needy, giving them a little and demanding a large return. Thus he injures them by the financial power which he wields, so that either they have to slave unremittingly to pay the usurer his interest, or their debt doubles itself year after year.

Such is the position of influence which the wealthy man occupies; he does not work other than being a man of property; he drinks blood and sweat in his greed, voracious in his idleness. But it is to work that Islam gives religious sanction, making work the primary ground of possession; and it does not permit wealth to grow through idleness, nor will it allow wealth to beget wealth. Only effort can beget wealth, otherwise such wealth is unlawful.

Islam has an interest also in the effect on the purity of the individual's nature, and on the fellow-feeling between the members of society. No man can live off usury and still have a true nature and conscience; and usury on the other side does not encourage or perpetuate fellow-feeling and sympathy in society. Anyone who gives me one dollar in order to demand a return of two dollars from me is my enemy; I cannot have any friendly feeling for him, nor can I bear him any affection.

Mutual help is one of the fundamental principles of the Islamic
society, but usury destroys mutual help and vitiates it at the
very root. Therefore Islam is opposed to this practice.

Furthermore in this present age there is apparent another
reason for prohibiting usury, a reason which was not formerly
apparent. This is that usury represents a method of amassing
a vast amount of capital wealth which does not depend on effort or labor; this is brought about by the existence of non-
workers who rely only on this means of increasing and multi-
plying their wealth. Thus idleness and luxury are encouraged
at the expense of the toiling masses, who need money and
have to borrow it at interest in the critical hour. From this
situation there arise two dangerous social ills: one is the
amassing of unlimited fortunes, and the other is the wide-
spread division of society into two classes, an upper and a
lower. So there appears an idle, lazy, and luxury-loving
class which does no work and yet has everything. The money
which they possess is like a net to entrap more money, except that there is no necessity to put a bait in the net; for
the poor fall into it only too readily; their steps, driven by
necessity, lead them straight into it.

Money should be loaned to those in need freely and without interest; this is the way to increase affection, to benefit
the sense of independence, and to create a sense of mutual
responsibility between rich and poor, between powerful and
weak. For there is no intrinsic excellence in property, but
only an enjoyment and an effort. And the mere possession
of money does not entitle a man to make a profit out of it
alone. It is the borrower who must put out the effort, and
therefore all profit resulting from that effort should accrue
to him who makes the effort; the capital of the loan should
be returned alone, that is to say without interest, to its
owner.

According to Islamic usage it is right that loans should
be made either to meet a need or to encourage production.
In the former case, where the loan is to be used for the
provision of material necessities, the borrower must not be
oppressed by having to pay interest on the loan, and the custom is that the principal sum shall be repaid alone when the
borrower is in better circumstances. In the latter case, the
principle is that the profit is made rather by the effort expended than by the money borrowed; for money cannot make

profits except by effort, and it is that effort which is the
important thing in the eyes of Islam. Accordingly Islam
forbids usury in all cases; but it holds that a loan must
be made freely to anyone who has to meet needs of any kind.

When a man borrows money and then falls on evil circumstances, "Then let there be indulgence until better times."[26]
It seems that the form of this command is really that of a
conditional sentence: "If he be in adverse circumstances,
then let there be indulgence until better times." This gives
it the form of a command rather than that of an exhortation.
And besides this, affection is encouraged by help and forbearance, as the Messenger said: "Allah will be merciful
to a man who is forbearing when he buys or sells or exacts
payment." Forbearance in collecting a debt preserves the
self-esteem of the borrower, and encourages in his heart
an affection for the lender; it gives him an incentive to work
hard in order to repay his loan as far as he can. So Muhammad said: "Anyone who rejoices that Allah has saved him
from the pains of the Day of Resurrection should attempt to
ease the pain of anotherwho is in evil circumstances, or
should remit his debt." Or again: "He who grants indulgence
to one in evil circumstances or who remits a debt--Allah
will grant him shelter."

On the other hand Islam commands the borrower to spare
no effort to pay back his debt, to clear his obligations, to
set against the grace of a loan the equal grace of repayment,
and thus to foster mutual trust in dealings between individuals.
"If anyone takes the money of others with the intention of repaying it, Allah will repay him for it; but if anyone takes
such money with the intention of destroying it, then Allah will
destroy him." Anyone who accepts money with the intention
of repaying it works unceasingly to earn and to support himself; thereby he gains for himself generally true greatness
and strength of character. But anyone who accepts money
with the intention of not repaying it desires to live on the
money of others; so he ceases to work altogether and becomes
lazy, till ultimately his ambition fails and he degenerates into destruction and ruin of character. So the Messenger said:
"Yes." But when the man turned away the Messenger called
him back, and added, "Allah will forgive--everything except
debts." Thus, for a debtor who is able to repay, it is not
enough to fight in the way of Allah and to be killed, not enough

to be a man of endurance, patient, always advancing and
never retreating; despite these things a debt still hangs about
his neck; for it is a duty, not only to Allah, but also to others,
so long as he is able to repay. One who has no means to discharge his debt is permitted to do so by the use of alms which
he receives. Abu Sa'id al-Khadri said: A contemporary of
the Messenger came into difficulties through his commercial
transactions, and had a huge debt. So the Messenger commanded: Give alms to him. The people gave him alms, but
still the amount could not discharge the debt. Then the Messenger said to the man's creditors: Take from him what you
can get, and let that be enough for you.

The Prophet also took another step forward when wealth
accrued to him after the conquests, in that he formed the
habit of settling the outstanding accounts of debtors after
their death out of the public funds. It is related on the authority of Abu Huraira as follows: When they brought to the Messenger of Allah a man who had died owing money, he would
ask, "Has he left enough to pay his debt?" If he was told
that such was the case, he would pray for the man; otherwise
he would say to the Muslims, "Pray for this, your comrade."
But after Allah granted him the conquests, he stood up in
public and said, "I have more love for the Muslims than they
have for themselves; so if any Muslim dies owing money,
the discharge of the debt shall be my duty. If any such man
leaves sufficient money, the discharge shall be the duty of
his heirs."

In this way Islam insists that every man be paid in full;
it demands this with the same insistence with which it demands that the needy be helped, and that there be indulgence
in the matter of repayment. Thus it takes a comprehensive
view of all the aspects of the matter, in order to guarantee
the general welfare, and holds an impartial balance between
privileges and responsibilities.

Ways of Spending

Such are the limitations which Islam lays down for the increasing of wealth by business dealings. But in the case of
spending money, the matter is not thus organized, without
general laws; the wealthy man is not free to be sparing of his
property, or to spend it as he wishes, even though there may
be a natural appearance of such freedom of disposal. In Islam

the individual is not left to himself to do with his property as
he wishes; he has his degree of freedom, but it is bounded by
a hedge of limitations. In addition, there can seldom be a
purely personal disposal of property which does not in some
way affect other people, even though such effects may not be
material or in any way apparent.

The man who is niggardly is similar to the man who is
wasteful; neither of these is approved by Islam, because both
of them are harmful to themselves and to society. "And do
not keep your hand chained to your neck that it cannot spend;
neither spread it wide open to squander, so that you are left
censured and in poverty."[27] "O sons of man, take your adornment at every mosque; eat and drink, but do not be wasteful;
verily He does not love those who are wasteful."[28]

"Chaining the hand" in niggardliness is forbidden to people,
so far as concerns the legal enjoyment of their property;
Islam commands the individual to enjoy what he possesses
within legal limits, and it is opposed to people who forbid
that which is not forbidden. For life should be made pleasant
and agreeable and cheerful, without wantonness or waste;
and Islam does not command austerity or asceticism or
abstinence from the good things of life. Therefore He commands the sons of man to adorn themselves with suitable
adornments in the above verse; and the Qur'an goes on after
this verse to say in disapproving accents: "Say: Who has
forbidden the adornments of Allah, which He has provided
for His servants, and the good things which He has provided?
Say: On the Day of Resurrection these will be exclusively
for those who have shown belief during the life of this world.
Thus do We make the signs distinct for people who have knowledge. Say: My Lord has forbidden only indecencies, both
open and secret, crime, and unjustified greed; He has forbidden that you should associate with Him anything for which
He has revealed no authority, and that you should say against
Allah things which you do not know."[29]

Islam desires that all men should have enjoyment of the
worthy pleasures of life, old and young, rich and poor alike;
hence the form of address in this passage, "Sons of man."
So when it happens that Islam summons men to endurance and
obedience, this summons does not entail asceticism or self-
denial; rather it is a summons to keep oneself in tranquility
of mind and to endure adversity until it passes away or is re-

126

moved. Beyond this, every individual wants to enjoy all permissible things, and society wants to encourage its members
to enjoy such things. So it will never forbid them to enjoy
the things which Allah calls them to enjoy in this life.

Accordingly it is laid down that a portion of the poor-tax
shall be given to the poor; by the "poor" are meant those
whose possessions are not sufficient to make them liable to
pay the tax. By this donation they may be given a comfortable
living, rather than the bare livelihood which they already possess. That is to say, Islam advocates not merely a bare
existence, but rather an enjoyment of life which is better
than a bare existence. So when Islam gives a gift to a poor
man out of the poor-tax money, it is giving him comfort and
the enjoyment of more than the bare necessities; it is better
for him to spend what he has, to enjoy the worthy pleasures
of life, and not to forbid himself the many goods things of
life. Thus his life may become pleasant and agreeable, and
thus the soul may find a freedom from purely material cares
to think great thoughts, to formulate lofty ideals, to ponder
the problems of the universe and human nature, and to take
up the search for truth and beauty. So the Messenger says:
"Allah loves to see the results of His beneficence to His servants." Hardship and poverty constitute the greatest possible
denial of the beneficence of Allah, and He disapproves such
a denial.

All this from only one point of view; but there is another
point of view which Islam has in mind, namely the undesirabil-
ity of money being kept out of circulation, and never being
spent. Such restriction of money nullifies its function; for
society requires that money be kept in general circulation,
so that the various aspects of life may be encouraged, so
that the widest fertility may be guaranteed in all fields, so
that work may be provided for the workers, and an incentive
kept before human nature. The restriction of money nullifies
all of this, and therefore in Islam such restriction is forbidden, because it militates against the welfare of the individu
and of society in general.

At the opposite extreme from niggardliness we have waste-
fulness, which is a corrupting influence alike on the individua
and on society. But let us first hasten to emphasize that the
spending of money--even the whole of one's money--in the way
of Allah is not waste. The basis of this belief is in the traditi

about the Messenger and the mountain of gold, in which he
desired that if he had the value of two cents left, he might
spend it all in the way of Allah. Waste is constituted only
by wasteful spending on oneself, and such is the meaning
Islam gives it.

Waste in this sense means that luxury of which Islam
disapproves so strongly; it hates wealth to be confined to
the rich, so that its total is not lessened by being spent in
the way of Allah; this it holds to be a source of injury both
to the individual who possesses the wealth, and to the society
in which he lives. Such misuse is therefore an evil thing
which it is incumbent on society to change in order to avoid
its own ruin by this means.

The passage of the Qur'an and the Traditions of the
Prophet which disapprove and forbid luxury are frequent
and numerous; they are clear and definitive, teaching that
this is the worst of unlawful things in the eyes of Allah and
His Messenger. Islam certainly urges men to enjoy the good
things of life, and disapproves of men denying themselves
those things which are lawful for them; it calls on men to
make life pleasant and agreeable, and not gray and drab.
Yet it is the same Islam which disapproves waste and luxury
so strongly and even violently.

The Qur'an characterizes luxury-loving people sometimes
as those whose ambition fails, whose strength disappears, and
whose liberality vanishes. "When a Sura is revealed which
contains the command, 'Believe in Allah, and fight his battles
along with His Messenger.' those who have long purses call
on you; they say, 'Let us be among those who stay at home.'"[30]
When we remember how Islam insists on holy war and urges
men to share in it, and honors those who take part in it, we
see how much it must despise by contrast those who have the
long purses for turning away and refusing to join the ranks
of those who fight. This is not in the least strange; for the
lover of luxury is flabby and weak-willed, soft, and with little
virility; he cannot rely on his strength, his ambition has failed,
and his generosity has vanished. To take part in a crusade
would hinder the gratification of his petty desires, and would
forbid him his creature comforts for a time; he recognizes no
value in life except these corrupt and disgraceful things.

Furthermore, many times in history mention is made of
the lovers of luxury as always impeding not only themselves

but also their followers in the way of truth; for so long as there are such, there will also be weaklings who will flatter their pride, minister to their desires, and lose their personality like insects. "We have never sent anyone as a warner to a town, but the men of luxury have said, 'We do not believe in your message.'"[37] "Then said the chief men of his people, who disbelieved and dismissed as false the idea of meeting the Last Day, men to whom We had given luxury in the life of this world: 'This is only a man like yourselves; he eats what you eat, and he drinks what you drink. If you obey a man like yourselves, surely you will lose by it.'"[32] "And they said: 'O our Lord, we obeyed our chiefs and our great ones, and they led us from the Way; O our Lord, bring upon them a double punishment, and lay on them a mighty curse.'"[33] Nor is there anything strange in this; for lovers of luxury must have their easy, selfish and idle life; they must gratify their desires and have their pleasures; they must have around them followers and courtiers who are submissive. But truth and religion and faith forbid them most of the things which they must have, and limit the number of their permissible possessions. Truth and religion and faith appear to them to be slight and insignificant things, in which their weak minds and jaded appetites can find no pleasure. Truth and religion and faith raise the status of the common man, so that the luxurious can no longer have an absolute authority over their weaklings, cannot make out of them obedient instruments and willing tools. Truth and religion and faith forbid their having the clever, imaginative, legendary tales with which they have surrounded themselves, and which they enjoy in their misguided, ignorant and subservient circles. Thus they are hostile to all truth and to all knowledge. All this takes no account of the effect which luxury has on the conscience, or of the atrophy of the senses which is produced by excessive indulgence. "And on the Day of His gathering the peoples, together with that which they have worshipped apart from Allah, He will say: 'Did you lead these My servants astray, or did they by themselves err from the Way?' They will say: 'Glory be to Thee. It was not right for us to take any patron apart from Thee; but to these and to their fathers Thou hast given a perpetual enjoyment, till now they have forgotten Thy reminder, and are become a ruined people.'"[34] So wealth and excessive property inherited from

a previous generation make one forget the reminder of Allah,
and thus issue in barrenness and drought. For the explanation
of the phrase, "They have become a ruined people" is one
which is pictorial, strange, and full of significance; land
which is "ruined" is barren land which cannot produce or
bear fruit; similarly the hearts and minds and lives of such
people are barren, smooth, and hard; in them no real life can
flow.

The Messenger describes the houses of the luxurious as
houses of the Satans, because of the corruption which springs
up in them, and because of the temptation which issues from
them. "There are camels which belong to the Satans, and
houses which belong to the Satans. The former I have seen
when one of you brings out his pedigreed camels which he has
been fattening, and on which he will not mount; he passes by
one of his fellows who is exhausted, and he will not give him
a lift. The latter I see only in the lattices which people have
screened with brocade." The Messenger of Allah saw camels
belonging to the Satans, which their owners had no need to
ride, while exhausted wayfarers could not afford a beast to
carry them. We see the same thing here in the shape of the
huge automobiles which come and go on small and trifling
errands, while thousands cannot afford a tram-fare; and
other hundreds have not even the use of their legs to travel,
having lost them in some calamity. As for the houses which
Muhammad saw in the lattices which people screened with
brocade, we still see them, and in them forms of luxury which
never occurred to the mind of man in that earlier age.

Undoubtedly luxury is the cause of destruction in the course
of history, as it is the cause of insolence. "How many towns
have We destroyed which were insolent because of their prosperity. These are their dwellings, almost uninhabited since
then."[35]

And equally certainly luxury is a reason for punishment
in the world to come, because it results in rebellion. "Those
on the left hand, what are they? They live now in hot wind
and scalding water, in the shadow of black smoke, neither
cool nor elegant; yet they were previously in luxury and persisted in grievous sin; they would say: 'When we are dead
and turned to dust and bones, can we really be raised up
again? And also our fathers and the men of old?'"[36]

But it is not only the individual who loves luxury who will

suffer destruction and punishment; the community which permits the existence of such luxury will be similarly afflicted. "And when it is Our will to destroy a town, We command its luxury loving citizens, and they deal corruptly in it; thus the sentence upon it is justified, and We destroy it utterly."[37] The "will" here referred to is not the "sovereign will of Allah" in the commonly accepted sense, but rather the law of cause and effect, or of reason and result. If there are luxury loving individuals in a community and the community suffers them to remain so, doing nothing against them; if it refrains from checking the causes of luxury; if it leaves the luxury loving to pursue their corrupt way; then all these factors are causes which will inevitably issue in the destruction and the downfall of the community, because of their very existence. Such is the meaning of "will" in this verse. That is to say, the results are related to the reasons, and the effects must follow where the causes occur; for such is the natural law which Allah has laid down for the universe and for all life.

The community will be held responsible for this evil which existed in its midst; for luxury must inevitably lead to evil by reason of its very existence in the community. As we have already seen, there must be some outlet found for excessive resources. Here in Egypt we have excessive wealth, which is a resource. We have also an excessive physical vitality, which is again a resource. We have an excess of spare time, not filled by work or thought, and this too is a resource. Accordingly young men and women who love luxury, who have youth and leisure and wealth inevitably go astray and seek extra outlets for their excess of resources in body, wealth, and time. Generally these outlets are trivial, and take their form from the period and the social environment; but there comes a time when they pass this limit of triviality and take the form of license and depravity, both physical and mental.

And on the other side there is exploitation, and profiteering, and destitution; these produce the slave traders, the toadies, the courtiers and hangers-on of the wealthy, all of whom spread the spirit of laxity and dissipation; they cheapen the true values of life which do not appeal to luxury loving men and women. Thence the disease extends outwards to all the other classes of the community; until finally there comes the inevitable result, namely the wide spread of immorality

throughout the community, the growth of license, the weakening of body and of mind, and the decline of moral and
spiritual powers. At this point the command of Allah is fully
justified, and such a community is utterly destroyed.

This is what Islam saw in the crime of luxury; it is a
crime which is basically individual, but when the community
acquiesces in it and does not check such an evil with hand
and voice and heart, then it is a crime which produces its
own fruits. The disease extends to the whole body of the
community and issues ultimately in its destruction; for
the results are dependent on the reasons, the effects on the
cause. "And you will not find any change in the custom of
Allah."[38]

But what, then, is the limiting factor in both luxury and
privation, and what is the just middle course between them?
It is our belief that environment and common usage provide
the most equitable criterion. So if we go back to the first
age of Islam, we find a poverty-stricken country in which
hardship and penury were common; it is for this reason that
we find the Messenger saying, as he limits luxury, "No son
of man has any right to possess any more than three things:
the house in which he lives, the garment which covers his
nakedness, and a crust of bread (that is, with nothing to
accompany it) and water." So too he forbids the wearing of
silk: "He who wears silk in this world will have no clothing
at all in the next." And Ali relates that the Messenger forbade also the use of Egyptian cloth, and of clothes dyed yel-
low. He forbade also the wearing of gold rings. All these
were forbidden to men. But women were permitted the use
of silk and gold, although he himself disliked his daughter
Fatima to wear gold. But this was a personal matter, in
that the Prophet enjoined it on his own household, but did not
apply it to the people in general.

It is our belief that we do not permit anything which should
be forbidden when we say: This was the logical outcome of
the Prophet's environment; but Islam does not demand hardship so long as that hardship is not necessitated by the conditions of the environment or by the state of the community.
It is true, none the less, that the wearing of silk and saffron-
dyed clothes, or of embroidered garments is harmful to the
status of men; it encourages them to become soft and cowardly
in time of war; and such softness cannot exist in a community

where there is to be economic equality. But the Messenger
did not carry the idea of hard living to the point of neglecting
and overlooking one's dress. Jabir told this story of him.
The Messenger of Allah came to visit us once, and seeing a
dishevelled man with untidy hair he said, "Could this fellow
find nothing to keep his head in order?" Then, seeing a man
wearing dirty clothes, he said, "Could this fellow find no way
of washing his clothes?" In the same strain Abu al-Akhus
al-Jashmi tells this story on the authority of his father. The
Prophet once saw me wearing old clothes, and said, "Have
you any property?" I said, "Yes." He asked, "Where did
you get your property?" and I said, "From all that Allah
has given me in the way of sheep and camels." He said,
"Then, since Allah has given you property, let Him see
you wearing some of the results of His favor and honor."

We have already noticed Allah's commandment to the
sons of man, to take their adornment, and not to forbid the
good things which He has permitted them. The meaning that
we take from all of this is that the condition of one's environment is the criterion in this matter, and that it is the general
standard of living in the community which must be the limiting
factor in both luxury and privation. For when Allah granted
to the Muslims the conquest of the neighboring countries,
when the general wealth increased and the standard of living
rose, clothes became more elaborate, and the Muslims enjoyed things that they had never known before. Yet no one
reproved them for such conduct, so long as they did not exceed a reasonable limit.

We can find many illustrations of this in the conditions of
our present age. For when the American working man, for
example, has his radio set and his private automobile, when
he may, if he is able, make a weekly excursion with his
family, or visit a cinema; when these things are so, it is
not luxury that the White House should be the home of the
President. But when millions of a nation cannot find a mouthful of pure water to drink, it is undeniably luxury that some
few people should be able to drink Vichy and Evian, imported
from overseas. And when there are millions who cannot afford the simplest dwelling, who in the twentieth century have
to take tin cans and reed huts as their houses; when there
are those who cannot even find rags to cover their bodies, it
is an impossible luxury that a mosque should cost a hundred

thousand guineas, or that the Ka'aba[39] should be covered
with a ceremonial robe, embroidered with gold. And it
makes no difference that it is the Ka'aba, or that it is a
mosque. For it is the public who have to provide the money
which is spent in this way.

From such examples it is possible to lay down limits for
luxury and for privation. The conditions of our environment
must be the criterion; and such conditions will generally
prove a reliable guide. The general wealth of the community
and the standard of living in each period and in each district
will limit the incidence of luxury, by showing it up; for the
social conscience seldom errs in its estimation of such
things. Such is the Islamic limitation for all changing conditions and in every age.

* * * * * * *

The Poor-Tax

Now let us consider the poor-tax, which is the outstanding
social pillar of Islam; a discussion of the poor-tax is the
most essential part of the economic theory of Islam.

Payment of the poor-tax is a duty which is laid on property;
in one aspect it is a form of worship, in another it is a social
responsibility. When we remember the Islamic theory of
religious and social affairs, we may say that the poor-tax is
a social responsibility with a religious significance. Hence
it is called zakat, which means purification and growth. It
is a purification of the conscience and of the moral sense, because it means paying the ordained due. It is a purification
of the soul and the heart from the natural instinct of avarice,
and from the disposition to love wealth; for money is powerful, and possession is an enviable thing, so that when a man
can give away his money generously to others, he cannot but
be purified, and elevated, and improved. And it is a purification of property itself, because it means paying what is due
on the property, after which its possession is legal. Again,
because there is a religious significance in the poor-tax, it
is a mark of the sympathetic understanding of Islam that
protected people who are "scripturaries" are not required to
pay it; instead of it they pay a land-tax, so that they may
contribute to the general expenditure of the state, without
being liable to a religious duty which is specifically Islamic.

The poor-tax is a right which the community claims from
the individual, either to guarantee a competence to some of

its members, or to provide some little enjoyment over and
above a bare livelihood. For this reason Islam decrees this
contribution, in accordance with its general principle, "In
order that property may not be passed around between the
rich among you." In other words, Islam disapproves of
people being in poverty and need; it decrees that every man
earn his living by his own work so long as he can, but that
he receive his share from the public monies when for any reason
he is unable to work.

Islam disapproves of people being in poverty or need, because it wishes to preserve them from the material cares
of life and give them leisure for better things, for things
which are more suitable to human nature, and to that special
nobility with which Allah has endowed the sons of man. "We
have given nobility to the sons of man, and have carried them
by land and sea; We have given them provision of good things,
and have given them great preference over many of the things
which We have created."40

And indeed He has given men a nobility through their minds
and their emotions, and through their spiritual yearnings for
what is higher than mere physical needs. But when men have
only the bare necessities of life, they cannot gain any respite
from labor in which to satisfy these spiritual yearnings or
these intellectual capacities; then they have been robbed of
their nobility, and are reduced to the level of animals. More
than that, even. Even animals generally find their food and
drink, and some animals can have pride and energy and
cheerfulness. Some birds can sing, and can rear a brood
into life, since they have a sufficiency of food and drink. But
the case with man, the noblest creation of Allah, is that the
material needs of food and drink keep him too busy to rise
even to this level which the birds and animals achieve, much
less to the level which is proper to man, to whom Allah has
given nobility. And even when he has done his allotted work,
he does not receive a competence; this is the disaster which
makes him many degrees lower than the state which Allah
purposed for him; this is the disaster which also ruins the
community in which such a man lives. For such must be a
degraded community, which does not ratify the nobility which
Allah has given, and which by that fact is disobedient to the
will of Allah.

Man is the vicar of Allah in His world; He appointed him

as such to encourage life in the earth, to elevate it, and to
make it a beautiful and pleasant thing; He appointed him to
have the enjoyment of its beauty and loveliness, and to give
thanks to Allah for His favors. But man can never achieve
any of this so long as his life must be spent in the pursuit of
his daily bread--even if through this pursuit he gains a sufficiency. How, then, can he fare if he has to spend his life
in labor, and cannot even then earn a sufficiency?

Islam disapproves also of the existence of class distinctions
in a community where some live on a standarad of luxury,
and others on a standard of hardship; it disapproves even more
of hardship becoming privation and hunger and nakedness.
Such a community cannot be truly Muslim; for the Messenger says, "He does not believe in me who sleeps full-fed while
his neighbor is hungry and he knows it." Or again, "Not one
of you will be a Believer until he loves his brother as himself."
Islam disapproves of such class distinctions because of the
rancors and hatreds which lie behind them, sapping the very
foundations of society; because they contain elements of selfishness and covetousness and harshness which will corrupt
the soul and the conscience; and because they compel the poor
either to steal and rob, or to humble themselves and to sell
their honor and their nobility. All these are degrading things,
from which Islam would deliver a community.

For all these reasons the poor-tax is prescribed as a compulsory duty on property; it as much the right of those who
receive it as it is the duty of those who pay it. Islam lays
down a statutory level of property, and all who are above that
level must pay the tax. This means that the most that a man
can have and still be exempt is four onces of gold, which is
equivalent to twelve guineas in current money, or twenty-five
ounces of silver, which is equivalent to six guineas. The com-
putation of this must be over and above a man's living expenses,
and must also be over and above any debt or obligation. This
is essential, because no man must be called on to pay the
poor-tax when he is in fact eligible to claim from it. Crops
and fruits are estimated and assessed at the time of harvest-
ing, and come under the heading of merchandise, being valued
in gold or silver. The case of livestock is governed by specific percentages which are equivalent in monetary terms to one
fortieth of their face value.

Those who may claim from the poor-tax as laid down in the
Qur'an are as follows:

First, the poor. That is, those who possess less than
the statutory amount, or those who have that amount but are
overburdened with debt. It is held that such people do possess something, but that it is very little, whereas Islam holds
that everyone should have a competence and something more,
so that as far as possible all may enjoy some of the good
things of life.

Second, the destitute. That is, those who possess nothing
at all. By the nature of their case they are more worthy
recipients than the poor. But my personal opinion is that the
poor are mentioned before the destitute in the Qur'anic verse
because the little that the poor do possess is not nearly enough,
and therefore they are on a level with the destitute. For the
aim of Islam is not merely a bare material living, but something in advance of that, as we have seen.

Third, those employed on the tax itself. That is, those
who collect it. These, even though they may be rich, are
given a proportion of the proceeds. This is the salary attaching to their position, and hence it must come under the
heading of labor and pay, rather than under that of need and
its remedy.

Fourth, those who are to be converted. That is, those who
have recently entered Islam. Here the purpose is to strengthen
their convictions, and to rescue them from their enemies.
But this practice has fallen into desuetude since Allah gave
strength to Islam after the Wars of Apostasy[41] in the days of
Abu Bakr, and Islam has never since then known the need of
making converts by means of money. None the less, such
persons are mentioned in the text of this verse from the Qur'an
and Abu Bakr saw nothing wrong with such a practice. So we
may bear this example in mind, and use it if need arise.

Fifth, slaves. That is, slaves to be ransomed. These
desire to regain their freedom in exchange for a sum of money
which has been arranged with their owners, in order to facilitate that freedom. This practice also has now disappeared,
owing to the circumstances of our time.

Sixth, debtors. That is, those whose wealth is submerged
by debt. This holds so long as such debt is not sinful, and so
long as luxury or some similar thing is not the cause of it.
To give to bona fide debtors out of the poor-tax is just, because it means the cancellation of their debts; it means that
they are freed from their burden, and are helped towards a
more ample form of life.

Seventh, in the way of Allah. This is a universal outlet for wealth, the conditions of which must be dictated by circumstance. It entails equipping a crusade, caring for the sick, teaching the ignorant, and performing all the other tasks of which the Muslim community stands in need. Expenditure under this head covers all social work in every country and under all conditions.

Eighth, the wayfarer. That is, one who carries no money, and who has nothing to spend. Such cases today are refugees in time of war, of raiding, or of persecution, who have had to leave their money behind them, and who have no way of recovering it.

These classifications, both private and public, cover all the aspects of social need in life. Islam assigns to these groups a share of the poor-tax--but only after they have exhausted their private means of support. Islam is insistent on the nobility of human nature; yet despite this, it gives allocations from the poor-tax as a right, and not as a gift or favor; for it is still mindful that "A generous hand is better than a stingy hand." But inevitably the giver confers a favor, and the recipient accepts a favor. Hence Islam insists that men cannot dispense with the method of work, and hence it lays on the community the prime responsibility of providing work for each of its individual members. Once a beggar came to the Prophet for charity; the latter gave him a small coin, and bade him buy a rope to use for collecting firewood, so that he could live by the work of his own hands. And as he gave it he said: "It is better for one of you to get a rope and collect firewood, carrying it on his back and selling it, than to beg from the people, who may give to you or may refuse you."

Such assistance from the poor-tax is the ultimate social benefit, and constitutes a guarantee for the man who is without resources; such a man may have exhausted his powers and got no return; or he may have got a return which is under the subsistence level; or he may have gained a bare subsistence. In this matter Islam has a synthesis of two points of insistence; one that every individual shall work as far as he can, and shall not rely on social assistance while remaining idle himself; and second, that the needy must be helped in order to avoid destitution, in order to relieve him of the weight of necessity and the pressure of need, and in order to set him free for a nobler form of life.

Other Statutory Taxes

But the poor-tax is not the only duty on property.

We must here look at the almost general agreement among those who discuss the poor-tax in these times that it represents the extreme limit of the demands which Islam can regularly make on capital. For this reason we must examine this agreement, to which the professional theologians have come.

For in fact the poor-tax is the lowest limit of the statutory duties on property, and it stands alone only when society does not require any additional income. But when the poor-tax is not enough, Islam need not feel that its hands are tied; on the contrary, it gives to the head of the administration wide powers to assign levies on capital--that is to say, forced contributions from capital at a reasonable rate--subject always to the permanent limitations of its own welfare.

The subject of "public interest" and of "blocking of means," the limitations of which we shall trace later, is a broad subject; it includes the care of all the aspects of communal welfare, and it guarantees the prevention of all want, in any form.

And we shall see that the occurrence of the problem in the history of Islam has provided examples in this field, as the community has from time to time felt the need. For the basic principle on which it rests is flexible enough to embrace all states and conditions.

VII. The Historical Reality of Justice in Islam

The material under consideration here may safely be called "The Spirit of Islam."

This spirit will be immediately perceived by anyone who studies the nature or the history of Islam; it is to be found implicitly in all Islamic law and exhortation. Yet, although this spirit must be very clear wherever men are not biased against recognizing it and against losing themselves in its depths, it is difficult to define in precise terms, as indeed must be the case with every deep universal feeling and every lofty universal philosophy. It is clearly discernable in objective and aims, in incidents and occurrences, in customs and rites, but it is difficult to define in exact terms.

It is this spirit which dictates the very high standard required by Islam as the objective to which its adherents must strive and seek; not merely by the observance of obligations and rites, but even more by that fundamental obedience which is greater than any obligation or rite. This standard is difficult of achievement, and still more difficult of permanent retention. For the needs of human life and the tyranny of human necessity do not permit most people to achieve such a high standard, or, if in a moment of high ambition and aspiration they do reach it, to remain long on it. For such a standard involves difficult responsibilities, duties of life and property, of beliefs and habits. But perhaps the most burdensome of these duties is the constant watchfulness which Islam enjoins on the individual conscience, and the keen moral sense which it evokes in a man; it gives him a clear view of his rights and his responsibilities, to himself and to the community in which he lives, to the human race to which he is related, and to the Creator who watches over him in small things and great, and who knows his most secret and inner thoughts.

None the less, the difficulty of such achievement and the impossibility of long maintaining it do not mean that Islam is a purely mental and imaginative philosophy or idealism to which men's desires may reach out, but short of which their

achievements must always fall. For the achievement of this
standard of which we have been speaking is not the responsibility of all men at all times. Rather it is the prescribed
objective for men to aim at today, as they will tomorrow,
and as they did yesterday, the objective which they have
sometimes attained, sometimes missed. There is in this
an example of the Islamic faith in man, in his conscience and
in his ability which is of great scope; there is also a belief
that there need be no despair of the human race in the near,
or even the remote, future. There is, besides, a wide range
for the labor and the life of those who are fit for greater
things; "Allah lays no responsibility on any man beyond what
he can accept." Thus the tolerance of Islam accepts gladly
from all men what they can achieve within their own limits,
below which the level of their life must not fall; "all men
have degrees of accomplishment," but the road to the highest
standard is always open.

This spirit to which we have referred has left its mark on
the historical course of Islam; this faith, which is at once a
philosophy and a theology, has taken various personal and
historical forms, but never has it been merely a set of barren
theories, a collection of maxims and warnings, of stories and
fables. Rather it has taken the form of living human examples
and proven historical events, customs and habits, which can
be seen by the eye and heard by the ear; and which have left
their traces on the course of life and on the events of history.
Hence has come the attraction of the Islamic spirit, because
it has manifested itself in persons whom it has changed and
renewed by a process of rebirth.

This is the most acceptable explanation of that galaxy of
remarkable characters whose recollection Islamic history
has preserved as it grew through the ages. It is also the
explanation of those events and occurrences which one would
almost regard as legends created by some fertile imagination,
were it not that the records of their happening have been ac-
curately kept and preserved by history. History can scarcely
record all the examples of spiritual purity and psychological
courage, or moving sacrifice and of death for an ideal, all
the flashes of spiritual and intellectual greatness, and the actual deeds of heroism in the various fields of life.

There must be a connection between all these deeds of
heroism and achievement which are scattered through the

pages of history, and the spirit of Islam which supplied a
motive for them. It was this spirit which provided the source
for the power discernible in all these manifestations. The
study of these deeds of heroism and achievement is mere
confusion if they are not connected with one fundamental
source; and it is to be feared that it is unsatisfactory and
false to the real truth of the universe and of life to refer the
secret of all greatness in personality to some individual
virtue, and thus to neglect the primary spirit which impels
and inspires a man. Such a spirit it was which influenced
not only the course of the times and the nature of events,
but also the spirits of heroes, sending them forth as a living
wave of powerful armies, in the deeps of which all personal
virtues and all events and circumstances were submerged.

We shall not go far wrong if we refer the occurrence of
all these personal virtues and all these deeds of heroism to
the action of that powerful spirit, which was a universal and
all-embracing movement. It inspired all those abilities which
appeared on the surface to be personal, but which were essentially universal. And the measure of all individual greatness is its ability to bear comparison with that universal inspiration. It was this office of prophecy which enabled him
to meet and to sustain continually that inspiration; it was
strong enough to keep him at his high standard throughout
his whole life, except on one or two chance occasions, when
Allah had to remind him with a harsh censure. Thus even
in these circumstances this mortal soul was enabled to match
that universal inspiration, because essentially his was a universal strength rather than an individual ability.

Other examples of greatness are thus to be graded down-
wards from the standard of the Prophet, as they occurred
in the Companions of Muhammad or in the adherents of his
faith, during the course of history. Each example must be
assessed according to its ability to bear comparison with
that underlying inspiration, within this massive faith.

It is a wide view such as this which can give us an understanding of how the spirit of Islam has touched mortal spirits,
how it has awakened virtues and inspired heroic deeds, and
how it has, in the broadest sense, changed the course of
human history.

The results of the activity of this spirit are to be clearly
seen alike in the great events of history and in the happenings

of everyday life. Spiritual greatness is not to be judged in
terms of quantity or measure, but rather in terms of quality
and influence. Thus the greatness shown in the conquest of
the Empires of Persia and Rome by a handful of Arabs in an
incomparably short space of time loses none of its value when
it is compared with the greatness displayed in the endurance
of Bilal, the Abyssinian slave. The Quraish persecuted him
beyond mortal endurance to make him abjure his religion,
but he would not; they burned him with red-hot stones placed
on his stomach and chest, they left him hungry and without
water, and they tortured him; yet even in the heat of that
unbearable torture he would say no more than, "Allah is One,
Allah is One."

It is the same spirit which inspires the "man in the street,"
without wealth or influence, to stand before the almighty and
all-conquering Caliph, and boldly to speak the word of truth
to him, not fearing to incur censure in the cause of Allah. It
is to be seen again in the case of the Orthodox Caliph, [1] who
could receive the submission of empires and yet remain un-
moved, who could be exalted and yet humble. Both of these
cases draw their inspiration from the same source, the
powerful, influential, and profound spirit of Islam.

In the matter of the Arab conquest of the Persian and
Roman Empires, we must reckon with the influence of the
spirit, and with its conquest of the gross materialistic powers
which lay in its path. These powers were mustered in the
two great Empires, and they were such that the Arabs could
never have matched them, had they lacked that spirit of Islam.
The victory of Islam here was the victory of a spiritual philosophy embodied in mortal men, and this fact gives powerful
support to the spiritual ideology before which materialistic
ideologies cannot stand, for they cannot possibly explain away
such a surprising victory.

It was a far-reaching spiritual change which Islam made
in the Arabs, in their thought and their behavior, in their
aims and their objectives, in their social and their economic
system. The evidence of this change is not less clear than
is that of the conquests; rather it is clearer and stronger.
What economic revolution, taking place in the life of Arabia
between the call and the death of Muhammad, could possibly
have effected this complete change in thought and mind, in organization and in objective? The only thing which could possibly have had these amazing results is a spiritual philosophy.

It is difficult for us of this present day to understand this
change; we may estimate its size from the following description, which was given by a witness from among the Arabs of
that very time, and which was given in the presence of other
witnesses who were opposed to this faith; yet this speech was
neither challenged nor contradicted. This incident took place
when some of the Muslims emigrated to Abyssinia, taking
their faith with them. They were fleeing from the persecution
of Quraish, and thus they became the first missionaries of
Islam. The Quraish were afraid that this emigration might
prove a source of strength to the Muslims, and so they despatched two of their number as envoys to the Negus of Abyssinia to bring back the emigrants; these two were Amr ibn-
al-As, and Abdullah ibn-Abi-Rabi'a. These two spoke something as follows: "O King, there have recently taken refuge
in your country some foolish youths who have abandoned
the religion of their people and who will not join your religion. They have brought with them a religion which is of
their own making, one with which neither we nor you are
familiar. So we' have been sent to you in this matter by the
chiefs of their people, who include their fathers and kins-
folk and relatives; we would restore them to their families
who are most highly regarded at home. Therefore you may
know what shame and what disgrace this has inflicted upon
them."

Then the Negus asked the Muslims, "What religion is this,
on account of which you have left your people, for which you
will not enter my religion, and which is a faith strange to all
known faiths?" The reply was given by Ja'far ibn-Abi Talib
thus: "O King, we were a people of ignorant barbarity. We
used to worship idols and eat carrion flesh; we practiced
immorality, we disregarded family ties, we neglected the
duties of hospitality, and the strong among us ate up the
weak. Thus we continued until Allah sent us a Messenger
of our own number, of whose descent we know, and whose
truthfulness, faith, and chastity are unquestioned. He summoned us to Allah, to believe in Him as One God, to worship
Him, and to repudiate what we and our fathers worshipped
apart from Him in the way of stones and idols. He bade us
tell the truth in our conversation, observe good faith and
ties of kindred, be faithful to our hospitable duties, and
avoid forbidden things and bloodshed. He forbade us to prac-

tice immorality and to use obscene speech, to eat up the property of orphans, and to slander chaste women. And he bade us worship Allah and associate nothing with Him, he ordained for us the prayers, the poor-tax, and fasting... etc."

Now the two Quraish envoys were present and one of them was Amr, who was neither unable to speak nor deficient in shrewdness; yet neither of the envoys contradicted Ja'far's description of the state of Arabia before Islam, or of the nature and form of the new religion. Therefore this must be a true and reliable description of the former state of affairs and of the new.

That is evidence from history itself, the history of Arabia. And here is another piece of evidence from one who is not a Muslim, and who lives in the modern age. J.H. Denison speaks of the world in general when he says in his book, "Emotion as the Basis of Civilization"[2]: "In the fifth and sixth centures the civilized world was on the brink of total collapse, because the cultures which had made the establishment of civilization possible had already collapsed, and there was nothing else to take their place. It was then apparent that the great civilization, the rearing of which had occupied the labor of four thousand years, was on the point of dissolution and disintegration, and that mankind would be forced to return to its former barbaric state wherein one tribe fought and killed another, where law and order were unknown. The system set up by Christianity was creating division and destruction, rather than unity and order.[3] Civilization was like a huge tree with spreading branches whose shade extended over the whole world; now it stood tottering, eaten away to the core by rot. And in the midst of such an aspect of general corruption there was born the man who was to unify the whole world."[4]

* * * * * * *

But we must proceed; for this discussion grows too long, and the subject of this book is not "Islam," but "Social Justice in Islam." It is our purpose now to turn to examples of this question taken from history.

* * * * * * *

Yet we shall not commence our examples of social justice until we have first looked at some examples of another matter

still more essential in Islam, and upon which all the foundations of Islam depend.

We spoke a short time ago of the constant watchfulness
which Islam enjoins on the individual conscience, and of the
keen moral sense which it inculcates. The course of Islamic
history has preserved examples of these qualities in larger
numbers than we can quote here, but a few typical examples
will serve to represent the whole field.

The following story comes from Buraida. Ma'iz ibn-Malik
came to the Prophet, saying, "O Messenger of Allah, purify
me." "Woe to you," answered the Prophet, "Turn and ask
pardon of Allah, and repent towards Him." So Ma'iz went a
short distance apart, then came back and repeated his request. The Prophet reiterated his former instructions, and
again Ma'iz followed them. But at the fourth time of asking
the Prophet said, "From what am I to purify you?" "From
fornication," he answered. The Prophet asked, "Is this man
mad?" and was told that he was not; "Has he been drinking?"
he asked; whereupon one of those present arose and smelled
Ma'iz' breath, but could detect no trace of drink. Muhammad
said to him then, "Have you really committed immorality?"
"Yes," he answered. So the Prophet gave the order, and
Ma'iz was stoned to death. Two or three days later the Messenger said in public, "Intercede with Allah for Ma'iz ibn-
Malik; for he has made such a repentance that if it had been
on behalf of a whole community it would have been effective
for all." Thereupon there came to him a woman of the
Ghamidi clan of Azd, and said, "O Messenger of Allah, purify
me." "Woe on you," he said to her, "Go and ask pardon of
Allah, and repent towards Him." She said, "Do you intend
to repulse me as you did Ma'iz ibn-Malik? For I am with
child by fornication with him." "You!" said the Prophet,
and she answered, "Yes." Then he commanded her, "Wait
till you have brought forth your child," and one of the Helpers
volunteered to care for her until the time of the birth. When
this happened, he came and told Muhammad, "The Ghamidi
woman has had her child." Then said the Prophet, "We cannot stone her, and leave her helpless child without a nurse";
but one of the Helpers at once said, "I will be responsible
for a nurse, O Prophet of Allah." So they stoned the woman
to death. Another version of the story relates that Muhammad said to the woman, "Go away until your child is born";

then, when the child was born, he said, "Go and nurse your
child until it is weaned." When the child was weaned, the
woman came back with her child, and with a piece of bread
in her hand, saying, "Now, O Prophet of Allah, I have
weaned him and he can eat solid food." So he gave the child
to one of the Muslims then gave the command, and a sword
was plunged into her breast; then Muhammad commanded
the people to stone her. Khalid ibn-al-Walid took up a stone
and threw it at her head, so that the blood bespattered his
face, and he cursed her. But the Messenger of Allah said
to him, "Softly, Khalid. For by Him in whose hand is my
life, she has made such a repentance that had it been made
even by a tax-gatherer, all would have been forgiven him."
Then he gave orders about the woman and prayed over her;
and she was buried.

Now neither Ma'iz ibn-Malik nor his partner in crime were
ignorant of the dreadful penalty which they would have to pay,
or of the shameful end which they would have to face. No one
had seen them, to establish the fact of their crime. Nevertheless they pressed Muhammad importunately, no matter
what was dictated by his mercy and by that of Islam, to deny
them the benefit of any doubt; they closed all possible ways
against their own escape; indeed the woman even taunted
Muhammad, the Messenger of Allah, with wanting to repulse
her as he had repulsed Ma'iz. Almost she accused Allah's
Messenger of neglecting his own religion.

Why did they do these things? The answer lies in their
request, "Purify me, O Messenger of Allah." This betrays
the true impulses which was strong enough to overcome the
love of life--a watchful conscience and a keen moral sense.
It was the desire to be purified of a crime of which none save
Allah was cognizant; it was the shame of meeting Allah un-
purified from a sin which they had committed.

This is Islam. Its keen moral perception appears in the
conscience of the offender, and its profound mercy appears
in Muhammad's repulsion of these two people and in his effort to provide a way of escape for them. Its resolution appears in the carrying out of the stipulated punishment when
the charge had been proven, despite the nobility of the con-
fession and the intensity of the repentance; for on this point
the sinner and the Prophet find common ground--that the
faith must stand by its basic tenets.

So much for the personal aspect. But how stands the matter with regard to the social consequences which must follow the action of such a conscience from time to time in the course of life?

An illustration of this is provided by the story of the deposition of Khalid[5] from the command of the Syrian expedition, and his replacement by Abu-Ubaida. Khalid was the general who had never yet been worsted in any engagement, an Arab, proud of himself, of his lineage, and of his victories. Such a man was Khalid who was deposed from his command; yet he bore no malice, nor was he so much the slave of power as to withdraw from the force--far less did he dream of rebelling. On the contrary he remained in the army because of his great resolution, and because of his eagerness for the success of Allah's faith, and for martyrdom in the way of Allah. He paid no heed to all the other factors in the situation, holding them to be subordinate to that watchfulness which Islam enjoins on the individual conscience, and to the keen moral perception laid upon him.

This event has a significance on the other side also; that is, as it affected Umar ibn-al-Khattab. For his deposition of Khalid was itself a product of that same keen moral perception. During the caliphate of Abu-Bakr he had been offended at Khalid for a number of things which had pricked his conscience and outraged his moral sense. He had been offended at Khalid's ready killing of Malik ibn-Nuwaira, and at his marriage to the latter's wife; he was offended again by another similar act, when Khalid married the daughter of Maja'a during the war against Musailima the Liar, on the day following that on which twelve hundred of the chief Companions of the Prophet were killed in the same campaign. Umar believed that Khalid had sinned, and it made no difference to him that this was Islam's finest and most victorious general; it made no difference that the Islamic community stood on the threshold of immense wars in Syria and Iraq; it made no difference that Islam had a supreme need of the valor of the unconquered Khalid. None of these things was able to silence the conscientious conviction of Umar that Khalid had sinned, and that therefore he must be removed from the command of the army, and ultimately from the army itself. As a result of all these considerations, even the measure of Khalid's success in all that he had had to do was as

nothing compared with the nature and character of Umar, and
his propensity for taking account of minute details.

But the question may be asked: "Why, in view of these
sins, did Abu-Bakr retain Khalid? Abu-Bakr's opinion of
Khalid was not as low as Umar's; he knew that Khalid had
made an error in speech; but Abu-Bakr was not looking out
for sins or faults, and so he pardoned Khalid freely. None
the less he was offended with him, especially on the second
occasion, when he wrote to him a letter "sprinkled with blood."
Yet, because he believed that Khalid had acted in error rather
than maliciously, he pardoned and retained him.

This is surely the true explanation of this incident, an
explanation which accords with the moral standards of Islam
at this period. It is therefore the more surprising that a man
like Dr. Haikal should propose an explanation of the positions
of Abu-Bakr and Umar which does an injustice to the spirit
of Islam, though it may well be in conformity with the un-
scrupulousness of modern politics. In his book, "Al-Siddiq
Abu-Bakr," pp. 150-152, he says:

"The difference of opinion between Abu-Bakr and Umar
in the matter of Malik ibn-Nuwaira had reached the level
which we have seen. Both men undoubtedly desired to
serve the best interests of Islam and of the Muslim community. But that aside, was this difference of opinion
due to differing estimates of Khalid's deed? Or did they
disagree about the policy which it was necessary to follow
at such a critical juncture in the life of Islam, when apostasy and rebellion were rife throughout all Arabia?

"My own opinion is that their difference was based on
disagreement about the policy which should be followed in
such a situation. Such a difference of opinion is in general
agreement with the characters of the two men. Umar was
a pattern of inflexible justice; he held that Khalid had killed
a Muslim, and had consummated a marriage with the latter's wife before the completion of her legal term.[6] Hence
it was not right that he should remain as commander of
the army, where he would be able to do the same thing
again, and thus bring a corrupting influence into Muslim
affairs. This would be bad for Muslim standing in the eyes
of the Arabs; and in any case it was not right that Khalid
should go unpunished for the wrong which he had done with
Laila. And even if it were true that Khalid had simply

made an error of speech in the case of Malik--which Umar
did not believe--Umar held that his treatment of Malik's
wife still brought him under the ban of the law. Umar
would not extend pardon to him because he was the "Sword
of Allah," or because he was the general to whom victory
always came. For if such a pardon was granted, then
Khalid and his like would be able to do what was forbidden,
the worst possible example of reverence for the Qur'an
which could be given to the Muslims. Hence Umar cease-
lessly urged and begged Abu-Bakr to recall Khalid and to
reprimand him for his actions.

"Abu-Bakr on the other hand perceived that the situation
was too dangerous for weight to be given to such matters.
What was the killing of one man, or even of a number of
men, through an error in speech or even on purpose, when
danger encompassed the entire state, when rebellion was
aflame from end to end of Arabia, and when this general ,
now accused of sinning, was one of the strongest forces
to save the state from ruin and avert the menace? What
did it matter that Khalid had married a woman contrary
to Arab custom--even that he had consummated the marriage before her legal term had elapsed? All this was
done in war, and the rules of war permitted Khalid to
possess all the women whom he captured. Granted that
it was necessary to apply the law, it was not necessary to
enforce it on eminent and powerful men such as Khalid,
especially since such a proceeding would injure the state
and expose it to danger. The Muslims stood in need of the
sword of Khalid, and at the moment when Abu-Bakr sent
for him to censure him, they needed him more than ever
before. In Yamama, Musailima was already in the vicinity of Khalid's camp at al-Bitah with forty thousand men
of the Banu Hanifa, thus constituting a dangerous threat
to Islam and its adherents; he had already defeated Ikrima
ibn-Abi-Jahl, one of the Muslim generals, and the only
remaining hope of overcoming him seemed to rest on the
sword of Khalid. Was Khalid, then, to be deposed because
of the killing of Malik, or because of Laila the beautiful
who had tempted him? Were the Muslim armies thus to
be exposed to defeat by Musailima, the faith of Allah to
be exposed to the possible results of such a defeat? Khalid
was the instrument and the sword of Allah. Therefore let

the policy of Abu-Bakr be to recall Khalid, and satisfy
Umar by reprimanding him; but at the same time to order
Khalid to march immediately to Yamama against Musiali-
ma.

"This is, to my mind, the true reconstruction of the
difference of opinion between Abu-Bakr and Umar on this
matter. Perhaps it was at that moment, when the false
prophet of the Banu Hanifa had defeated Ikrima, that Abu-
Bakr ordered Khalid to march against Musailima simply
for this reason: that the people of Medina, and especially
such of them as were of Umar's opinion, might see that
Khalid was a man condemned; that they might know that
in sending him into the fire of war Abu-Bakr was actually
punishing him. On the field Khalid might be surrounded
and killed, which would be the most suitable punishment
for his treatment of Umm Tamim in marrying her; or he
might gain a victory, which would cleanse his reputation
and make him out a victorious leader who had rescued the
Muslim world from a terror beside which his own doings
at al-Bitah were as nothing."

And this is "the true reconstruction" of the matter, according to Dr. Haikal. Here is a man whose mind and soul
are steeped in the atmosphere of that period of Islamic history, a man whose mind lives in the shadow of the keen and
intensely perceptive conscience of the men of that age; and
yet such a man cannot get his own mind away from explaining
events on such a level as this, which is obviously based on
an acquaintance with the political expediencies of the present
age of materialism, rather than on the spirit and the history
of Islam in that age. It is a theory peculiar to the present
day that the end justifies the means, a theory which degrades
the human conscience to the level of a temporary expediency,
a theory which reckons the supreme virtue to be a certain
dexterity in the manipulation of affairs. How petty does Abu-
Bakr appear in this reconstruction which Dr. Haikal calls
the true one. If Abu-Bakr-had not been much greater and
nobler than in this estimate made by a man living in a de-
generate age, he could not possibly have justified the exalted
estimation which he has always enjoyed.

Dr. Haikal returns to the question in "Al-Faruq Umar,"
part I, where he reconstructs the thought of Umar, seeking

to depose Khalid. The degeneracy of the age in which he lives again affects the writer, as does the fact of being the leader of a party which advocates temporary advantages and local gains; such a man can never understand the spirit of Islam at its highest levels. Thus he says (pp. 99-100):

"How could Umar insist on the deposition of Khalid, when the latter was the commander of the Muslim forces in Syria, especially when these forces were in such a critical situation? They stood at that time face to face with Rome, yet without active hostility, for neither the Muslims nor the Romans had any excess of strength over the other. Such was the position before Khalid left Iraq to join the Syrian forces, and such the position remained even after his arrival, both sides looking for an opportunity of breaking the stalemate and attacking the enemy. Would not the Caliph be afraid to compromise the situation by striking Khalid off the Muslim strength, and thereby increasing the critical nature of the position? Was it not rather the expedient course to delay until Khalid had extricated the Muslims from their predicament, and after that to give what orders he wished?

"These were undoubtedly weighty considerations in view of the impending struggle, and, as we shall see, Abu-Ubaida gave them full force; but he was afraid of the displeasure and the anger of the Caliph. Umar, however, saw the matter from a different angle, and even if he had postponed the matter of Khalid's deposition until after the Roman struggle, even that would have been against his policy and contrary to his character. The struggle could only have one of two issues; the Muslims would be defeated, or they would be victorious. If they were defeated, the deposition of Khalid would not then retrieve the defeat; while if they were victorious under the command of Khalid, Umar would not be able to effect the deposition of such a general in the hour of his victory. On the other hand, if the deposition were carried through now, the difficulty was resolved. Hence Umar was insistent that Khalid should not be left in the command, either in Syria or elsewhere. For these reasons Umar hastily gave the order for Khalid's deposition, making the excuse that Khalid had not fulfilled the duties assigned to him by Abu-Bakr. Then, when the Muslims proved victorious, no blame could attach to Umar, who

had done what he was satisfied was right, while Khalid
was in the position of having suffered nothing from the
man who had deposed him. "

Thus would "Haikal Pasha" argue in the twentieth century.
It is his own argument which he transfers back to Umar at
the beginning of Islam, just as he has previously carried out
the same process with Abu–Bakr. These are the words of a
man whose spirit has no affinity with that of Abu–Bakr or that
of Umar; even the fact that he has for long lived in the atmosphere of early Islam cannot sever him from the conditions of
the twentieth century. All he does is to twist and distort
facts to give opportunity for an attack on conscience, virtue,
and religion.

What does Haikal think of Umar? Would Umar have retained Khalid in his office if the time and the situation had
been different? And the more so when he was convinced in
his own conscience--as even Haikal admits--that Khalid had
sinned in the matter of Malik, sinned against Allah and against
the faith. Was Umar the man to give weight to such considerations, and to bow before them? Was this the Umar who
crossed mountains without deviating from the straight path,
who faced the tempest in faith, without bowing to it? Such a
course as this was often taken by Mu'awiya, [8] in whom it is
regarded as the fruit of shrewdness and craftiness; but with
Umar or with Abu–Bakr it is impossible. Such an opinion of
these two can be held only by the shallow spirit of this age,
and by the degeneracy of its standards of judgment.

But we must proceed; for we have spent too much time in
pointing out and rebutting this kind of argument. But it was
necessary to rectify the profound error which has overtaken
those who seek to reconstruct the thought and the morals of
the age which produced the spirit of Islam in terms of the
thought and the morals of this material age which is far removed from that fine spirit. This is an error which only
publicizes a misunderstanding of the nature of the human conscience and its ability for growth and for sensitivity. We
have no desire to clothe these men in garments which are
too ample, or to portray them as completely devoid of all
human weakness. But we do desire to restore to mankind
a faith in the human conscience, and to portray this period
of Muslim life in its true colors, as marked by the strong

effort of the individual conscience to achieve to this lofty standard.

And now we may proceed to mention examples of this moral sensitivity in other directions.

This same Caliph, Umar, went out one day carrying a skin of water, and his son asked him disapprovingly, "Why are you doing this?" Umar replied, "I have been too self-satisfied, and I must humble myself." What moral perception is there! For here is a man who can recognize in the depths of his own soul a pride in his office as Caliph, in his conquests, and in the greatness which he has attained; and unwilling that such pride should continue, he determines to humiliate himself, and that in the sight of all his subjects. It made no difference to him that he was the Caliph, ruler of a territory which embraced not only Arabia as a whole but also the major parts of the Persian and Roman Empires.

So also the Caliph Ali used to shiver with cold during the winter; he wore only a summer cloak, and would have no other protection, though he had control of the public treasury. He was unable to draw on that treasury because of that same watchfulness of conscience and that same keenness of moral perception.

Similarly with Abu-Ubaida and his army in Emmaus, where they were caught by the fatal plague. Umar was afraid for "the servant of the community," and attempted to get him out of the danger by sending for him in a letter, in which he said: "To proceed; I need your presence here concerning an urgent matter which I wish to discuss with you personally; I command you, as soon as you have read this letter, not to lay it down until you have come to me." Abu-Ubaida read the letter and recognized Umar's purpose; he knew that Umar only wanted to get him out of the way of the deadly plague, and he said, "May Allah pardon the Commander of the Faithful." Then he wrote to Umar, thus: "I know what matter you need me for, but I am with a Muslim army and I have no pleasure apart from them. I have no desire to leave them until Allah brings an end in death to me and to them. Therefore release me from your order, Commander of the Faithful, and leave me with my army." When Umar read the letter he wept, so that those who stood by asked if Abu-Ubaida were dead. In a voice choked with tears Umar replied, "No; but it is as if he were." And in fact he did die.

What was it but profound faith in the power of Allah which sustained the courage of Abu-Ubaida? And with that faith went the moral perception that he could not take to flight alone, leaving the army; for he and they together formed an army fighting in the way of Allah.

Or there was Bilal ibn-Rabbah, the Messenger's muezzin. After the birth of Islam his brother Abu-Ruwaiha besought him to act as his agent in arranging a marriage for him with a Yemenite family. So Bilal said to them: "I am Bilal ibn-Rabbah, and this is my brother Abu-Ruwaiha; he is a man of evil nature and no religion. If you will have him for a marriage arrangement, well and good; but if you do not wish it, then let him be."

Thus he refused to deceive them, or to conceal anything about his brother; he could not bear in mind that he was an agent, and at the same time forget that he was responsible before Allah for all that he said. But the Yemenites gladly took Abu-Ruwaiha in marriage, because of such candor of speech; for they had formed a worthy estimate of the agent who thus asked the hand of their daughter for his brother.

Then there was the famous Abu-Hanifa, who "sent goods to Hafs ibn Abd-al-Rahman, his business associate, and informed him that there was a fault in one of the garments; and he showed the fault in public. Hafs sold the goods, and, forgetting that the fault had been pointed out, demanded the full price for the imperfect garment. It is said that the price was thirty or thirty-five thousand dirhams.[9] But Abu-Hanifa refused to accept the money, and sent a message to his partner, making him responsible for finding the customer. The partner would not make any restitution to the buyer, and Abu-Hanifa would only be satisfied with the dissolution of their partnership. And so it had to be. Furthermore he disdained to add this tainted money to his honest money, and so gave it all away in alms."[10]

"It is related that Yunus ibn-Ubaid had in his shop suits of clothes at different prices; one kind was priced at four hundred per suit, and another at two hundred. When Yunus went to prayers he left his nephew to keep the shop, and during his absence a Bedu[11] came in, looking for a suit at four hundred. The nephew showed him one of those priced at two hundred, which met with his approval; he bought it, and went away with it over his arm. Yunus met him, and, recognizing the

suit, asked him, "How much did you pay for this?" "Four
hundred dirhams." "It is not worth more than two hundred,"
said Yunus. "Come back with me till I give you back the
extra money. "But," said the Bedu, "In our district even
this is worth five hundred, and I am satisfied with it." "Never
mind that"; replied Yunus; "Sincerity in religion is worth
more than this world and all that it contains." So he took
the Bedu back to the shop and returned to him two hundred
dirhams. When his nephew remonstrated with him, he said:
"Are you not ashamed? Have you no reverence for Allah?
You make a hundred per cent profit, and you leave honesty
to Muslims." "By Allah." protested the nephew, "He would
not have taken it had he not been satisfied with it." But
Yunus answered him: "Did it not seem satisfactory to him
simply because you made it appear so?"

It is related also of Muhammad ibn-al-Munkadir that in
his absence one of his slaves sold a piece of cloth to a Bedu
for ten dirhams, though it was of a type which was worth only
five. All day long Muhammad searched for that Bedu, until
at last he found him. "The slave made a mistake," he said,
"and charged you ten dirhams for what is only worth five."
"O man" said the Bedu, "I am quite satisfied." But Muhammad retorted, "Even if you are satisfied, I will not be satisfied for you to have anything which does not satisfy me." So
he repaid him the five dirhams.[12]

The key to these three stories is in the question of Yunus
to his nephew, "Are you not ashamed? Have you no reverence
for Allah?" And indeed the answer is in fact in these two
things; shame arising from the conscience, and reverence
for Allah. That is the result which Islam can have on human
nature when the power of its spirit is acknowledged, and
when its nobility is widely assimilated.

Beyond these stories which we have quoted there are scores
and hundreds of similar instances, drawn from every aspect
and sphere of life. We have recorded these few merely to
demonstrate the level of purity and exaltation to which Islam
seeks to raise the human conscience, a level far above all
worldly and material things, above the love of self and the
love of life, the love of wealth and of influence. It seeks to
empower the individual conscience to uphold the responsibilities of that constant watchfulness which is enjoined on it, to
maintain the duties of that keen moral perception which is

laid on the ethical sense. And thus it seeks a guarantee of the achievement of this standard.

Now we may safely proceed to draw attention to some aspects of the historical experience of Islam as they relate to social justice, in the way of those brilliantly high standards which characterize Islam.

* * * * * * *

The absolute equality of all mankind was the gospel of Islam, that and an absolute freedom of conscience from all values and considerations which would detract from such equality. We have already discussed the Islamic theory of equality and freedom; we have seen the Qur'anic passages which leave no room for doubt that this theory is profound and fundamental to the construction of Islamic thought on human society. Now we may see how that theory has been applied in practice.

In all parts of the world the slave was regarded as being different by nature from a free man. The same belief was held in Arabia; yet Muhammad married his niece Zainab bint-Jahsh, a daughter of the Hashemite clan of Quraish, to his client Zaid.[13] That marriage was an instance of moral perception which raised the question of human equality to a level far above any other. No man except the Prophet, and no power except that of his religion, could have sufficed to bring about such an impossibility--a thing which is not yet possible in any country outside the Muslim world. In the United States we see today that a slave is still discriminated against by law; a negro cannot marry a white woman--any white woman; he is forbidden by law to sit beside a white in public vehicles; he may not live beside a white in an inn or a hotel; he is not allowed to sit beside a white in a college classroom.

When Muhammad instituted a brotherhood between individua Emigrants and Helpers at the beginning of the Muslim era, his uncle Hamza and his client Zaid were brothers; Abu-Bakr and Kharija ibn-Zaid were brothers; Khalid ibn-Ruwaiha al-Khath'ani and Bilal ibn-Rabbah were brothers. This relationship was no mere matter of words, but was a life-long connection, just as strong as blood relationship. It was a tie of relationship which embraced the persons, their property, and all the other features of their lives.

Further the Messenger appointed Zaid his client as leader of the expedition against Muta, and he later appointed Zaid's son Usama as leader of an expedition against the Roman Empire; he gave him command of an army which included a great number of Emigrants and Helpers, among them being Abu-Bakr and Umar, who were the two lieutenants of the Messenger and his closest friends, later to be the first two Caliphs by the common consent of all the Muslims. Among the members of the army also was Sa'd ibn-Abi-Waqqas, a near relative of Allah's Messenger since he belonged to the family of the Bani Zuhra, who were the Prophet's maternal uncles. Sa'd was one of the first members of Quraish to come over to Islam, which he did under the guidance of Allah at the age of seventeen. He was wealthy and influential, a skilled warrior of great bravery.

When the Messenger died before Usama's expedition set out, Abu-Bakr resolved to despatch the army, and he kept in command of it the man whom the Messenger had chosen. He went personally to escort Usama out of Medina, the latter riding while Abu-Bakr, the Caliph, walked on foot. Usama was ashamed to ride, he being a young man, while the Successor of Allah's Messenger walked afoot, and he an old man. "O Caliph of the Messenger," he said, "By Allah do you ride, else I shall walk." But the Caliph replied with an oath, "By Allah, you will not walk, and by Allah I will not ride. Would you forbid me to soil my feet with dust for one hour in the way of Allah?" Later Abu-Bakr found that he need Umar at Medina, for he had been carrying the full weight of the Caliphate on his own shoulders. But Umar was then no more than a common soldier in Usama's army; the latter was the commander, and therefore his permission must be sought. So the Caliph wrote to him in these terms: "If you please, will you appoint Umar to my service."

This is the level of the spirit of equality to which neither words nor writing can do full justice.

Then with the passage of time we find Umar himself as Caliph, appointing Ammar ibn-Yasir, another former slave, as governor of Kufa. And while Suhail ibn-Amr ibn-al-Harith ibn-Hashim and Abu Sufyan ibn-Harb together with a company of Quraishite nobles stood waiting at Umar's door, Suhaib and Bilal were admitted before them. These two were clients and poor, but they were of those who had fought at Badr, and

were of the number of the Companions of the Messenger.
Abu-Sufyan was furious at such treatment, and gave vent to
barbarous curses, saying, "Never have I seen anything like
this. He admits these slaves, and leaves us standing at his
door."

Umar was one day passing near Mecca when he saw servants sitting, not eating with their masters. His anger was
kindled, and he said reprovingly to the masters: "What is
to be done with those who think themselves better than their
servants?" Then he summoned the servants to eat out of the
same dish as their masters.

Umar had appointed Nafi ibn-al-Harith governor of Mecca,
and, meeting him one day at Usfan,[14] he asked, "Whom did
you leave as your regent over the people of Mecca?" "I left
Ibn-Abza." "Who is Ibn-Abza?" asked Umar, and was told,
"One of my clients." Then said Umar, "You left a client as
your regent?" "He is a Reader of Allah's Book," responded
Nafi, "He is skilled in the law and a judge." "Of a truth"
cried Umar, "Your Prophet once said that by this Book Allah
raises some and puts down others."

Umar's question was not asked in a spirit of censure; simply he wanted to know where lay the qualifications of Ibn-
Abza, since he was not acquainted with him. Otherwise he
would have spoken openly, for it was he who commanded the
six members of the council which was to nominate his successor: "If Salim the client of Abu-Hudhaifa had been alive,
I should have myself nominated him as my successor."[15]
For in his eyes Salim was preferable to any of the six members of the council, though they included Uthman, Ali, and
Sa'd ibn-Abi-Waqqas.

A certain client once asked a man of Quraish for the hand
of his sister in marriage, and gave valuable gifts to the
woman. Her brother refused to let her marry him, and
when Umar heard of it he said to the Quraishite, "What prevented your giving her to him? He is an upright man, and
he has given your sister fair gifts." The Quraishite replied,
"Commander of the Faithful, we have a certain standing, and
he is not her equal." "He has standing both in this world and
in the next," said Umar, "For in this world he has his money
and in the world to come he has his piety." So the Quraishite
promised his sister if she herself was willing; when she was
asked she agreed, and so she married the client.

We have already seen how Bilal the client was an agent for Abu-Ruwaiha the Bedu in a marriage negotiation with a Yemenite family; and we saw how they honored Abu-Ruwaiha and received him because of Bilal.

The way was always open for clients to attain to the highest positions of honor in every field. "When we hear of Abdullah ibn-Abbas we hear of his client Ikrima along with him. So with Abdullah ibn-Umar and his client Nafi, Anas ibn-Malik and his client Ibn-Sirin, and Abu-Huraira and his client Abd-al-Rahman ibn-Hurmuz.

"In Basra there was Hasan al-Basri, while in Mecca there were Mujahid ibn-Jabar, Ata ibn-Abi-Rabah, and Tawus ibn-Kisan, all jurists.

"In Egypt the commander of the corps d'elite in the days of Umar ibn-Abd al-Aziz was Yazid ibn-Abi-Habib who was a black client from Dongola."[16]

It is still in this same spirit that the Muslim world regards the working man. He has in his own hands the power of advancement and dignity; such power is not purely theoretical and ideal, but lies within the realm of practical possibility. There is no trade which can lower the status of the man who exercises it; for work of all kinds is a source of nobility, and no man's trade can disqualify him to acquire learning and thereby to gain increased status and regard.

"Abu-Hanifa was a silk-merchant, just as many of the exponents of canon law after him were merchants or tradesmen."

"The father of this Imam, Ahmad ibn-Mahir, the cobbler, had been a pupil of Muhammad and of Al-Hasan, both of whom were friends of Abu-Hanifa. 'The Cobbler' it was who edited the 'Book of the Land-Tax' for the Caliph Al-Muhtadi; he wrote his great works on the canon law while earning his living by repairing shoes. Similarly Al-Karabisi sold 'karabis' or cotton cloth, and the famous Al-Qaffal used to stretch out his hand and show the marks on the back of it, saying 'These are the marks of my original trade (that of a locksmith).' So Ibn-Qatlubugha worked as a tent-maker, and Al-Jassas, the doyen of his age, was so named because he worked with plaster. Thus too we have Al-Saffar, one who sells brass-ware, Al-Sidalani, one who sells perfume, Al-Halwani, whose father sold sweetmeats. Al-Daqqaq (the flour-merchant), Al-Sabuni (the soap-merchant), Al-Na'ali (the sandal-maker),

Al-Baqqali (the green-grocer), Al-Qaduri (the pot-man), and many others. All these cases are illustrations from various periods of history, and they indicate just this: that from the very dawn of Islamic civilization and from its earliest times this community established a principle which the Western world has sought for ten centuries to establish almost without success, namely that there are not some trades which are estimable and others which are degrading; rather there are some men who are estimable, and others who are not."[17]

* * * * * * *

But this standard of equality cannot be considered perfect until we have discovered how Islamic society treated its exalted members. For it is not enough to show regard for the humble and promote them to high position; the exalted must also be brought down to the same equitable level. They must be permitted no preeminence save through their work, and through it alone, not through social standing or lineage, influence or wealth.

Abu-Yusuf[18] in his book on the land-tax says: It is related by Abd al-Malik ibn-Sulaiman on the authority of Ata as follows. Umar once wrote and directed his governors to come to him for a conference. When they came he stood up in public and said: "O people, I sent out these men as my governors, to wield a just authority over you. I did not make them your governors to strip you of your flesh, your blood, and your wealth. So if any man here has been wronged by one of these, let him now stand forth." Only one man got to his feet, and he said: "O Commander of the Faithful, your governor gave me a hundred lashes." Umar said to him, "Would you give him a hundred lashes? Come, then, and take your vengeance." Then Amr ibn-al-As[19] spoke up: "O Commander of the Faithful, if you start dealing thus with your governors, it will go hard with them; for this will be taken as a precedent after your time." But Umar replied, "Shall I not allow this man his retaliation, when I have seen the Messenger of Allah permit retaliation upon himself? Come, you, and claim your vengeance." Amr persisted: "Let us then make some accomodation in the matter," and Umar said, "As you will." So they compromised to settle the matter for two hundred dinars--two dinars per lash.

Amr ibn-al-As thus protected someone else, but he could

not prevent the same thing happening to his own son for striking Ibn-al-Misri. In this case Umar permitted the injured man to retaliate, and even said to him, "Strike hard on this son of a nobleman." And even Amr himself would have tasted the same experience if Al-Misri had not relented and remitted the penalty.

Umar was one day sitting making the division of the public funds among the Muslims, with the people jostling around him, when Sa'd ibn-Abi-Waqqas, whose lineage and courage in the service of Islam we have already noticed, approached him; he fought his way through the people and forced a clear space round Umar. The Caliph thereupon set about him with his whip, crying, "If you do not respect the authority of Allah in this land, I must teach you that the authority of Allah does not respect you."

But it may perhaps be objected that this only refers to one Caliph. So let us look now at how much freedom of speech and conscience the Caliphs and kings were granted by their subjects; for rulers owe their position to that freedom of conscience which Islam bestows, and to that absolute equality which it establishes in word and deed.

Umar once as Caliph said to the people in the course of a sermon: "If you see any evil thing in me, then set it right." Whereupon one of the ordinary members of the Muslim community answered him: "If we had found any evil thing in you we would have set it right with the edge of our swords." And ever after that Umar used to say: "Praise be to Allah that He has given Umar one subject who would set him right with the edge of his sword."

The Muslims once captured a number of Yemenite scarves,[20] of which Umar got one as his share of the booty, as did his son Abdullah, in common with every other Muslim. Now because Umar needed a cloak, Abdullah gave him his scarf, so that by joining it and his own together Umar might make a cloak. When this was done, Umar was standing one day delivering the sermon, attired in this cloak; in the course of the sermon he said: "O people, hear and obey." A certain man immediately jumped up and cried, "We need neither hear nor obey you." "Why?" asked Umar. "Where did you get that cloak?" asked the man; "All you got was one scarf, and you are a tall man." "Not so fast," replied Umar, and shouted, "Abdullah." No one answered, so he cried again,

"Abdullah ibn-Umar!" "Here, Commander of the Faithful," answered his son. "I adjure you by Allah," said Umar, "This scarf which I wear at my waist--is it yours?" "By Allah it is," replied he. Thereupon the objector said, "The matter is settled. We hear and we obey."

But let us proceed; for still the objection might be raised that this is only the case of Umar.

The famous Abu Ja'far al-Mansur[21] built up his position by means which we would call today arbitrary. One day Sufyan al-Thauri came to him and said: "O Commander of the Faithful, how can you justify your expenditure of the wealth of Allah and of the community of Muhammad without their permission? Umar once was making the pilgrimage and had spent sixteen dinars on himself and his company, and said, 'I cannot but think that we have ruined the public treasury.' You know what Mansur ibn-Ammar told us, for you were there, and your chief secretary wrote it down at the time. He told us on the original authority of Mas'ud that the Messenger of Allah once said: 'A ruler who plunges deep into the public treasury to meet his own desires will tomorrow be in Hell.'" Then Abu-Ubaid the secretary--one of the personal attendants in the royal place--cried out: "Must the Commander of the Faithful hear such stuff as this?" But Sufyan gave him only a reprimand in answer, saying, "Quiet. Pharaoh and Haman destroy one another."[22] And so saying he left, after making a powerful and honest protest, because tyrants, be they never so autocratic, dare not attack those whose heart is pure, who are above material interests, and whose souls are unspotted in the sight of Allah.

Or again Al-Wathiq,[23] another of the despotic rulers, was visited one day by a venerable scholar who gave him the greeting of "Peace." as he entered. Al-Wathiq did not return the greeting, but said only, "May Allah give you no peace." Then the old man took him to task: "Evil was the training that your teacher gave you. Allah the Exalted says, 'When you are greeted, return the greeting with a better, or at least in the same terms.'[24] Yet you did not return a better greeting; you did not even reply in the same terms."[25]

As Abu-Yusuf sat giving judgment, there came before him a case involving a garden, which concerned a private individual and Al-Hadi,[26] the Abbasid ruler. Abu-Yusuf perceived that the right was on the side of the individual, but that the king had witnesses against him. So he said: "The case necessitates that Al-Hadi take an oath to the veracity of his witnesses." Al-Hadi shrank from taking such an oath, for he had arranged that his witnesses would perjure themselves for him; so he had to give back the garden. Similarly Abu-Yusuf made Al-Rashid[27] take such an oath in a case where he saw it to be necessary. Al-Fadl ibn-Rabi'a once gave evidence before him, and he rejected the evidence. When the Caliph remonstrated with him, asking, "Why did you reject this evidence?" the judge answered: "I heard him say that he was your 'slave.' If the matter is true, we do not need the evidence of a slave; if it is false, then his evidence is the same."[28]

This flame which Islam kindled in the human conscience has not failed even in the darkest passages of history, and during its lifetime has illuminated various examples of a free conscience, and a spirit raised above all worldly values, all temporal powers, and all worldly considerations.

"In Egypt Ahmad ibn-Tulun[29] paid great respect to Bakkar ibn-Qutaiba, the Hanafite judge, and used to come and hear him teach; Bakkar never knew of his arrival until the ruler stood by his side. But when Ibn-Tulun desired him to curse Al-Muwaffaq, the power behind the Abbasid throne, he refused, saying, "Surely the curse of Allah is already on evil-doers.' It was suggested to Ibn-Tulun that this remark was actually an attack on him, and he demanded the return of the gifts which he had given Ibn-Qutaiba. They were returned to him new and unopened. Then Ibn-Tulun imprisoned him, but as the result of an appeal on his behalf, placed him in a hired house where he could sit at a window and teach the people. When Ibn-Tulun was attacked by the disease of which he was to die, he repented and asked pardon of Ibn-Qutaiba. But the judge said to the messenger: "Say to him that I am a very old man, and he is ill; so the time is near when we shall meet, and it is Allah who will interpose between us. So Ibn-Tulun died, and Ibn-Qutaiba remarked, 'So the poor wretch is dead.'"[30] "Poor wretch" because of the pride which Ibn-Qutaiba discerned in him, and because of the evil of his character, even though he had acquired power.

So in the time of the Ayyubid dynasty, "King Isma'il made an agreement with the Franks during the Crusades, and handed over to them Sidon and other fortresses, in order to

gain their support against Najm al-Din Ayyub. But Iaa al-
Din ibn-Abd al-Salam took him to task for such an act. This
angered Isma'il, and he deposed him from office and imprisoned him. But later he sent him a message, setting him
free and promoting him. This the messenger told him in
these word: 'All your honors shall be restored to you, and
more also, on the sole condition that you humble yourself
before the sultan.' But the old man answered only: 'By Allah it is not my will that he should ever again receive my
allegiance. O people, you and I are in the same strait.'"[31]

Recent history has also afforded examples of this nobility
of character, and we shall look at two instances which the
present writer heard at first hand, but which he does not
recollect ever to have seen in print. The first was told me
by the late Ahmad Shafiq Pasha, the famous historian, concerning the age of Isma'il,[32] and the second, which I have
heard from many sources, concerns a period close to it, that
of the Khedive Tawfiq.

The first incident relates that when the Sultan Abd al-Aziz
visited Egypt in the days of Isma'il, the latter was somewhat
anxious about the visit, because part of the business of the
visit was to secure for himself the title of "Khedive," together with a number of other important matters connected
with the administration of Egypt. Part of the program for
the visit was a reception for the ulama in the palace; but
various customs attached to such solemn receptions, among
them that of all who entered the Caliph's presence bowing to
the ground, using the Turkish form of address three times,
and all the rest of those ancient customs--which are so foolish and so contrary to the spirit of Islam. So it became the
duty of the palace staff to drill the ulama in the procedure of
receptions for several days, so that they should not make any
blunders in the Sultan's presence.

When the time came, the leading and most eminent ulama
made their entry; they put aside their religion and paid court
to the world; they bowed low in their prostrations before one
who was created like themselves; they greeted him by touching earth to their brows, their mouths, and their breasts;
and they retired, keeping their backs to the door and their
faces to the Caliph--all just as their ceremonial instructor
had bidden them. All but one, the Shaikh Hasan al-Adawi.
He retained his religion and spurned worldly customs; he

knew that Allah alone is truly great. So he made his entry
with head erect as free men do; he greeted the Caliph with
the Islamic formula, "Peace be upon you, Commander of
the Faithful"; he talked to him with sincerity as wise ulama
should, exhorting him to show piety towards Allah, and to
use justice and mercy in dealing with his subjects. And
when he had finished, he gave him the greeting of "peace"
again, and retired with his head erect as free men do.

The Khedive and the palace staff were horrified, thinking
that all their plans would be frustrated, for the Sultan would,
of course, be furious; all their efforts would be wasted, and
all the hopes lost that they had built up. But true and faithful speech is never lost, nor can it fail to touch the heart
with force and power; for it is delivered with such force and
power. Thus it was in this case; for the Sultan said, "This
is the only man among you." And it was he and no other whom
the Sultan honored.

The second incident took place in the Dar al-Ulum between
the Khedive Tawfiq[33] and Shaikh Hasan al-Tawil. The latter
was a professor in this college, and he always dressed in informal clothes. One day the Principal learned that the Khedive
was going to visit the college, so he made his preparations
to put the best appearance upon the establishment; and one of
his ideas was that the Shaikh al-Tawil should change his
clothes and dress in formal attire, so that he might be suitably garbed to meet the dignitaries.

The Shaikh listened to the Principal's request, and agreed
with the suggestion. The next day he appeared in his usual
garb, but carrying a handkerchief in which was a bundle of
clothes. When the Principal saw him, his face registered
his displeasure, and in obvious anger and disappointment he
said, "Where are your formal clothes, Professor?" "Here,"
said the Shaikh, pointing to the handkerchief. So the Principal left him, satisfied that he would change into formal wear
when the distinguished visitor arrived, and quite content with
such a strange proceeding.

Time passed, and at length the pillars of the college shook
with the arrival of the long-expected visitor. But now came
a tremendous surprise for Principal, Professors, and everyone; for al-Tawil advanced to meet the Khedive, with a bundle
of clothes in his hand, and with an assured and confident air
he said: "I was told that I must have formal clothes, so I

brought them. If you want the clothes, here they are; if
you want Hasan al-Tawil, here he is."

The Khedive characteristically preferred to have Hasan
al-Tawil.

Such believing souls as these respect no greatness save
that of Islam; hence they know a freedom of mind and conscience from all false values, and from all worldly considerations. They have grasped the very essence of Islam, and
have comprehended its central treaching; they have found
their strength in its powerful and lofty spirit, and hence they
have no need of the influence of men. And that is Islam

* * * * * * *

In the same connection of human equality, freedom of
conscience, and absolute justice we may perhaps also discuss the historical experience of Islam in the administration of conquered territories, and of non-Muslim communities in Muslim territory. This is an aspect of equality and
justice in which individuals may go further than communities,
and in which the religious laws of Islam go further than
statutory man-made laws.

Any discussion of conquered territories must lead us to
discuss the nature, the causes, and the aims of Muslim
conquest. This is an immense subject, from which we shall
select only such few points as are indispensable, such points
as have a radical bearing on social justice in its universal
application.

The preaching of Islam has always been based on an appeal to the mind, the heart, and the conscience; it has always
dispensed with the method of conquest, even with that spiritual
form of conquest used by the earlier religions in the form of
wonderful miracles. Islam was the first religion to show
respect to the human faculty of perception and intellect, and
to content itself with an appeal to this faculty, rather than
an attempt to overcome it by producing supra-rational
miracles. And from the very outset it has never made forcible conquest one of its aims. "There shall be no compulsion
in religion."[34] "Summon men to the way of your Lord wisely
and with fair warnings; bring against them a better argument."[35]

It was the Quraish who were the first to put physical force
in the way of the new religion, by maltreating those whose
hearts Allah had turned to Islam; they drove out the few Muslims from their lands, their houses, and their families; they

attempted to cut off the Muslims as a body, and to destroy them by hunger. There was not a single method of physical violence which they did not use to turn men away from this religion. Thus it became inevitable that Islam should use the same methods, and should turn force against those who had first used it. "Permission is given to those who have been opposed by force, because they have been wronged; verily Allah is able to help them"[36] "Fight in the way of Allah against those who oppose you by force; but do not open hostilities, for Allah does not love those who do so."[37] This is defensive warfare, aimed at guaranteeing freedom of worship and preventing injury to Muslims; it does NOT aim at compelling anyone to adopt Islam.

Finally the whole of Arabia was Islamized, and the conquests spread to the lands outside Arabia. Of what nature were these conquests?

As we have seen, Islam reckons itself to be a world-wide religion, and a universal system; therefore it could not confine itself to the limits of Arabia, but naturally desired to spread over the whole world in every direction. However, it found itself opposed by political forces in the Persian and Roman Empires, which were its neighbors; these stood in the way of Islam, and would not allow its missionaries to travel through their countries to inform their people of the nature of Islam, this new faith. Therefore it followed that these political forces had to be destroyed, so that there might be toleration for the true faith among men. Islam aimed only at obtaining a hearing for its gospel, so that anyone who might want to accept it would be free to do as he wished, while anyone who wanted to reject it could be the master of his own destiny; this was possible only when the political and material forces of the Empires had been removed from the path.

The Islamic conquests, then, were not national wars of aggression, nor yet were they a system of colonization for economic gain, like the colonizing ventures of later centuries. They were simply a means of getting rid of the material and political opposition which stood between the nations and the new faith which Islam brought with it. They were an "intellectual war" on the peoples, and a physical war on the powers which held these peoples, and which denied them access to the new religion.

The consequence of the Islamic doctrines, first that Islam is a universal religion, and second, that it must not employ physical or spiritual conquest, is this: Three possibilities are placed before the people of a conquered country, one of which every one must choose; Islam, the poll-tax, or war.

Islam: this is the true way, being the pefect philosophy of the universe, life, and mankind. It is like a strait over which a non-Muslim may pass; then, from the first moment of his crossing, he is a brother to all Muslims; he has all that they have, and he must do all that they do; they cannot be superior to him in rank or in lineage, in wealth or in influence. He is one with them, irrespective of race or community or tribe.

Or the poll-tax: individual Muslims must pay the poor-tax to the state, and thus bear their share of the expenses of society. Individual non-Muslims also enjoy the security afforded by the Islamic state, its protection at home and abroad, and all the other benefits which the state extends to its citizens; so in all equity non-Muslims must bear their share of the state's expenses. But since the poor-tax is a form of religious duty for the Muslim, besides being a statutory duty on wealth, Islam has a fine perception for the susceptibilities of those who do not belong to it, and is therefore unwilling to force them to fulfill a Muslim religious duty. So it imposes the statutory duty on their wealth in the form of a poll-tax, rather than in that of a poor-tax. Thus the poll-tax is a symbol of submission; that is to say it is a sign that there is here no opposition to the doctrines of Islam; but it is also a symbol of Islam's universal tolerance. Which is the aim of Islam.

Or war: for to refuse both Islam and the payment of the poll-tax argues that a man seeks to serve the material forces which intervene between Islam and the minds of men. Hence such a one must be disposed of by physical force, which is ultimately the only way.

Thus Islam completely established its universal aims in the conquered territories. It gave the conquered peoples absolute equality with the native Arabs, on condition that they chose Islam. It gave them their full human rights if they chose to pay the poll-tax. And it gave them just and humane treatment if they chose war.

Islam confirmed in their office some of the governors of the conquered territories, if they became Muslims. Such a one was Bazan the Persian, whom Abu-Bakr confirmed in his office in the Yemen. He also installed Firuz as governor of San'a, and when Qais ibn-Abd Yaghuth the Arab chief expelled him, Abu-Bakr sent him back, thus aiding a Persian Muslim against an Arab.

Similarly Muslim governors confirmed lesser officials in the positions which they had previously held in their native countries, now conquered. These might stand by their former religion, without professing Islam; the only qualification necessary was that they should be willing to work honestly for the general welfare.

The tenets of Islam actually allow the conquerors to appropriate everything that formerly belonged to their opponents, if these have refused to accept either the poll-tax or Islam, and if they have fought against the Muslims. Yet Umar had assimilated so much of the spirit of Islam that, when a country was conquered in his times, he used to leave the land in the possession of its owners, merely laying on them land-tax. Two benefits accrued from this system: The people of the subjugated territories benefitted, for even though they had fought against the Muslims, they still had their livelihood and their work. And subsequent generations of Muslims benefitted, for it meant that they were not excluded from the benefits of the conquest in favor of the one generation which had achieved it; rather the tax arising from these lands was there for the benefit of coming generations, to the general advantage, and to meet public needs for a long time.

This is a significant indication of the manner in which Islam dealt with the conquered territories; it administered them according to humane principles, permitting all that was best for them, and allowing them the exercise of all their prerogatives, without limit or condition. Indeed it enjoined upon them by all means to make good use of all their benefits, and to exercise their prerogatives. It would not place one color or race or religion or tongue before another; all had the opportunity of exerting their natural zeal for the common good. We have already noticed how clients and natives of the conquered territories acquired prominence in matters pertaining particularly to Islam, such as canon law and ecclesiastical law. There was not one of the high positions in public life which was restricted to the Arab conquerors; even the office of governor of a province was within their

reach in many periods. In the same way the taxes gathered
in each country were used primarily for the welfare of that
country; only what was left over afterwards was sent to the
public treasury. The conquered territories were not treated
as colonies, where the conquerors lived off the blood and the
wealth of the native population.

Also connected with this subject is the freedom which Islam gave to conquered peoples to preserve their own religious
beliefs, and the protection which it afforded to their synagogues
and churches, their sanctuaries, their priests, and their
monks. And it is to be noted how Islam fulfilled the promises
which it had made, a rarely parallelled phenomenon, and
one unknown to humanity in its experience of empires ancient
or modern. And to this day the tradition of Islam is still
to conduct its administration in the same way.

So in every age Islam wears an aspect of outstanding
grandeur and high nobility, when it is contrasted with present
day Western civilization and its practices in countries whose
backwardness brings them into the toils of colonial administration. Such countries are denied the true prerogatives of
Western civilization, such as education, commerce, and
trade, to the end that they may remain as long as possible in
the role of milch cattle for the colonizing nations. In addition
to this there is entailed the degradation of all human nobility,
both individual and social, the corruption of morals which
arises from such a frank opportunism, the rivalries of party
and sect whose seeds are sown and whose growth is encouraged,
and all varieties of theft, robbery, and plunder on the part of
individuals, societies, and nations.

As for the freedom of religious belief, of which so much
is often made in this age, the horrors of the Spanish Inquisition
hardly bear out such a claim, nor do the horrors perpetrated
by the Crusaders in the East. And this kind of religious
"freedom" is still an issue today; Christian missionaries in
the Southern Sudan are supported by all the power of the government, while Muslims are forbidden to enter the country,
even to trade. And Allenby, the famous English general of the
First World War, spoke for every European when he exclaimed
as he entered Jerusalem, "Only now have the Crusades come
to an end."

Islam has always represented the highest achievement in
universal and comprehensive social justice; European civili-

zation has never reached the same level, nor ever will. For it is a civilization founded on pure materialism, a civilization of murder and war, of conquest and of subjugation.

* * * * * * *

We have already discussed the Islamic theory of benevolence and charity, of that mutual responsibility which makes common cause between the strong and the weak, the rich and the poor, the individual and the community, the ruler and his subjects; in a word it embraces all men. Now we must turn to some illustrations from the course of history, selected from the great number of such afforded by the long story of Islam.

At the time when he became a Muslim, Abu-Bakr had a fortune of forty thousand dirhams, amassed from the profits of his trading; and after becoming a Muslim he still made a great deal through trade. Yet when he accompanied Muhammad on the Emigration to Medina all that was left of his fortune was five thousand dirhams. The remainder he had spent in two ways: First, in ransoming the slaves who through him became Muslim clients; these had formerly suffered various kinds of afflictions at the hands of unbelievers who owned them. And second, in charity to the poor and the destitute.

So too when Umar, who was himself a poor man, received a gift of lands at Khaibar, he went to the Messenger and said to him: "I have received a gift of lands at Khaibar, but no money, which I would have preferred. What do you advise me to do with the land?" The Messenger told him: "If you wish you may keep it, but give away the income from it in alms." So Umar made the lands a charitable foundation for the poor and for his relatives, for slaves, for use in the way of Allah, and for the weak. Thus he did not offend the donor, who had given it to him that he might live suitably off it, and so that he might have a good living without undue wealth. Thus too he avoided letting his property get a hold upon him, and proved the truth of the verse, "You will never be really charitable until you spend what you love."[38]

Before Uthman became Caliph one of his caravans returned from Syria at a time when the Muslims were hard pressed by famine by reason of a drought; the caravan was composed of a thousand camels loaded with corn, olives, and raisins. So the merchants of Medina approached him with a request that he would sell them some of the goods, since he knew the straits that the people were in. He assented gladly, and asked, "What profit will you give me over my buying price?" They offered double what the goods cost, but Uthman said that he had a better offer than that. The merchants protested: "But, Abu-Amr, there are no merchants in Medina except ourselves, and no one can have approached you before us. Who has made you this offer?" "Allah offers me ten times the price of the goods," said Umar; "Can you go higher than that?" "No," they confessed. Then he swore by Allah that the caravan and all its contents should be given as alms to the destitute and the poor among the Muslims.

Ali and his household gave away in alms three loaves of barley bread which they had, to relieve the destitute, the orphan, and the prisoner; they themselves had to sleep hungry, but the recipients were satisfied.

Husain[39] was heavily in debt, but though he owned the spring of Abu-Naizar he would not sell it; for the poorer Muslims used to draw their water from it, and it was reserved for them. So he decided rather to bear the weight of his debt, for he was a nobleman of noble descent from the best of the clan of Hashim.

In the same way the Helpers in Medina shared with the Emigrants their property and their houses; they took them as brothers, paid their ransoms, and redeemed their captives, treating them in all things as themselves. As the glorious Qur'an describes them, "They found no desires in their hearts for the share which had fallen to others; they preferred them above themselves, though among themselves there was poverty."[40]

The spirit of Islam continues to be thus active as long as the Islamic world is free from the influence of materialistic Western civilization. This is well shown by this account of the Touareg tribes, given by Professor Abd-al-Rahman Azzam in his book, "The Eternal Message."

"I have known Touareg tribes in North Africa who live this happy life of mutual responsibility; none among them lives for himself, but all for the community. The greatest source of pride and glory among them is how much they can do for this community. The first thing that attracted my attention to this system was when a certain man who came from the urban area fled from the French and came to the

Touareg at Fazzan, where he claimed the hospitality of the community and lived off their bounty. He afterwards returned to his native place, to look for some means of earning money with which to repay the Touareg in full; but his family he left in the protection of this Islamic community. Ill luck, however, pursued him, and he was unable to make any money. He came to me in his distress, to ask for help, and I advised him to go back to his family. About a year later he came back to see me a second time, and I imagined that in the interval he had been with his family. But he said, 'No. Only now can I return to my family.' When I asked, 'How is that?' he said to me: 'After I saw you last time I used all my available money in a business venture, and now I have enough to take back with me to the Touareg community.' I asked him, 'Are you taking it to your children, or to the community?' and he replied: 'To the latter in the first place; for they have given hospitality to my children during my absence. So I will make myself responsible for the children of any other man whom I can find to be away from home. I shall divide what Allah has granted me between my own children and those of my neighbor.' Then I asked him, 'Does the whole community live in the same way as you with your neighbor?' and he replied: 'All of us are equal in good times or in evil; all extra can go to him who wants it. So any member of our community would be ashamed to return purely to provide for his own; he must look after, not only his own family, but also that of his neighbors, who have awaited his return just as eagerly as his own household.'"

This piece of evidence the author follows with a general statement which explains the underlying truth.

"Such a communal spirit is not peculiar to this Touareg community or to others similar to it among the desert and wilderness dwellers; nor is this spirit one of the prerequisites of their solidarity. In effect it is no more than the spirit of Islam, which is more clearly apparent among such people who are still uncontaminated by modern materialistic life. I have found this spirit in those Muslim villages and hamlets which are still characteristically Islamic, no matter whether their inhabitants are Arab or otherwise, white or black, Eastern or Western. In most of these I have found a Muslim community still living a life of virtue and fellowship, of mutual responsibility, and mutual help, inspired by charity.

Such people are closer to the ideal society as envisaged by
the founder of Islam than the tens of millions who are attracted
by materialistic Western civilization. The latter live for
themselves, even though their society may be on the verge
of destruction; they prefer the satisfaction of their own desires
to charity towards their own families, let alone towards
their neighbors."

This mutual responsibility inculcated by the spirit of Islam is not left solely to the discretion of the social or of the
individual conscience; a ruler also has his necessary part to
play. Thus Umar instituted a payment from the public treasury to all who were very young or very old, and to all who
were sick; this was not a recognized use for the public monies,
but was an aspect of his perception of social responsibility
in the conditions of his time. And in fact this dispensation
made the law concerning theft unnecessary during the "Year
of Ashes,"[41] when the people were starving. And that, although starvation constitutes almost a compulsion to theft,
and under such circumstances laws are commonly disregarded.

Perhaps the following story about Umar is most significant
for the practical application of the thought of mutual responsibility; it also concerns the right of individual possession,
and its laws in relation to society.

"They say that some of the slaves of Hatib ibn-abi-Bati'a
stole a camel from a man of the Muzaina; Umar caught them,
and they confessed the crime, so he ordered Kathir ibn-al-
Salt to cut off their hands. When the latter refused, Umar
insisted. Then Kathir said to Hatib: 'I would indeed have
cut off their hands; but I knew that you made these slaves
work hard, and that you kept them so hungry that if one of
them had eaten anything forbidden by Allah he would have
been pardonable.' This remark reached the ears of Abd
al-Rahman, the son of Hatib, who exclaimed: 'I swear by
Allah although I had no part in this deed, yet I will discharge the obligation of the complaint.' So he demanded of
the Muzainite, 'How much was your camel worth to you?'
'Four hundred dirhams,' answered the man. But Umar said
to Abd al-Rahman, 'Go and pay him eight hundred.' Then
he remitted the penalty of the slaves who had committed the
theft, on the grounds that Hatib had driven them to such an
act by keeping them hungry, so that they had to have enough
to stave off starvation."

Thus in historical practice there was implemented that far-reaching precedent which was accorded by Islam to the right to live, and to the right to possess a competence; this it held to be greater than the right of individual possession. Here also there was a clear and distinct ratification of the principle of mutual responsibility in society, between the "have's" and the "have-not's" within the community.

This conception of social responsibility is made even more famous in the history of Islam by the fact that it passed beyond the limits of the purely Islamic world, and was applied to mankind in general.

Umar once saw an old blind man begging at a door; he asked about him, and learned that he was a Jew. Then said Umar to him: "What has brought you to this state?" "The poll-tax, penury, and age." Umar took him by the hand, and brought him to his own house, where he gave him sufficient to satisfy his immediate needs. Then he sent a message to the keeper of the public treasury: "Look after this man and others such. For by Allah we have not given him justice if we have profited from his youth, only to desert him now in his old age. Alms are only for the poor and the destitute; and this man is in destitution, and is one of the scripturaries." So he remitted the poll-tax to him and to others like him.

Similarly, while on his way to Damascus Umar passed a piece of land belonging to some Christian lepers, and commanded that a gift be made to them out of the alms money, and that food be supplied to them.

Thus Umar raised the spirit of Islam to this universal level more than thirteen centuries ago. He made social security a universal right, independent of religion or creed, and not to be precluded by any religious doctrine or belief. Surely this is a supremely high level which mankind is still striving unsuccessfully to achieve.

* * * * * * *

When we come to discuss political and economic theory from the practical point of view of the state, we find that the course of history shows an exemplary failure in the life of Islam, a failure which has had lamentable results. The reason for this we shall see in what follows. For we must discover whether the reason for the failure was some integral part of the nature of the Islamic system of politics and economics, or if it was the outcome of chance occurrences of evil, unconnected with the nature of the system.

We shall start with a consideration of political theory, because economic theory follows political in the course of history, and is formed by it.

When the death of the Prophet drew near, he appointed Abu-
Bakr to lead the prayers. A'isha protested, because Abu-
Bakr was a tender-hearted man, and when he stood up to lead
the prayers his voice would not be heard for sobs. But Muhammad fell into a rage, and recalled the foolish women in the
story of Joseph,[42] insisting that Abu-Bakr be appointed to
lead the prayers.

Does this, then, mean that the Messenger appointed as his
successor his former companion in the cave?[43] And if so,
did the Muslims clearly understand that fact?

We must reject both of these ideas. If Muhammad had
wished to appoint a successor, and if such an appointment had
been one of the ordinances of Islam, he would have declared
the appointment publicly, as was his custom with all the other
ordinances of the faith. And if the Muslims had clearly understood that he had appointed Abu-Bakr as his successor, the
following dispute would never have taken place between the
Emigrants and the Helpers; for the latter would never have
disputed any matter which was governed by a command from
Allah's Messenger.

The matter, then, was one for the council of Muslims to
decide to the general satisfaction which of the people had the
best right to the caliphate. And when within the council there
was a dispute as to whether or not the Caliph should be one of
the Emigrants, that matter was not one of the ordinances of
Islam, but rather a matter for agreement and accommodation
among the Muslim community. The Helpers could have rejected a Caliph, and were not liable to censure for so doing;
but actually they approved Abu-Bakr because of the local hostility between the Aus and the Khazraj, the two main tribes
of Helpers, and because both of these parties were unwilling
that the caliphate should fall to the other; both preferred that
under the circumstances it should go to the Emigrants.

When agreement was reached, it was settled that day that
the Caliphate should belong to the Emigrants; but there was
nothing in that to necessitate that the caliphate should become
the prerequisite of the Quraish. Had it been so, Umar, when
he named the council to appoint his own successor, would
never have said, "If Salim, the client of Abu-Hudhaifa had

been still alive, I should myself have nominated him as my successor." For Salim was certainly no Quraishite. The spirit and the principles of Islam alike forbid that the Quraish should have any status above that of ordinary Muslims, simply because they are the Quraish, or because they have a blood connection with the Prophet.

Abu-Bakr certainly appointed Umar as his successor; but this involved no compulsion on the Muslims, since they were free to reject the appointment. Therefore Umar became Caliph, not because Abu-Bakr had appointed him, but because the people took the oath of allegiance to him. In the same way Umar himself named a council of six, that after his death one of these should be chosen. Yet the Muslims were not compelled to accept one of these six; the only reason was that experience had shown that the six in question were the best fitted for the office, and thus Umar's choice was in line with experience. From this fact there arose all the compulsion that there was.

As for the oath of allegiance to Ali, there were some who were willing to take it, while others refused to take it; and so for the first time civil war was known in Islam. From that fact there came all the disasters which have encompassed the spirit and the principles of Islam in politics, economics, and in other regards.

This brief review has shown us the fundamental political theory of Islam; namely, that the unfettered choice of all Muslims is the only warrant for authority. This was clearly apparent to the Muslim community when it passed over Ali, the nephew and son-in-law of Allah's Messenger and his nearest kinsman. Ali was defrauded when he was passed over, especially after the death of Umar; the worst thing that could have happened in the history of Islam, as we see it, was the neglect of Ali after the death of Umar. Yet this same neglect had a certain value as a practical illustration of Islamic political theory, with its insistence that authority is not subject to the right of inheritance in any way; such an idea is completely foreign to the spirit and principles of Islam. Thus, although the great Imam personally was defrauded in this way, yet the emphasis on the preceding fact was from every point of view infinitely more important.

With the coming of Mu'awiya the caliphate in Islam became a monarchy, or a tyranny, confined to the Umayyad family.

This was characteristic, not of Islam, but of the pre-Islamic age, just as the common verdict on the Umayyads is that they had no deep-seated religious beliefs; Islam for them was a cloak which they assumed to cover their preoccupation with material and worldly prosperity.

It will be sufficient at this point to quote as proof of this the account of the oath of allegiance as it was taken to Yazid.[44] From this we may discover the foundation of Umayyad power, and find out whether Mu'awiya, who established that power, was true to the spirit of Islam, or to some other ideal. Mu'awiya summoned delegates to represent all the provinces at the taking of the oath of allegiance to Yazid. Then Yazid ibn-al-Muqaffa stood up and said: "The Commander of the Faithful is here," and he indicated Mu'awiya. "If he dies, his successor is here," and he indicated Yazid. "And if anyone refuses--here." and he pointed to his sword. Then said Mu'awiya, "Sit down, O best of preachers."

After the oath was taken to Yazid in Syria, Mu'awiya gave to Sa'id ibn-al-As the task of gaining the acceptance of the people of the Hejaz. This he was unable to do, so Mu'awiya went to Mecca with an army and with a full treasury. He called together the principal Muslims, and addressed them thus:

"You all know that I have lived among you, and you are aware also of my ties of kindred with you. Yazid is your brother and your nephew. It is my wish that you take the oath to Yazid as the next Caliph; then it will be you who will bestow offices and depose from them, who will collect and apportion money." He was answered by Abdullah ibn-al-Zubair, who gave him a choice of three things to do: First, he might do as Allah's Messenger had done, and appoint no successor; second, he might do as Abu-Bakr had done, and nominate a successor who was not of his immediate family; third, he might do as Umar had done, and hand over the whole matter to a council of six individuals, none of whom was a member of his own immediate family. Mu'awiya's anger was kindled, and he asked, "Have you any more to say?" "No." Mu'awiya turned to the remainder of the company: "And you?" "We agree with what Ibn-al-Zubair has said," they replied. Then he addressed the meeting in threatening terms: "I excuse him whom I warn. I was speaking among you, and one of you was bold to get up and call me a liar to my face. That I will bear and even forgive. But I stand to my words, and I swear by Allah that if any of you speaks one word against the position that I take up, no word of answer will he receive, but first the sword will take his head. And no man can do more than save his life."

In the further course of events, Mu'awiya set a warder with two guards over each one of the principal men of the Hejaz who opposed him, and to each warder he said: "If your man leaves his guards to speak one word, either for me or against me, then let the guards strike off his head with their swords." Then he mounted the pulpit, and proclaimed: "These men are the leaders and the choicest of the Muslims; no matter can be successfully handled without them, nor can any decision be taken without their counsel. They are now satisfied to take the oath to Yazid, and indeed have already taken that oath by the name of Allah." So the people took the oath.

It was on such a basis, completely unrecognized by Islam, that the royal authority of Yazid stood. And what was this Yazid?

He it was of whom Abdullah ibn-Hanzala said: "We had hardly left the presence of Yazid when we feared to be struck down by lightning strokes from Heaven. For men were marrying their mothers or their daughters or their sisters, they were drinking wine, and omitting to say the prayers. By Allah, had not one of the people been with me, I would have called him to a fair trial before Allah."

Even if this represents an exaggeration due to hostility towards Yazid (though there is probably no exaggeration in it), it remains a fact that he was a youth devoted to drinking and pleasure, which he pursued to the limit of folly; it is true that he cared more for the keeping and the rearing of monkeys than he did for ruling and caring for his subjects; he was a man of levity, lightmindedness, and pleasure.

This was the "Caliph" whom Mu'awiya imposed on the people, forcing them to accept him by a means which Islam does not recognize, namely the force of family and tribal solidarity. This was neither difficult nor strange in the case of Mu'awiya; for he was the son of Abu-Sufyan, and his mother was Hind, the daughter of Utba. Mu'awiya was in all respects a son worthy of such a family, and supremely so in the extent to which his spirit differed from the true nature of Islam. No one can judge Islam by Mu'awiya, or by

any of the Umayyads; and Islam can bear no responsibility
for him, or for any of them.

In order to acquit Islam, its spirit and its principles,
from this hereditary system which Mu'awiya introduced into
it. we must digress a little to discuss Mu'awiya and the clan
of Umayya, purely for the purpose of establishing the truth.

Abu-Sufyan was the man from whom Islam and the Muslims
received such treatment as has filled the pages of history.
He did not embrace Islam until its victory was assured, and
even then his conversion was a thing of words rather than of
faith in heart and conscience; for Islam never penetrated to
his heart. Accordingly he was always watching for the defeat
of the Muslims; he expected it at the battle of Hunain, [45] and
again during the Muslim attack on the Roman Empire. He
was all this time ostensibly a Muslim himself, but the old
loyalties of the pre-Islamic age still had control of his heart.
Thus when he stood one day at Umar's door with Suhail ibn-
Amr ibn-al-Harith and a number of other nobles and saw Umar
admit Bilal and Suhaib before them, because these two had
been early Muslims, Abu-Sufyan was particularly enraged,
and in an effort to stir up discontentment he said: "Never
have I seen anything like this; he admits these slaves, and
leaves us standing at his door." But his companion reproved
him in these words: "O people, by Allah I can see what is on
your faces. But if you are going to be angry, then let your
anger be against yourselves; you were summoned to become
Muslims at the same time as others, but the others went
over quickly, and you slowly. How will it stand with you on
the Day of Resurrection, when others are called and you are
left?"

But Abu-Sufyan still nourished a rancor against Islam and
against the Muslims, and he saw no opportunity of rousing
discontent without eagerly availing himself of it. When Ali
was passed over in favor of Abu-Bakr for the caliphate, Abu-
Sufyan spoke up in these words: "By Allah I foresee here a
flame of trouble which will only be quenched in blood. O
family of Abd Manaf, what has Abu-Bakr to do with your affairs? Where are the two weaklings, the humble Ali and Al-
Abbas?

> "None bear the evil blow of fate save two
> Most humble, cord and peg their tribe to raise;
> Yet this in ignominy silent sits,
> The other dead without a word of praise."

Ali realized what Abu-Sufyan was aiming at, and he fore-
stalled him by saying: "By Allah, your whole object in this
is to rouse discord; as indeed you are constantly planning
evil against Islam." He is also reported to have said: "O
Abu-Sufyan, Muslims are those who give honest counsel to
one another; but hypocrites are those who deceive one another,
who deal treacherously between themselves, even though
their homes and their persons are near neighbors."

Abu-Sufyan was, of course, dreaming of a monarchy which
would be hereditary among the Umayyads ever since Utha-
man became Caliph, and indeed on that day he said: "O
Umayyads, take the power now, once for all. For by Him
in Whose name Abu-Sufyan swears, I have always hoped for
this on your behalf--that this power might be yours and your
children's by right of inheritance." Authority among the
Muslims was always referred to as "kingship" until the time
of Muhammad, when he stood reviewing the Muslim army
on the day of the conquest of Mecca. On that occasion he
said to Al-Abbas, his uncle: "By Allah, Abu-al-Fadl, the
royal power of your nephew has today become great." But
when Al-Abbas reminded him, "It is rather a prophetic
power," he agreed, "You are right."

"Your are right." For "kingship" was a word heard only
with the ears, rather than a term accepted by the heart.
For such a heart as that of the Prophet could accept only the
meaning of such a term as kingship and royal authority, not
the actuality of it.

Such, then, was the father of Mu'awiya. His mother was
Hind, the daughter of Utba; she it was who stood at the battle
of Uhud and lapped up the blood as she bit into the liver of
Hamza like a fierce lioness. Even this shocking deed was
not too much to satisfy the hatred of the dead Hamza which
had been kindled in her by a blood feud.

She it was too who stood firm after her husband had embraced Islam; she still held out against it, even when the
success of Islam was assured. Then she cried aloud: "Kill
this mischievous rascal in whom there is no good. A ruffian
is he who spies upon his people. Will you not, then, fight
these fellows to repulse them from your persons and your
lands?"

The Umayyads under Islam were exactly the same as they
had been before Islam; they alone had refused during the pre-

Islamic age to take the Oath of Fudhul.[46] This oath had
touched a humane note which the Umayyad nature could not
show; for it was phrased thus: "To stand up for the oppressed
until he is given his rights, to take from our own possessions
and to share our own property to satisfy those rights, to prevent the strong from oppressing the weak, and the native
doing violence to the stranger." The Umayyad nature made
it impossible for them to take such an oath; their inherited
family characteristics forbade it.

The aunt of   Umar ibn-Abd al-Aziz,[47] herself an Umayyad,
perceived that there was in Umar a strain not native to the
Umayyads when he succeeded to the caliphate and embarked
on a course foreign to the nature of that family. He was distinguished for his humane nature; he redressed the wrongs
which had been done by the hands of his own kinsmen; and
he prevented the latter from carrying on their illegal plundering of the public treasury. So when his aunt was brought
into his presence, she addressed him thus: "Verily your
kinsmen are complaining about you, and saying that you have
taken from them everything except what you give them yourself."" I have taken nothing from them that is their right,"
he replied, "And nothing which belongs to them." She answered: "I have heard their talk, and I fear that they will
inflame an evil day against you." Said he: "Allah can guard
me from the evil of every day which I fear, save only the
Day of Resurrection."

Upon this she realized that Umar had in him a strain
foreign to the Umayyad nature, and one of which she disapproved. When she returned to her own family she told
them: "See how things turn out for you as a result of marrying into the family of Umar ibn-al-Khattab."

Yes indeed; see how things turn out for you. For it was
a crime in Umayyad eyes for a ruler to show piety towards
Allah, to withhold perquisites and easy riches, to stand for
the right, and not to exercise the power of his authority to
fill his coffers and to sate his appetites. Yes indeed; this
was a crime brought on by an alliance with the family of Al-
Khattab; for the great Umar was the grandfather of Umar II
on his mother's side. And it was his influence which disturbe
the rooted and inherited mode of Umayyad life.

The erroneous fable still persists that Mu'awiya was the
scribe who wrote down the revelations of Allah's Messenger.

The truth is that when Abu-Sufyan embraced Islam, he be-sought the Prophet to give Mu'awiya some measure of position in the eyes of the Arabs; thus he would be compensated for the disgrace of being slow to embrace Islam, and of being one of those who had no precedence in the new religion. So the Prophet used Mu'awiya for writing letters and contracts and agreements. But none of the Companions ever said that he wrote down any of the Prophet's revelations, as was asserted by Mu'awiya's partisans after he had assumed the throne. But this is what happens in all such cases.

We cannot condemn Mu'awiya for instituting a new system of political theory including the idea of hereditary succession, or for forcing the people to accept it. But we can condemn him strongly for suppressing all moral elements in his struggle with Ali, and throughout the course of his reign thereafter; for this was the first time that any such suppres-sion had taken place in the history of Islam. For in Islam politics, like life in general, had always been the expression of those moral feelings which lie deep within life, and which are rooted in its very nature. The existence of these feelings was a natural consequence of that constant watchfulness which Islam enjoined upon the individual conscience, and of that keen moral perception which it awakens in the souls of its adherents; of this we have seen examples at the beginning of this chapter. The greatest crime of Mu'awiya, therefore, was that he de-stroyed the spirit of Islam at the very beginning of his reign by a complete suppression of its moral elements.

It was doubly unfortunate that such a calamity should be-fall Islam thus early, when no more than thirty years of its first life had passed; thus it was given no opportunity of be-coming permanently established, or of settling the profound traditions which are so difficult to regain once they have been deserted. This was undoubtedly a stroke of ill luck. Yet in actual fact Mu'awiya was not the prime originator of the evil; rather it was the passing over of Ali and the election of Uthman, a weak old man, to the caliphate, and the fact that the management of affairs was handed over to Marwan ibn-al-Hakam, the Umayyad. If fortune had decreed that Ali be elected Caliph after Abu-Bakr and Umar, then the traditions of Islam would have continued unbroken for a further period, and it would have remained on a steady course for a third term; then there would not have followed the obliteration of the spirit of Islam which did actually take place.

In order to appreciate the full significance of this statement we must examine the form of political theory in the
different periods; under Abu-Bakr and Umar, under Uthman
and Marwan, under the Imam Ali, and finally under the
Umayyad, and later the Abbasid, kings, when the spirit of
Islam had been completely crushed by Mu'awiya and his
nephews.

When the Muslim community invited Abu-Bakr to become
the Successor (i.e., Caliph) of Allah's Messenger, his status
in his own eyes was not increased because he was now responsible for enforcing on the Muslims the observance of the
faith and the law of Allah. It did not occur to him that this
new position might permit him anything which was not permitted to him when he was a private individual, that it might
allow him any new right which he had not previously enjoyed,
or that it might absolve him from any one of his former re-
sponsibilities--to himself, to his people, or to his God.

After the oath of allegiance had been taken, he stood in
the courtyard and thus addressed the people: "Now O people,
I am your ruler, though I am not the best among you. If I
do what is right, support me. If I do what is wrong, set me
right. Follow what is true, for it contains faithfulness; avoid
what is false, for it holds treachery. The weaker among
you shall in my eyes be the stronger, until, if Allah will, I
have redressed his wrong; the stronger in my eyes shall be
the weaker, until, if Allah will, I have enforced justice upon
him. Let the people cease not to fight in the way of Allah,
lest Allah abase them; let not evil practices arise among the
people, lest Allah bring punishment upon them. Obey me as
I obey Allah and His Messenger; if I disobey them, then do
you disobey me."

Abu-Bakr lived at al-Sunh, a suburb in the vicinity of
Medina, in a small and humble house; when he became Caliph
he changed neither his house nor his mode of living. He used
to walk on foot from his house at al-Sunh to and from Medina,
morning and evening, though sometimes he rode a horse which
was his private possession, not supplied out of the public
treasury. Finally, when the pressure of his work grew too
great, he moved into Medina.

He lived off his earnings as a merchant; but when he
sought to go and attend to his business, the Muslims restraine
him, saying: "This office does not go well with business." So

he asked them, as one who knew of no other way to earn his daily bread, "Then how shall I live?" Thereupon, after deliberation on the question, they assigned him an allowance from the public treasury, to feed himself and his family; this was in the nature of a recompense for having had to give up his business and confine himself to his official duties.

Despite this, when he was at the point of death, he commanded that all that he had received from the public monies should be counted up and repaid out of his property and his lands, so that he might spare the property of the Muslim community. He always held himself personally responsible for the needs of every individual among his subjects, because he believed strongly in that constant watchfulness of conscience which Islam lays upon both ruler and ruled, and in that keen moral perception which it kindles in the conscience of all and sundry. This he carried to the point of drawing milk for the poor from the flocks and herds of his neighbors at al-Sunh. For when he came to the caliphate he had heard a servant girl say: "The ewes of our household will give no milk for us today." Abu-Bakr, hearing it, said: "Nay, by my life, but I will milk them for you." And so he did. Sometimes he would ask the girl: "Girl, do you want the milk frothing or clear?" Sometimes she would say one, and sometimes the other, but whatever she asked, he milked accordingly.

During the caliphate of Abu-Bakr, Umar took in hand to look after a blind woman of Medina, and assumed the responsibility for her affairs; but when one day he came to see her, he found that her needs had been met. Umar kept watch for a day, and found Abu-Bakr supplying her; he was not too busy with the cares of the caliphate to do such a things. Then, seeing him, Umar cried aloud: "By my life, it was you, then."

This is a sketch of Abu-Bakr's habits while he ruled. When Umar succeeded him these habits remained unchanged; for Umar also believed that his new position brought him no new privileges of any kind, except that it increased his work by making him responsible for the enforcement of the law of Allah.

In his sermon[48] after the oath of allegiance he said: "O people, I am no more than a man like yourselves; and had it not been that I was unwilling to refuse to assume the task of Successor to Allah's Messenger, I would never have taken the responsibility of ruling you."

In a second sermon which he gave he said: "O people, it is your duty, if I show any evil qualities, to reprove me for them. You must see that I do not exact from you any tax or anything of what Allah has given you, except that which He allows. You must see that when I have supreme power I do not take from you more taxes than are due. You must see that I do not keep you too long in posts of danger, or detain you unreasonably on the frontiers; for when you are away on military service I must be the father of your families."

He also used to say: "Public property has the same standing with me as that of an orphan; if it is much, it must be conserved, and if it is little, it must be used with care."

When he was questioned one day about how much of the public funds he was entitled to, he replied: "I will tell you how much of it I am entitled to. I am entitled to two suits of clothes, one for the winter, and another for the summer, enough to perform the Pilgrimage and to observe its ceremonies, and sufficient to provide food for myself and my household on the level of a man of Quraish who is neither over rich nor over poor. Beyond that I am an ordinary Muslim, and I share the lot of all Muslims."

In this spirit he lived, but as far as possible he refused to accept even what he was entitled to. One day he was not feeling well, and they prescribed honey for him; now there was a skin of honey in the public treasury, so he mounted the pulpit and announced to the people: "If you permit me to take it, then I shall do so; but if you do not permit me, then I shall not touch it." They gave him permission.

The Muslims perceived what straits he was in, and some of them went to his daughter, Hafsa, the "Mother of the Faithful," and said: "Umar refuses all things save the most exiguous allowance. But Allah has enlarged our resources, so let him take as much as he wishes out of the treasury; for he has the full permission of the whole Muslim community." But when Hafsa mentioned it to him, his answer was: "Hafsa my daughter, you have been faithful to your family but unfaithful to your father. My family have a right only to my person and my property; to my religion and to my faith they have no right."

Umar had a profound understanding of the implications of

the equality which existed between himself and each of his
subjects; thus when the people were starving during the
"Year of Ashes" he took a private oath that he would not
touch butter or meat until the people were in better circum
stances. This oath he kept faithfully until his skin grew
dark and he grimaced if he ate an olive. It happened that
there came into the market a skin of butter and a skin of
milk, and one of Umar's servants bought them for forty
dirhams. The servant went to Umar to tell him what Allah
had granted to him; how this skin of butter and skin of milk
had come into the market, and how he had bought them. But
when Umar heard the price he said: "It is too dear; go and
give them away as alms. I cannot bring myself to eat what
is bought extravagantly." He sat silent for a space and
then added: "How can the state of my people be of concern
to me if what touches them does not affect me?"

Thus he saw to it that he denied himself what was denied
to his subjects, in order, as he said, to experience what
had touched them; also because, from the bottom of his
heart he could not see that his status as ruler gave him any
rights or privileges which the remainder of the people did
not have; and thirdly, because he held that if he did not act
with fairness here, he had no claim on the obedience of his
subjects. We have already mentioned the story of the two
Yemenite scarves; the emphasis of this is on the fact that
the people were not bound to obey him until Umar's equity
was established. This is an emphasis on one of the main
principles of authority in Islam; the unjust ruler has no
claim to obedience.

This understanding of Islam was profound within Umar,
and it governed his actions in all matters. He once bargained
with a man for a horse, and rode it in order to try it out.
The beast was foundered, and he wished to return it to its
owner, but the latter refused to have it. So the two of them
took the matter for decision to Sharih, the Iraqi. He heard
both sides of the case, and then said: "Commander of the
Faithful, either keep what you bought, or else return it as
you got it." Said Umar: "Could there be a better decision
than that?" So he made Sharih judge over Kufa as a reward
for such a fair and honest decision.

Since Umar interpreted his authority in this manner, it
was impossible that his relations should have priviliges greater

than those enjoyed by the remainder of Umar's subjects. So
when his own son Abd al-Rahman was at fault in the matter of
wine-drinking, there could be no doubt but that he would be
punished. This story is well-known, as is that of Amr ibn-
al-As oppressing Al-Misri, in which case again it was inevitable that Umar should permit retaliation against him. In
the matter of money all of Umar's governors were held accountable for any increase in their possessions following the
tenure of an office; for he feared that such an increase might
have been made at the expense of the public monies or by
the arbitrary exercise of official power. "Where did you get
this?" was the law by which he judged his governors individual
whenever he had occasion to take them to task. So he compelled restitution in the case of Amr ibn-al-As, his governor
in Egypt, in the case of Sa'd ibn-Abi-Waqqas, his governor in
Kufa, and so he froze the assets of Abu-Huraira, his governor in Bahrain.

Umar's conception of the nature of political authority was
briefly this: obedience and advice in the realm of faith on the
part of the subject, and justice and beneficence on the part of
the ruler. We have seen how one of his subjects once said to
him: "If we had found any evil thing in you, we would have set
it right with the edge of our swords." Such a story gives expression to the principle that the subject has a right to correct
his ruler. In the same strain Umar once said in a sermon to
the people: "I do not appoint governors over you to scourge
your bodies, or to revile your honor, or to take your wealth.
I appoint them to teach you the Book of your Lord and the Custom of your Prophet. If any man is oppressed in any way by
his governor and has not access to me, then let him have the
matter brought to my notice, that I may punish the governor
for him." Thus he gave emphasis to the strict limits set to
the ruler's power over the people.

It was because of his profound understanding of the responsibilities of a ruler that Umar did not wish these to be borne
by two members of the family of Al-Khattab. Thus he prevented his son Abdullah from being prepared for the office,
even though he did make him one of the elective council. It
was then that Umar made his famous remark, still quoted as
the truest description of the caliphate; "We have no incentive
to undertake your affairs, and I have never estimated them
so highly that I would desire to see one of my family concerned

in them. If he be good, then he has already made his contribution; if he be evil, then it is enough for the family of Umar
to be represented by one."

* * * * * * *

This description of the nature of the tenure of authority
undoubtedly suffered a change under the rule of Uthman. It
was an evil chance that Uthman should come to the caliphate
when he was already an old man whose resolution of character
was less than his faith in Islam, and whose will was too weak
to oppose the craftiness of Marwan and the other Umayyads.

Uthman held that his office of Imam permitted him free
disposal of Muslim funds in gifts and allowances, and his frequent retort to those who found fault with him in this matter
was: "Then for what am I the Imam?" Similarly he held
that he had the power to promote his immediate family and
clan to positions of authority over the people, among them
Al-Hakam, who had formerly been expelled by Allah's Messenger. It was, he held, his simple right to accord to his
own people honor, advancement, and protection.

On the day that Al-Harith ibn-al-Hakam married Uthman's
daughter, the latter gave him from the public treasury two
hundred thousand dirhams. The next day the treasurer, Zaid
ibn-Arqam, came to the Caliph with grief written large on
his features, and with tears sparkling in his eyes. He asked
Uthman to accept his resignation from his position, and when
the Caliph discovered that the reason was his gift to his new
son-in-law out of the public funds, he asked in astonishment:
"Ibn-Arqam, are you weeping because I give gifts to my family?" "No, Commander of the Faithful," returned this man
who understood the keen spirit of Islam, "I am weeping when
I think of you taking this money which formerly, during the
life of Allah's Messenger, I used to spend in the way of Allah.
Even if you had given him only a hundred dirhams, by Allah
that had been too much." Uthman was enraged at such a man
whose conscience could not accept such liberal expense out of
public funds on the relation of the Muslim Caliph, and he said:
"Leave your keys of office, Ibn-Arqam, and we will find some
other to take your place."

Examples of such prodigality are numerous in the life of
Uthman; he gave Al-Zubair 600,000 one day, and Talha 200,000,
and he presented Marwan ibn-al-Hakam with one fifth of the
revenues of the province of Ifriqiya. When some of the Com-

panions of the Prophet, chief among whom was Ali, expostulated with him about this, his answer was: "I have relatives and kinsmen." But they still reproved him, asking: "Did not Abu-Bakr and Umar also have relatives and kinsmen?" He answered: "Abu-Bakr and Umar were concerned to deny their relatives; I am concerned to give to mine." So they left him in agner, saying: "By Allah what Abu-Bakr and Umar gave was better for us than what you give." Yes; and better for Islam; and also more true to Islam.

Even apart from money there were also the governoships which Uthman scattered profusely among his relatives. Among these was Mu'awiya, whose power Uthman expanded considerably, giving him control of Palestine and the district of Emesa; he granted to him the single control of four armies, and thus made it the easier for Mu'awiya later to aspire to royal power during the caliphate of Ali, by which time he had acquired money and built up armies. Among the relatives whom Uthman thus favored were also al-Hakam ibn-al-As, who had been expelled by the Messenger, Abdullah ibn-Sa'd ibn-Abi-Sarh, his foster-brother, and many others.

The Companions noticed such a deviation from the Islamic spirit, and they roused the city to restore Islam and to rescue the Caliph himself from disaster; for due to his great age and infirmity Uthman was unable to protect his own interests against Marwan. It is hard to doubt that Uthman had in his heart the spirit of Islam; but it is equally hard to find an excuse for his errors. The mistake from which all the evil emanated was his acceptance of the caliphate when he was already an old man and exhausted, surrounded by the evil influence of Umayyads of an inauspicious nature.

At a public meeting Ali was deputed to visit Uthman and to interview him. When he entered Uthman's presence Ali spoke thus: "I bring to you the opinions of the people who have charged me with this message. By Allah I do not know what to say to you; for I know nothing that you do not know, nor can I tell you anything of which you are unaware. You know what we all know, and we cannot speak to you of anything of which we have a superior understanding. We have no private information to which we can make you party, and we have no facts inaccessible to you. You have seen and heard and companied with the Messenger of Allah, and you even became his son-in-law. Neither Abu-Bakr nor Umar

was better fitted than you to do right; for you were more
closely related to the Messenger than were they; by your
marriage to his daughter you had an advantage which they
did not have, while they had nothing that you did not have.
By Allah the spirit must be in you, for you are not renowned
for blindness, neither are you famed for ignorance; the way
of Islam is clear and definite, and the characteristics of the
faith are plain. You know already, Uthman, that the worthiest
servant of Allah in His eyes is the just Imam, one who is
guided himself by Allah, and who in his turn guides others,
who preserves worthy customs and destroys unwanted heresies;
by Allah all this is explicit, and the established customs are
well-marked. But the most evil of the people in the sight of
Allah is the unjust Imam, who, himself in error, leads
others into error, who destroys worthy customs and intro-
duces unwanted heresies. I myself once heard the Messenger say: 'The unjust Imam will be arraigned on the Day of
Resurrection; he will have no helper and no advocate, but
will be flung into Hell where he will be whirled around like
a mill; then he will be plunged into the depths of Hell.'"

    Then Uthman replied: "By Allah I knew that they would
say just what you have said. In truth, were you in my place,
I would never have upbraided you nor betrayed you; I would
not have found fault with you nor come to reprove you because
you had been generous to your relatives, because you had
given posts of command to such persons as Umar had given
them to. O Ali, I adjure you by Allah, are you aware that
Al-Mughira ibn-Shu'ba is no longer here?" "Yes," said
Ali. "Are you aware that Umar appointed him to a command?"
"Yes." "Then," said Uthman, "Why blame me for giving a
command to Ibn-Amir, together with his relatives and kinsmen?" Said Ali: "I will tell you. All Umar's governors went
in fear of him; if there came to his ears even a hint of a
crime committed by them, he visited the utmost severity upon them. But that you do not do. You are soft and compliant
to your relatives." "And to yours also," retorted Uthman.
"By my life," said Ali, "They should have no preference from
me, simply because of their relationship. Rather would the
preference go to others." "Are you aware," asked Uthman,
"that it was Umar who appointed Mu'awiya to the whole of his
present command, while I did not more than confirm the
appointment?" Said Ali, "I adjure you by Allah, do you not

know that Mu'awiya was more in awe of Umar than was the
most terrified of Umar's servants?" "Yes," replied Uthman. "But," said Ali, "Now Mu'awiya does as he pleases
without reference to you, and without your knowledge. So
the people say: 'It is only Uthman'; and even when you hear
about it, you do nothing about Mu'awiya."

Finally the revolt against Uthman came to a head; it contained elements both of right and of wrong, of good and of
evil. Yet to one who views matters through the eyes of Islam, and who seeks to interpret events by the spirit of that
faith it must be apparent that the revolt was more akin to the
spirit and purposes of Islam than was the position of Uthman;
or rather, than was the position of Marwan. And behind
Marwan stood the Umayyads, who had never at any time been
inspired with anything of the spirit of this faith.

The only possible defense of Uthman is that it was his
evil fortune to come to the caliphate too late; the Umayyads
surrounded him, while he himself was approaching the age
of eighty, with his powers sapped and enfeebled by senility.
His position was that described by his friend Ali: "If I sit at
home and do nothing, Uthman says that I have deserted him
and his relatives, and that I have denied him his rights. If
I satisfy him in this and do proffer advice, Marwan still
makes a puppet out of him. Thus he is driven hither and
thither as Marwan wishes, despite his great age and his
friendship with Allah's Messenger."

Indeed it was a stroke of ill fortune. It was one of the
first misfortunes of the infant faith of Islam to fall into the
hands of the Umayyad family by the agency of the third Caliph
in his old age. Hence the practical application of Islamic
theory was a long time in taking root in the soil of Arab culture
Had Uthman come to the Caliphate earlier it would have been
better; for then his natural strength would not have been failing. Or if he had been Caliph later it would have been better;
then Ali would have held office   after the two older men.
In that case the prodigality of the Umayyads could not have
gained force and taken root as it did in Syria and elsewhere;
those vast fortunes could not have been amassed as they were
under the administration of Uthman, as we shall see when we
come to discuss economic theory under his rule; and the revolt against Uthman would not have shaken the structure of
the Islamic community and endangered its dependence on the

spirit of the faith. Had all this been the case, the aspect of the entire history of Islam would have been changed, and it would have followed an entirely different path.

The vitality of the Islamic spirit and of the Islamic social system merited some result other than that which actually took place. But this consideration will be dealt with in due course. In the meantime we may proceed to notice the development of political theory after Uthman.

* * * * * * *

Uthman went to the mercy of his Lord, and he was succeeded by the Umayyad state on a de facto basis; this by virtue of the power which the Umayyads had achieved in the Muslim world, particularly in Syria, and by virtue of the power of the rooted Umayyad principles which were so much at variance with those of Islam. These principles comprised the appropriation of booty and property and profits, a complete absence of any attempt at a spirit of brotherhood or liberty or mutual responsibility, and the encouragement of an onslaught on the spirit of religion itself within the Islamic community. Not the least important factor was the growth-- rightly or wrongly--among the people of the feeling that the Caliph could give preference to his own family, and could allow them hundreds of thousands of dirhams; that he could depose from office the Companions of the Prophet, and replace them by enemies of the Prophet; or that he could persecute the like of Abu-Dharr for inveighing against the amassing of riches and against the luxury into which the rich were sinking, and for summoning men to follow what the Messenger had taught them about expending their money in alms, and about charity and frugality. The natural outcome of the rise of such ideas, whether right or wrong, was that some were opposed to, while others favored, Uthman. The former were those whose minds were imbued with the spirit of Islam; hence they disapproved and condemned. The latter were those who wore Islam as a cloak, those whose hearts had never been touched by accepting it truly, those who were swept away by worldly desires, and who clung to the crest of the wave. Such were the closing features of the reign of Uthman.

When Ali succeeded him it was not easy to bring matters back to their true condition. Those who had made their fortunes under Uthman, and particularly the Umayyads, knew that Ali would not leave them undisturbed, and so they betook

themselves and their fortunes to Mu'awiya. If Ali had followed the example of Umar, they would not have been given
the opportunity to do so; for Mu'awiya's strength at that time
could not compete with that of the Caliph, nor yet with that
of the religious spirit in men's hearts. Nor yet was Mu'awiya
prepared to risk an open breach with the Caliph, as he was
later to break with him; for it was only the thirteen years of
Uthman's rule that had made Mu'awiya what he was; in these
years he had built up his economic, military, and political
strength throughout all Syria.

The real tragedy is that Ali was not the third Caliph.

Ali set himself to restore the Islamic conception of rulership in the minds of governors and people alike. He used to
eat barley-meal, hand ground by his wife, and he used to
seal the meal-bag, with the words, "I like to know what I am
putting in my mouth." Often he sold his sword to get money
to buy food and clothing, and he disliked living in the "White
Castle" in Kufa, preferring the lodging-houses where the poor
lived. He lived in the manner related by Al-Nasr ibn-al-Man-
sur on the authority of Utba ibn-Alqama in these words: I
once visited Ali and found him with sour curds set in front of
him. Their sourness and their dryness offended me, and I
said: "O Commander of the Faithful, do you eat this stuff?"
He answered me: "Abu-Janub, Allah's Messenger used to eat
it drier than this, and used to wear clothes coarser than
these"--and he pointed to his own clothes--"And if I do not
accept what he did, then I fear that I do not do what is right."
Or again there is the story told by Harun ibn-Antara on the
authority of his father: I visited Ali at Khawarnaq during the
winter, and found him wearing a shabby velvet cloak in which
he shivered. I said to him: "Commander of the Faithful,
Allah has granted a portion of the public funds to you and your
family, yet you treat yourself this way." "By Allah," he replied, "I will not deprive you of anything, and this is my own
cloak which I brought from Medina."

Ali did not treat himself and his family thus because he was
unaware that Islam allowed him more than he took; he knew
that Islam did not prescribe asceticism, self-denial, and hardship. He knew that his proper share from the public treasury
purely as a private Muslim was at that time double what he
was taking, and that his allowance as a ruler who had to pay
public servants was still more than that. If he had wished,

he could have taken the amount which Umar had specified to be given to some of his provincial governors; Umar had allotted to Ammar ibn-Yasir on his appointment to Kufa a sum of six hundred dirhams per month, for himself and his assistants; in addition he had the gifts, of which he got his share among his equals, together with half a sheep and half a measure of flour. Similarly Umar had allotted to Abdullah ibn-Mas'ud a hundred dirhams and four sheep, for teaching the people of Kufa and acting as keeper of the public treasury; and to Uthman ibn-Hanif he had allotted a hundred and fifty dirhams and a quarter of a sheep per day, together with the customary gifts, which, in his case, amounted to five thousand dirhams.

Ali did not treat himself as he did because he was ignorant of all this. It was simply because he realized that a ruler is at once an object of suspicion and an example; he is suspected of squandering the public monies which lie in his power; and to governors and people alike he should be an example of purity and frugality. So Ali modelled himself on the discipline of Abu-Bakr and Umar, rather than on the indulgence of Uthman. The reason was that the young faith of Islam and the new social order was more in need of discipline to compel obedience, than of any indulgence which the faith might permit. So only the highest level would suffice this best of the Caliphs; the indulgence was not permissible for him, though he could see that it was legal for others who were naturally inclined towards it. But discipline was needed in one who had to be a pattern and an example to others; for through such discipline he could encourage them to strive in emulation.

Thus Ali proceeded to restore the concept of rulership which the Prophet and the two first Caliphs had built up. "He once found his coat of mail in the possession of a Christian, whom he thereupon brought before Sharih, his judge, in a civil lawsuit, as if he had been a private citizen. His case was: 'This is my coat of mail; I did not sell it, and I did not give it away.' So Sharih questioned the Christian: 'What have you to say to what the Commander of the Faithful alleges?' When the latter answered, 'This is my own armor; and what a liar the Commander of the Faithful is.', Sharih turned to Ali and asked: 'Have you any proof, Commander of the Faithful?' Ali smiled and said, 'Sharih has found the point. I have no proof.' So Sharih gave his decision in favor of the Christian, who took the armor away, leaving Ali standing looking after him. But he had only gone a few steps when he came back and said: 'I must bear witness that this is of the teachings of the prophets; the Commander of the Faithful takes me to court before his own judge, and the case goes against him. I testify that there is no god but Allah, and I testify that Muhammad was His servant and His Messenger. By Allah the coat of mail is indeed yours, Commander of the Faithful. I used to follow the army, and when you went to Siffin I took the armor from your camel.' Said Ali: 'Since you have become a Muslim, I give it to you.'"[49]

The course which Ali followed was that which he had marked out for himself when, in a sermon following the oath of allegiance being taken to him, he had said: "O people, I am only a man like yourselves, with your endowments and your limitations; yet I will lead you in the path of your Prophet, and will enforce my commands upon you. All lands which Uthman assigned, and all money which he gave away out of the public funds shall be refunded. Nothing shall invalidate this promise; even if I find such money used as a dowry for women, for the purchase of slaves, or scattered world-wide, it shall be restored. For in justice there is an ampleness of life, and whoever feels that he is constrained by the right, let him remember that he would be more so by tyranny.

"O people, tomorrow when the world swallows you up, when you buy estates and open up water channels, when you ride horses and choose slave maidens, then let none of you say that Ali has forbidden you your rights; meaning that I have debarred them from what they have undertaken, or that I have restricted them to their basic rights. Nay, but if any one of the Emigrants or Helpers, the Companions of the Prophet, thinks that he has a claim to special consideration because of this circumstance, then tomorrow that claim shall rest with Allah, and upon Him shall be the responsibility for the clothing and the allowance of such a man. If any man has accepted Allah and His Messenger, if he has believed in our faith, entered our religion, and accepted our qibla, then he has taken upon himself the privileges and the responsibilities of Islam. You are the servants of Allah, and property is the property of Allah, to be divided equally among you,. so that no one has a better claim than any other. But those who show piety towards Allah shall have the best reward. "

As was but natural, the place-seekers were dissatisfied with Ali; those accustomed to preëminence were displeased by the regulations for complete equality, as were those accustomed to preferential treatment by the regulations for complete justice. Such betook themselves to the other camp where, among the Umayyads, they found their desires could be satisfied, and where they could trample on the elements of justice, right, and conscience, alike in life and in authority.

Those who see in Mu'awiya sagacity and merit do not find these qualities in Ali, and to these things they attribute the ultimate triumph of Mu'awiya. Such an opinion errs in its estimate of the conditions, as well as in its understanding of Ali and of the tasks which confronted him. The first and the greatest task which Ali had to face was to restore vitality to the duties of Islam and its true spirit to the faith, to take away the veil which had been thrown over that spirit by the Umayyads, through the age and the weakness of Uthman. If Ali had copied Mu'awiya in taking no account of any moral instinct, then he would have failed in his purpose, and there would have been no point in his tenure of the caliphate from the point of view of the life of this faith. And what profit could there have been in exchanging one Mu'awiya for another? Ali had either to be true to himself or let the caliphate pass from him, and with it his life. This is surely the true interpretation of the matter, and the one which he himself had in mind when he said: "Mu'awiya is not more astute than I; but he is prepared to be treacherous and faithless. Had it not been for my dislike of treachery, I could have been the most astute man alive. "

* * * * * * *

So Ali went to the mercy of his Lord, and was followed by Mu'awiya, the son of Hind and Abu-Sufyan.

Whatever faith and gentleness and piety Uthman had had, they had acted as a restraint on the Umayyads; but with the removal of this restraint and with the breaking down of this barrier the Umayyads went straight back to their pre-Islamic and early Islamic heritage. So Mu'awiya proceeded to promote that family loyalty which was part of his plan; the first example of it was Amr ibn-al-As. The Umayyads were a family united by their desires and their ambitions, but divided by their cupidity and their greed; they were without a trace of morals, religion, or conscience.

It was a calamity which broke the back of Islam.

The territory of Islam was certainly increased during the period which ensued, but the spirit of the faith was undeniably lost; and what is the value of territory if the spirit is lost? Had there not been a hidden strength in the very nature of Islam, together with an abundant source of spiritual power, the Umayyad period would have been instrumental in writing finis to its career. But the spirit of the faith endured, firm and unyielding, and its latent strength remained capable of the struggle for survival.

We need not speak at length of Mu'awiya, nor need we here record his reign; but we must consider his action in bequeathing the throne to Yazid, in order to discover what kind of a man he was. And we must consider the history of Yazid, in order to discover what a crime was perpetrated when the Umayyads gained control of the Muslim peoples and of Islam.

This we may say: From Umayyad times all restrictions on the public treasury were removed, and it became a legitimate source of plunder for the kings, their courtiers, and their sycophants. The bases of Islamic justice were destroyed, and the treasury became the perquisite of the ruling class, a source of profit for their followers, and a source of income to their hangers-on. The caliphate became a monarchy, and a tyrannical monarchy at that, as the Messenger once said that it would, in a sudden access of prophetic insight.

Frequently we hear of immense gifts being made to sycophants and jesters and musicians; one of the Umayyad rulers once gave twelve thousand dinars to Ma'bad the singer, while among the Abbasids Harun al-Rashid presented Isma'il ibn-Jami' the singer with four thousand dinars, a costly house and furniture, and rich clothing--all for one song. Thus the wave went on its way, arrested only now and again.

In this connection we must mention the reign of Umar ibn-Abd al-Aziz, which was a throw-back to the age of the Caliphs, a shining beacon casting light on the path. He began his reign by restoring authority to its original and rightful owners, from whom it had been wrested. He gave power back to the Islamic community, which has the duty of making a free and willing

choice of its leaders, unhampered by the might of an army,
or by the force of inheritance. Umar mounted the pulpit and
said: "O people, I have been put in this position without my
wish or my desire, and also without the Muslims being consulted. I hereby release you from any obligation to take the
oath of allegiance to me; you may choose your ruler for
yourselves." But the people cried aloud: "We choose you,
Commander of the Faithful, and we are content to have you.
So seal the matter at once with the oath and the blessing."

Thus the office was returned to him, but now it was no
longer a power without common consent, without acclamation
or acceptance. Thereupon he addressed the people again,
saying: "There have been rulers before me whose respect
you have gained by resisting any tyranny on their part; for
no obedience can be given to any created man who rebels
against his Creator. If a man obeys Allah, it is your duty
to obey that man; but when a man rebels against Allah, then
he need not be obeyed. So obey me as long as I obey Allah
regarding you; but if I rebel against Allah, then you need not
obey me."

Accordingly, when he set about his administration he
started by making compensation for all exactions; and first
of all in his own case. "I must," he said, "start at the beginning with myself." So he made an inventory of his possessions in land, in goods, and in the taxes which these
brought him; when he looked at a jewelled ring on his finger,
he said: "Walid[50] gave me that; but he had no right to it,
for it came from his estates in the West"; so he returned it.
There was also the income from his estates in Al-Yamama,
at Al-Mukaidas and Jabal al-Wars in the Yemen, and at Fadak,
from all of which he drew an income. All of them he returned
to the treasury. But he made an exception of the well at
Suwaida, which he had had dug with his own money; it brought
him an annual income of some hundred and fifty dinars.

"When he decided to restore all these possessions, he commanded that it be publicly proclaimed. Then at the Friday
prayers he mounted the pulpit, said the 'Praise be to Allah,'
and the ascription of glory, and then continued thus: 'These
people have given us gifts which it was not right for us to take,
nor for them to give. This matter is now in my power; I
have no interest in it except that of Allah, and I have already
restored all these things, making a start with myself and my

immediate family. Read, Mazahim.' Now a basket had already been brought in, containing the account books, and
Mazahim started to read from each book in turn; Umar held
the books, and with a pair of scissors which he held in his
hand he clipped out each entry, until nothing was left.

"Then he turned to his wife, Fatima, daughter of Abd al-
Malik ibn-Marwan; she had jewelry which had been the gift
of her father, and the like of which had never been seen.
Umar said to her: 'Choose whether you will return your jewelry to the treasury or consent to let me separate from you;
for if you keep them I cannot live together with you.' She
answered: 'Nay, but I choose you, Commander of the Faithful, rather than these; rather than twice these if I had them.'
So Umar commanded accordingly, and the jewels were taken
and placed in the public treasury. When Umar died he was
succeeded by Yazid ibn-al-Malik, who said to his sister,
Fatima: 'If you wish I will restore your jewels to you.' 'I
have no wish for them,' said she; 'I was happy without them
while Umar was alive, and shall I now have them again when
he is dead? Never, by Allah.' When Yazid heard this he
divided the jewels between his wife and his family.

"But Umar was not satisfied with restoring any exactions
which he held; they say that he would accept nothing from
the treasury, and would not take a single dirham from any
booty. Umar I used to take two dirhams per day from that
source, but when someone said to Umar II: 'Why do you not
take what Umar I used to take?' he replied: 'Umar ibn-al-
Khattab had no money, whereas I have enough to satisfy me.

"Similarly he compelled the sons of Marwan to disgorge
the possessions which they had acquired unjustly, and this
he returned to its proper owners. It is said that there came
to him a certain man who belonged to one of the protected
peoples, a native of Emesa, and complained: 'Commander
of the Faithful, I require of you the Book of Allah.' Umar
asked him what he meant, and the man said: 'Al-Abbas has
wrested my land from me.' Now Al-Abbas was sitting there
at the time, and Umar turned to him, saying: 'Abbas, what
have you to say?' Al-Abbas replied that Al-Walid had assigned to him the lands in question, and had given him letters
patent for them. Again Umar turned to the complainant:
'What have you to say to that?' 'Commander of the Faithful,'
he replied, 'I require of you the Book of Allah, Great and

Glorious is He.' Then said Umar: 'Yes. The Book of Allah is more worthy to be followed than any writing by Al-Walid. Abbas, you will restore his property to him.' And Al-Abbas did so.

"Al-Walid had a son named Rauh who had grown up in the desert and was almost a Bedu. A party of Muslims once came to Umar with a case against Rauh concerning some wineshops in Emesa. These belonged to them, but Rauh's father, Al-Walid, has assigned them to him. Umar said to him: 'Give them back their wineshops' but Rauh retorted that they were his by the authority of his father. Said Umar: 'The authority of Al-Walid is not sufficient; the wineshops are theirs, and the deeds are in their hands; now give them their shops.' Then Rauh and one of the men left the court together, and Rauh threatened him; the man promptly returned to Umar and told him: 'By Allah, Commander of the Faithful, that fellow threatened me.' Umar said to Ka'b ibn-Hamid, who was the commander of his guard: 'Go to Rauh, Ka'b, and if he hands over the wineshops, well and good; if he will not, then bring me his head.' Some of those who were friendly to Rauh heard this, and told him what Umar had commanded. His heart failed him, and when Ka'b came to him with his sword half-drawn and said: 'Come, give him his wineshops.' Rauh hastily agreed, and the shops were handed over.

"So people would come constantly to Umar bringing cases of injustice before him; no case was ever brought to him without being adjusted, whether it was a matter concerning himself or someone else. He took from the sons of Marwan and others the possessions which they had exacted; he restored wrested properties to their owners without demanding a written proof. He was always content with very little proof; if he recognized from the circumstances that a man had suffered injustice, he adjusted it for him without making him establish a legal proof; for he recognized the exactions which had taken place under previous rulers. They say that he exhausted the treasury in Iraq through this system, so that more money had to be brought from Syria.

"Sulaiman[51] had allotted to Anbasa, another Umayyad, twenty thousand dinars; the order went through all the offices until it was entered at last in the final register, and had only to be paid over. But Sulaiman died before it was paid. Now Anbasa was a friend of Umar, and on the following day he

decided that he would speak to Umar about the allotment which
Sulaiman had promised him. He found the Umayyads waiting
at Umar's door for an opportunity to talk to him about their
own affairs; when they saw Anbasa they said: 'Let us see
how Umar treats Anbasa before we speak to him.' So Anbasa
went in and found Umar. He said to him: 'Commander of the
Faithful, Sulaiman, the late Caliph, had promised me twenty
thousand dinars; the order went through to the final register,
and all that remained was for me to collect the money; but
Sulaiman died before I could do so. Now you, Commander
of the Faithful, are the fittest person to see to this matter
for me; for my relations with you are closer than ever were
my relations with Sulaiman.' 'How much was it?' asked Umar.
'Twenty thousand dinars.' 'Twenty thousand dinars' said
Umar, 'Is enough for four thousand Muslim households. And
I am to pay that to one man. By Allah I can never do that.'
Then, said Anbasa, I produced the letter containing the deed
of gift from Sulaiman. But Umar said to me: 'It is not necessary for you to have the letter with you; possibly you got it
from one who was more reckless with money than I, one
who would make you such a promise.' So I took the letter and
went out, to find the Umayyads still waiting; I told them what
had happened, and they said: 'After that there is no hope for
us. Go back and ask him if he will permit us to retire to our
homes.' So I went back to him, and I said: 'O Commander
of the Faithful, there are some of your family at the door,
requesting that they may continue to enjoy what they enjoyed
before your time.' 'By Allah,' swore Umar, 'I do not possess
so much money of my own, and other money I have no power
to put to such a use.' I went on: 'Commander of the Faithful,
they request, then, that you permit them to return to their
homes.' 'They may do as they like,' said Umar; 'That I will
permit them.' 'Will you permit me to do the same?' I asked,
and he said: 'I give you the same permission. But I know
that you will stay; for you are a man of great wealth. Now
I will sell you an heirloom of Sulaiman's and perhaps with it
you may be able to buy something which will bring you profit
in place of that which you did not get.' So I stayed and bought
an heirloom of Sulaiman's for a hundred thousand; I took it to
Iraq, where I sold it for two hundred thousand. And I also
kept the deed of gift; when Umar died and Yazid came to the
throne I showed him Sulaiman's letter, and he paid me the
stipulated sum."

"Umar gathered together the sons of Marwan and addressed them thus: 'You have been continually given favors and
honors and wealth, until by my reckoning a half or even two
thirds of the resources of this community are in your hands.
Restore, then, what you possess of the true property of the
people, and do not compel me to measures take such against
my will as you will suffer against your will.' Not one of them
answered him until he commanded them: 'Answer me.' Then
one of them replied: 'By Allah we will not give up the wealth
which came to us from our fathers; we will not pauperize our
children and dishonor our fathers until our heads are severed
from our bodies.' Then said Umar: 'By Allah, were it not
that you are protected from me by one to whom I have granted
such a right, I would speedily humble your family. But I
fear civil war; none the less, if Allah spares me, I will restore to every man his rights, if Allah wills.'"[52]

He did not live to restore to every man his rights, as was
his wish, and he was succeeded by others who followed the
courses of the Umayyads rather than those of Islam. When
the Abbasids grasped the succession, they did so as kings,
so that the Muslim world was corrupted and the people out of
touch with the duties of the faith. Such a divorce and such a
wide gulf had the Umayyads succeeded in placing between the
people and their religion. The Abbasid kings were no better
than the Umayyads, for one and all they represented a tyrannical monarchy.

* * * * * * *

But since we are not here writing a history of the Islamic
state, but rather a history of the Islamic spirit in relation
to authority, we shall content ourselves with a sketch of the
signs of change and deterioration in this spirit by quoting
from three sermons given by these kings; these may be compared with the other three already quoted from the Caliphs;
the profound difference will be immediately apparent.

First, the sermon of Mu'awiya to the people of Kufa after
the truce. "Men of Kufa, do you think that I fought against
you on account of prayers or taxes or pilgrimage? I knew
that you said the prayers, that you paid the poor-tax, and that
you performed the Pilgrimage. I fought you in order to have
control and mastery over you; now Allah has granted me that
mastery, though you may not like it. Now, therefore, all
the money and all the blood which I have had to expend in this

war is still to be repaid, and all the promises which I made
in the truce are under my feet here."

"All the promises which I made in the truce are under my
feet here." Yet Allah has said: "Fulfil your treaties if a
treaty has been necessary." Or again: "If they appeal to you
for help in a matter of religion, then you must help them, unless it be against a people with whom the Muslims have a
compact." Here it is stated that for Muslims to fulfill a compact to a non-Muslim people with whom a treaty exists is
preferable even to helping fellow-Muslims in a matter of
religion. Yet Mu'awiya was breaking a compact which he
had made with Muslims; and his offence becomes the more
notorious and shameful because he takes pride in it.

He was an Umayyad, a member of that family whose nature forbade their joining in the oath of Fudhul.

Or again in a sermon preached at Medina Mu'awiya spoke
in these terms: "But to proceed; by Allah I did not gain the
caliphate with any good will on your part, nor did you welcome
my coming to office; rather I had to fight you at the sword's
point. For myself, I longed for command over you in the
caliphate of Abu–Bakr, and I wished for the post in the caliphate of Umar, but I was forcibly kept from it; I wished it
under the rule of Uthman, but it was refused me. So now
you and I stand in what may prove to be a profitable position,
meat and drink to me. And if you do not find that I am the
best among you, you may find that I am the best governor
for you."

Indeed he did not gain the caliphate by their consent. Yet,
as is well known, the caliphate in orthodox Islam is an office
which can be conferred only by public approval. But Mu'awiya had little in common with Islam.

So also, after the influence of the Umayyads had done its
work of transforming authority until finally in the days of the
Abbasids it had become a theory of divine right, Al-Mansur,
the Abbasid Caliph could say in a sermon: "O people, I am
the Sultan of Allah in His earth; I rule you by His help and
in His strength. I am His guard over His property, with
which I may do what He wills and what He desires; I can give
it away by His permission, for He has made me the custodian
of it. If He wishes, He can empower me to take your gifts and
your offerings; or if He wishes, He may debar me from such
a course."

At this point political theory has completely parted company with Islam and with Islamic teachings.

* * * * * * *

Economic theory followed a course parallel to that of political theory, a course dependent upon the change in rulers
according to the nature and course of the political tendency,
and according to the rights of ruler and subject. During the
life of Muhammad and his two Companions, Abu-Bakr and
Umar, as well as during the caliphate of Ali, the ruling
theory was characteristically Islamic; property was communal, and neither the ruler nor his relatives had a right
to any share greater than that to which they were entitled as
individual Muslims; nor could they make gifts from it to any
other person, except insofar as such a person might have a
right to a gift. Even in the time of Uthman, when this practice began to be slightly relaxed, the people still retained
their rights. By this time the public funds were more than
adequate to meet the claims of the people, and the Caliph
conceived that he was permitted to dip his hand into the treasury and bestow gifts on his family or on any others whom he
considered worthy. But when the caliphate became a tyrannical monarchy, then all barriers and limits were removed,
and the monarch had absolute power to give or to withhold--
justifiably in a few cases, but generally the reverse. Thus
the public funds became the source of unlimited luxury for
monarchs and their children, their followers and their
courtiers. In this final stage such monarchs completely abandoned the laws of Islam.

This is a general statement of the case, for which we must
adduce examples from each of the different phases of the
course of history.

The sources of public revenue in the time of the Messenger were:

1. The poor-tax, which was obligatory on all Muslims
according to their property. The tax was reckoned on
the constituent parts of that property, gold and silver,
grain and produce, cattle, income from trade, and mining.
The general taxation level was one fortieth on such things,
and the resultant money was expended in the eight recognized ways.

2. The poll-tax, which was levied on each individual

of the protected peoples who lived under truce. This cor-
responded to the poor-tax as paid by Muslims, in order
that a share of the public responsibilities might be taken
by non-Muslims. If a man became a Muslim the poll-tax
was no longer levied on him, but was then replaced by
the poor-tax.

3. The booty.[53] This was what accrued to the state
from unbelievers who were granted an amnesty without
fighting. This belonged entirely to Allah and His Messenger, to the latter's family, to the orphan, the poor, and
the wayfarer, according to the Qur'anic precept.

4. The plunder. This was what the state acquired from
unbelievers in time of war. Four-fifths of it belonged to
those who had done the fighting, and the remainder was
disposable on the same terms as the booty mentioned above.

5. The land-tax, which was the money paid by those
lands which belonged to unbelievers who were conquered
by the Muslims in war. Or a truce might be granted to
the unbelievers, who might then be left in possession of
their lands. This, as we shall see, was Umar's practice.

In the time of the Messenger the sources of revenue were
not extensive. The Emigrants had left their houses and their
property, and the Helpers had been generous to them, had
shared their own possessions with them, and had treated them
as brothers. Besides, the number of the Muslims was limited,
so that before the conquests there was only one source of
revenue, the poor-tax, and it but slight; and the small numbers made it yet slighter. This revenue was expended in the
eight ways detailed in the verse, "The alms money is only
for..."[54]

But when the conquests started another source was added,
that of plunder. Four-fifths of this went to the fighting men,
and of this the Prophet used to give one share to each foot-
man, and two shares--though some say three--to each horse-
man. Similarly he used to give one share to a single man,
and two to a married man; thus he gave expression to the
important principle of the care of the family, and also to the
principle of "to each according to his need." The rest of
the plunder he disposed of in the ways which we have mentioned.

The first case of booty occurred in the expedition against

the Bani Nadir, and the whole of it was given by the Messenger to the Emigrants, except that shares were also given to two poor members of the Helpers. After this the Qur'an laid down the general Islamic principle, "that it may not be passed around among the rich among you."

After this the Muslim revenues commenced to expand along with the growth of Islamic territory, through the successive conquests; thus better circumstances began to spread gradually through the Muslim community, for all shared in the revenues of the treasury in the proportion to which Islam entitled them.

When the Messenger went to his Supreme Friend, there were some who rebelled and withheld the poor-tax. Then Abu-Bakr took his famous stand and spoke his immortal words: "By Allah, if they withheld from me even the halter of a camel which they had been paying to Allah's Messenger, I would fight them for it." Umar's opinion was different; he was inclined to treat the apostates easily, and to delay active hostilities. For Islam was young, its enemies were lying in wait for it, and in every quarter of Arabia the apostates were powerful. His opposition reached the point where he said in a fit of rage: "How can we fight these people when the Messenger himself said, 'I have been commanded to fight this people until they confess that there is no god but Allah, and that Muhammad is Allah's Messenger. Whoever confesses this is safe from me in property and in life, except for his obligations. His reckoning must be with Allah.'" But Abu-Bakr answered him resolutely: "By Allah I will fight against any infringement of the prayers and the poor-tax; for the latter is an obligation on property, and the Messenger said, 'Except for his obligations.'" Then Umar commented: "By Allah, then I saw that Allah had strengthened Abu-Bakr to fight, and I knew that he was right."

Thus in this famous decision there was finally and historically confirmed one of the principles of economic theory in Islam.

Abu-Bakr proceeded to distribute the poor-tax monies in the ways sanctioned by the practice of the Messenger; and he did the same with the one-fifth of the plunder, and with the remainder of the revenues. He took for himself only that meagre share which the community bade him take--said to be two dirhams a day, and he distributed their legal share to those who were entitled to it. What remained in the treasury he used to equip the armies for war.

In the time of Abu-Bakr there arose a question of precedence, on which he and Umar disagreed. Abu-Bakr held that
equal shares should be given to those who had been the first
Muslims and those who had come in later; that there should
be equal division between free men and clients, between men
and women. Umar, along with the majority of the Companions,
held that the earliest Muslims should have preferential treatment according to their standing. But Abu-Bakr replied: "As
for what you say about the precedence and the excellence of
the first Muslims, how well do I acknowledge it. Yet that is
a matter whose reward must rest with Allah alone, glorious
is His Praise. But this is a matter of livelihood, in which
equality is better than preference."

This equality continued to be observed, and prosperity increased among the Muslims as the revenues grew. But in
the time of Umar's caliphate he still held to his opinion: "I
will not treat one who fought against Allah's Messenger the
same as one who fought along with him."

It happened one day that Abu-Huraira, his governor in
Bahrain, came to Umar with a large sum of money. Here is
Abu-Huraira's account: I came from Bahrain with five hundred
thousand dirhams, and in the evening I went to see Umar. I
said to him: "Commander of the Faithful, take this money."
"How much is it?" he asked. "Five hundred thousand dirhams."
"Do you realize how much five hundred thousand dirhams is?"
said he. "Yes; a hundred thousand and a hundred thousand,
five times." "You are dreaming then. Go home, and come
back tomorrow." The next morning I went to see him again,
and said: "Take this money from me." "How much is it?"
"Five hundred thousand dirhams." Then he asked: "Is this
true?" "Certainly it is." Then said Umar: "O people, we
have acquired great wealth. If you wish me to weigh it out
for you, I will do so. Or if you wish, I will count it out for
you. Or if you wish me to measure it out to you, I will do
that." Then a certain man suggested: "O Commander of the
Faithful, draw up registers for the people, by which they may
be paid," a suggestion which Umar approved. He allotted
to each of the Emigrants five thousand, to each of the Helpers
three thousand, and to the wives of the Prophet twelve thousand. . . .

We have quoted this story here as illustrating the belief of
Umar that some of the people should take precedence over

others; we have quoted it also because of its description of the standard of wealth, according to which half a million dirhams appeared to be a dream, only conceivable to a man in his sleep. But that was to change entirely in the period following the great conquests.

Abu-Yusuf in his book, "The Land Tax," says: I was told the following by a certain Medinese shaikh on the authority of Isma'il ibn-Muhammad ibn-al-Sa'ib, quoting Zaid who had it from his father. I heard Umar say: "By Allah, than Whom there is no other god, there is no one who does not have a right to this money, either to give or to withhold; there is none has more right to it than any other, with the sole exception of a Mameluke slave; and in this respect I am but as one of you. But we have our stations in respect of Allah's Book, and we are differentiated by our relation to Allah's Messenger. Islam assesses a man by what he has suffered, by his precedence in the faith, by his wealth, and by his need. And by Allah, if there is any left over, then the very shepherd of San'a shall have his share of this money as his right, before his face reddens--that is, by having to ask for it."

"Then he allotted to every man who had fought at Badr five thousand dirhams per year. He allotted to every one who had come into Islam at the same time as the men of Badr, those who had been in the emigration to Abyssiania, and those who had fought at Uhud four thousand dirhams per year. To the sons of the men of Badr he allotted two thousand each, except for Hasan and Husain, the two sons of Ali; to each of them he allotted the same as was given to their father, because of their kinship to Allah's Messenger; thus each of them had five thousand dirhams. To every man who emigrated to Medina before the conquest of Mecca he allotted three thousand dirhams, and to every one who entered Islam at the time of the conquest two thousand. To the young children in the families of Emigrants and Helpers alike he gave the same allotment as that last named. He allotted shares to all the people according to their status, their knowledge of the Qur'an, and their participation in the wars. Finally he classed all the rest of the people together; to every Muslim who had come to Medina and had stayed there he gave twenty-five dinars; to Yemenites and Kaisites in Syria and Iraq he allotted varying amounts of two thousand, one thousand, nine hundred, five hundred, and three hundred; but none had less than three hundred. Umar himself said: 'If there were enough money I would allot four thousand dirhams to every man; one thousand for travelling, one thousand for weapons, one thousand for the care of his family, and one thousand for his horse and his mule.'"[55]

"But Umar did make exceptions to the principle which he had laid down for the organization of the stipends; to certain men and women he gave larger stipends than were given to others of the same standing and class. Thus to Umar ibn-Abi-Salama he allotted four thousand dirhams; for this Umar was the son of Umm Salama, the 'Mother of the Faithful.' Muhammad ibn-Abdullah ibn-Jahsh took exception to this and said to the Commander of the Faithful: 'Why do you give preference to Umar over us, when our fathers were in the Emigration and in the fighting?' Umar replied: 'I gave him preference because of his relation to the Prophet. Anyone who can claim a mother like Umm Salama has only to come to me and I will satisfy him.' Similarly he allotted to Usama ibn-Zaid four thousand dirhams; Abdullah, his own son protested: 'You have given me three thousand, and you have given Usama four thousand, although I have done more fighting than he.' Umar's answer was: 'I have given him a larger stipend because he was dearer to Allah's Messenger than you. And his father was dearer to Allah's Messenger than was your father.' He allotted to Asma, the daughter of Amyas and wife of Abu-Bakr, one thousand dirhams, to Umm Kulthum, the daughter of Uqba, one thousand dirhams, and to Umm Abdullah ibn-Mas'ud a like sum. He increased these stipends over those of their equals because of their personal greatness as the wives and mothers of men of outstanding status and excellence."[56]

There are, then, these two opinions on the division of the public monies, that of Abu-Bakr, and that of Umar. The latter found its support in, "I will not treat anyone who fought against Allah's Messenger the same as one who fought along with him," and in, "Islam assesses a man by what he has suffered...etc." This idea can find some justification in Islamic theory, because it does represent a fair balance between effort and reward. But the opinion of Abu-Bakr is not without support; "They have handed themselves over[57] to Allah, and to Him alone; He it is who will reward them, and will recompense them on the Day of Resurrection; for this world is no

more than a means of livelihood." And we must unhesitat-
ingly choose Abu-Bakr's opinion as being closer than the other
to the spirit of Islam, and as more fitted to express the
equality of all Muslims, which is the greatest of the principles
of this faith. It is also superior inasmuch as it does not give
rise to the evil consequences which arise from a discrimina-
tory system--the vast fortunes which are a dividing factor in
a people, and the growth of such fortunes year after year,
merely through their own productivity, a growth which mathe-
matically forms a geometric progression. We must reckon
also with the results of the existence of capital sums which
Umar saw at the end of his life, and which made him swear
that if he had time he would again equalize the stipends;
these are his famous words: "If I had foreseen the consequences of my action which are now apparent, I would have
taken their excessive wealth from the rich and given it to
the poor."

But unfortunately the time was past, the days of Umar
were finished, and the bitter fruits were already reaped
which were to poison equality within Muslim society; ultimately, thanks to their employment by the Umayyads and
their ratification by Uthman, they were to lead to civil war.

Umar, then, renounced his view that there should be discrimination between Muslims in the matter of stipends, when
he saw the results of such discrimination; it was then that he
came over to Abu-Bakr's position. Ali's opinion also agreed
with that of the first Caliph, and therefore we are inclined
to regard his caliphate as a natural continuation of that of his
two earliest predecessors, while the age of Uthman formed
an interregnum. So we may now continue our discussion by
dealing first with Ali's caliphate, after which we may retrace
our steps to deal with that of Uthman.

Ali supported the principle of equality in stipends, as he
indicated in his first sermon when he proclaimed: "Nay, but
if any one of the Emigrants or Helpers, the Companions of
the Prophet, thinks that he has a claim to special consideration because of his circumstance, then tomorrow that claim
shall rest with Allah, and upon Him shall be the responsibility
for the clothing and the allowance of such a man. If any man
has accepted Allah and His Messenger, if he has believed our
faith, entered our religion, and accepted our Qibla, then he
has taken upon himself the privileges and the responsibilities

of Islam. You are the servants of Allah, and property is the property of Allah, to be divided equally among you, so that no one has a better claim than any other. But those who show piety towards Allah shall have the best reward."

This is the authentic Islamic principle, in conformity with the Islamic spirit of equality; it lays on the Muslim communi- ty the duty of equity, and it permits the growth of fortunes only by means of effort and labor. It forbids such growth of wealth through any kind of preferential treatment; for such gives to one an opportunity denied to others, and for the same work it pays one more than another.

It was to this principle that Umar returned at the end of his life, but unfortunately for Islam his death followed almost immediately. He was unable to put his resolve into effect; yet it was none the less his resolve to take excessive wealth from the rich and give it to the poor. For such excess of wealth had grown up in most cases from the discrimination in stipends which he himself had established. It was also his resolve to equalize the stipends for the future, so that such differentiation should not recur, and so that Islamic society should not again be thrown into the confusion which it was then experiencing.

Then came Uthman. He saw no reason to follow either or both of these resolves. He left the excessive wealth in the hands of its owners, and took back none of it; he also left the stipends on the preferential footing on which they stood. But this was not all. He enlarged every one's stipend, and thus even increased the wealth of the rich, although at the same time he did slightly ameliorate the lot of the poor. Again, he started to permit those who had large resources to make huge loans; he allowed the Quraish to travel the world, using their amassed wealth in trade, so that their wealth was doubled and redoubled. He allowed the wealthy to acquire estates and mansions in Southern Iraq and elsewhere, he made assignments of lands, and thus by the end of his caliphate he had brought about the thorough corruption of the Muslim community.

Abu-Bakr and Umar had previously insisted that all the Quraish chiefs should be kept at Medina, and that they should not be allowed to travel the conquered territories; care should be taken because, when surrounded by the Helpers, the eyes of these chiefs would stray to visions of money and power, because of their preeminence through their relationship to

Allah's Messenger, or because of their sufferings for Islam
and their early conversion. In this insistence there was no
real contradiction of personal freedom as Islam understands
it; for this freedom must always be limited by the welfare
and advantage of society. But when Uthman came to power
he permitted the Quraish to travel the world. Nor was that
all; he encouraged and even urged them to lay out their money
on mansions and estates in various places; and to that end
he gave many of them gifts which ran into hundreds of thousands of dirhams.

All this might have been a charity and a blessing to the
Muslims and to their chiefs; but it gave rise to one immense
evil which had not been hidden from the insight of Abu-Bakr
or of Umar after him. It produced vast economic and social
cleavages in the Islamic community, and it brought into being
an idle aristocratic class whose income was derived from
every source except that of work of any kind. It gave rise
also to a spirit of luxury which Islam had fought by legislation and exhortation alike, and against which Uthman's two
predecessors had struggled in an effort to wipe it out.

An adequate description of the consequences of this policy
is to be found in passages from "The Great Civil War: Uthman" by Dr. Taha Hussein, and especially in the following:

"A section of the chief Companions controlled the major
part of the wealth, both capital and current, of the Hejaz.
This they hastened to spend in the purchase of land in the
provinces; for they knew that such land was richer and
more fertile than that of the Hejaz. Thus Talha ibn-Abdullah spared no effort to buy out all those who had shares
in the Khaibar property, either because they had fought
along with the Prophet and captured the place, or because
they had received their shares through inheritance. But
when Uthman gave him the chance, Talha sold all his holdings at Khaibar to Hejazis who had taken part in the conquest of Iraq at the price of their land holdings in that
province. Then, having additional money available, he
bought up also the holdings of other Hejazis in Iraq; and
even from Uthman himself he bought Iraqi land which the
latter held there, at the price of land which he himself still
held in the Hejaz. Everyone else did the same, and all who
had no desire to move from the Hejaz to live on their lands
in the provinces sold these lands and bought others nearer
home.

"From this practice there came for the first time the
growth of vast possessions in Iraq and other provinces.
The only people who could take advantage of the process
were those who, having large resources, could buy up the

small holdings, men like Talha, Zubair, and Marwan ibn-Hakam; and thus there was in that period great economic activity, in buying and selling, in borrowing, bartering, and trading. Later this was not confined to Iraq and the Hejaz, but came to include all Arabia on the one hand and all the conquered provinces on the other. There were vast assignments of land and broad estates on the one hand, while on the other hand the workers stayed on the land as slaves, as clients, or as free men. Thus there came into being in Islam a new social class, the 'plutocrats,' the nobility of whose birth[58] was increased by the extent of their financial means, their vast fortunes, and also by the number of their followers.

"In the second place there arose from this practice the fact that those who bought land in Arabia in general, and in the Hejaz in particular, wished to exploit that land. Therefore they imported slaves in far larger numbers than heretofore, until in a short time the Hejaz had become one of the most fertile districts of the country, one of the most fruitful and productive, yielding most wealth to its owners. The net result was that luxury and idleness followed in the train of wealth, and in the Hejaz itself, in Mecca, in Medina, and in Ta'if, there grew up a class of idle aristocrats who did nothing; all the work was done by their imported slaves, while they consumed their time in the distractions of sport, amusement, and frivolity."

But at this point there was a reaction towards the spirit of Islam in the minds of many people; the leader and instigator of this reaction was Abu-Dharr. This man was the famous Companion of whom the present-day Egyptian opinion is, either that he was honest but misguided, or that we today have a better understanding of Islam than he.

Abu-Dharr preached against the luxury of the rich, which he held to be unjustifiable in Islam, and against Mu'awiya and the Umayyads in particular, who encouraged such luxury, increased it, and themselves wallowed in it. He inveighed against Uthman personally for giving away hundreds and thousands of dirhams from the treasury, and thereby increasing further the wealth and luxury of the rich. He complained that Uthman had given to Marwan ibn-al-Hakam a fifth of the revenues of Africa, to Al-Harith ibn-al-Hakam two hundred thou-

sand dirhams, and to Zaid ibn-Thabit a hundred thousand.
The conscience of Abu-Dharr was not such as tamely to accept such things, and so in a public address he spoke freely,
in such terms as these:

"Things have now come to the position which we see. And
by Allah none of this is in the Qur'an or in the Custom of the
Prophet. By Allah I see right destroyed and wrong preserved,
truth called falsehood, and selfishness without piety, O you
crowds of rich who oppress the poor." So too he preached
against those who amassed gold and silver, and who would
not spend it in the way of Allah; he warned them that these
would be heated red-hot in Hell-fire and used to brand them on
foreheads, sides and backs.[59] "O you who amass wealth,
know that there are three who share in your wealth. Fate,
which may take away the good or evil of wealth by destruction
or death, before you are aware of it; your heir, who watches
only for you to lay down your head in order to seize your
wealth while you still hold it; and yourself, the third; and
since you cannot but be the weakest of the three, you will not
have it long. Is not this the word of Allah, the Great and
Glorious: 'You cannot know charity until you spend of that
which you love?'"

"You have acquired veils of silk and cushions of embroid-
ery, and you make sore trouble to recline on the finest wool;
yet the Messenger of Allah used to sleep on the bare ground.
You must have your delicate varieties of food; yet the Messenger used to eat but sparingly of barley bread."

A story is told about Abu-Dharr by Malik ibn-Abdullah al-
Ziyadi, thus: He came once seeking audience with Uthman
ibn-Affan, and when he was brought in, he had his staff in his
hand. Said Uthman to Ka'b: "If Abd al-Rahman dies and leaves
money, what do you think about it?" Ka'b answered: "If he
acquired it lawfully in the sight of Allah, then there is nothing
wrong with it." But Abu-Dharr lifted his staff and struck Ka'b,
saying: "I have heard the Messenger of Allah say, 'If this
mountain were of gold for me to spend as if it belonged to
me, I should not like to leave behind me six grains of it.' I
adjure you by Allah, Uthman, do you hear me?" This he repeated three times, and Uthman said, "Yes."

This was a type of preaching which Mu'awiya and Marwan
could not endure, and the two of them were continually urging
Uthman, until finally Abu-Dharr was sent to Rabadha, banished

from the country. Yet he had never opposed Allah or His
Messenger, nor had he ever striven to cause corruption in
the land, for which crimes alone Islamic law prescribes
banishment.

Abu-Dharr's protest was one of the reactions of the true
spirit of Islam, but it was unpopular with those whose hearts
had been corrupted; in the same way such protests are still
resented by the modern equivalents of these, the present-
day exponents of exploitation. But this protest did represent
the watchfulness of a conscience which could not be drugged
by desires; it saw all too clearly the disgraceful growth of
wealth which was splitting Islamic society into classes; and
along with that it saw also the breakdown of the fundamentals
which this faith had sought to establish for all men. It is
relevant here to consider some examples of the vast fortunes
of that age as given by Mas'udi.[61]

"In the caliphate of Uthman the Companions acquired
estates and wealth. On the day of his death Uthman held in
his coffers a hundred and fifty thousand dinars, and a million
dirhams. The value of his estates at Wadi al-Qura, at Han-
nin, and elsewhere was a hundred thousand dinars; he also
left a great number of horses and camels. The value of Zubair's estate at his death was fifty thousand dinars; he also
left a thousand horses and a thousand slaves. Talha's income from Iraq was a thousand dinars a day, and from the
district of Sirat he had still more. Abd al-Rahman ibn-Auf
had in his stables a thousand horses, and he also possessed
a thousand camels and ten thousand sheep; at his death a
quarter of his estate was valued at eighty-four thousand
dinars. Zaid ibn-Thabit left gold and silver in ingot form,
besides money and estates. Al-Zubair built a mansion at
Basra, and had palaces also in Cairo, in Kufa, and in Alex-
andria. Talha also built a mansion at Kufa, and he raised
a palace at Medina, using gypsum, baked brick, and teak.
Sa'd ibn-Abi-Waqqas built his palace with chalcedony, roofed
it, and included a large courtyard, placing on the top of it all
crenellated walls. Al-Miqdad built his mansion in Medina of
gypsum, both inside and out, while Ya'la ibn-Munbih left fifty
thousand dinars, together with property of various kinds to a
value of three hundred thousand dirhams."

This was a type of wealth which started in a small form;
some Muslims in the time of Umar had preferential treatment

in the matter of stipends; it was this preferential system which he would later have cancelled, and the evil results of which he sought to rectify, had not the blow fallen just then which struck, not merely at the life of Umar, but also at that of Islam. Thus the preferential system continued in force, and even grew in the hands of Uthman, extending its range to cover stipends, gifts, and the assignment of lands. Once started, the growth of wealth spread widely and swiftly, through the process of the amalgamation of properties, estates, and profit-making enterprises. It was encouraged by Uthman, who permitted the buying of lands in the provinces, and the amassing of wide-spread estates. And the process was even increased after the suppression of that deep and sincere protest which came from the heart of Abu-Dharr. If this protest had achieved its aim, if it had received a favorable hearing from the head of the state, it would sufficiently have set matters to rights; it would have accomplished what Umar wished to do at the end of his life, namely, to take from the rich their excessive wealth and to give it to the poor. This he was legally entitled to do by the authority of his office, in order to root out all evil from the community. More; this was his bounden duty as a method of ensuring the welfare of society.

But in proportion as wealth was heaped up and amassed on the one side, so on the other side poverty and misery inevitably increased, and with them a sense of grievance and discontent. This was not long in growing to such a height as to give rise to open civil war; this in turn was exploited by the enemies of Islam, and was ultimately responsible for the death of Uthman, and for the end of all trust and all peace in the Islamic community. It was this situation which gave the Islamic community over to tyranny and hatred, in a holocaust which was not to be extinguished before it had enveloped the whole spirit of Islam in its smoke. Through it the Muslim community was handed over to the power of a tyrannical monarchy which had no foundation in Islam.

It is not surprising, therefore, that there was considerable anger among the capitalists and those who found the preferential system of stipends to their advantage when Ali, succeeding Uthman, laid down a policy of equality and justice. Nor was it strange that such men should pretend that they advised him to give up this policy simply because they feared

that it would cause a rebellion. His only answer was that
the inspiration of his policy was his strong awareness of
the spirit of Islam. "Do you, then, advise me to seek success by the oppression of those who are under my rule? If
this money had been my own, I would have shared it equally
among them; how then can I do otherwise when it belongs to
Allah? Surely to dispose of money wrongfully is a form of
waste and squandering; it may raise a man in the estimation
of this world, but it lowers him in the world to come."

* * * * * * *

Mu'awiya, who succeeded Ali, followed the form of economic theory dictated by his own characteristics; he used
public money for bribes and gifts, for buying over supporters
for the oath of allegiance to Yazid, and for other similar
purposes. He used it also for purposes of statecraft, for
his armies and his conquests as circumstances dictated.

The other Umayyad rulers followed his example until the
time of Umar ibn-Abd al-Aziz, who did what we have already
seen to stop extortion and to check the scattering of public
money in a wrongful fashion. Then the Umayyads got no
more than anyone else; the court flatterers and sycophants
got no share at all, and the poets with their eulogies got no
reward from the public treasury.

There is a story about Umar and Jarir[62] which relates
that when the latter discovered a panegyric on him Umar
said: "O Jarir, are you one of the Emigrants? Tell me,
that I may know to give you what is due to such a man. Or
are you one of the Helpers, that your reward may be the same
as theirs? Or are you a poor Muslim? If so, I shall order
the almoner of your tribe to give you what he gives to others
of your people." "Commander of the Faithful," answered
Jarir, "I am none of these. I am one of the richest and best
situated of my people. All I ask from you is what the Caliphs
have been accustomed to give me--four thousand dirhams,
together with an accompaniment of clothes and pack animals."
Then said Umar: "Every man must produce his work, but
I see nothing on your part which would merit a share of the
public money. However, if you wait until my stipend is paid,
then I shall set aside enough to support my family in reduced
style for a year; then if there is any left over, it shall be
handed over to you." But Jarir refused, saying: "No. Rather
let the Commander of the Faithful take all of it, and do what

is right, and I shall go away content. That is what I would
rather do." So he went; but no sooner had he gone than Umar
said: "Verily this is doing evil that good may result. Bring
him back." When he was brought back Umar said to him:
"I have forty dinars and two ceremonial robes, of which one
is being washed and I am wearing the other. All this I will
share with you, though Allah the Great and Glorious knows
that I have more need of these things than you." Then said
Jarir: "Allah has returned your gift to you, O Commander
of the Faithful, for I am now content." But Umar insisted:
"Nay, for I have sworn it, and if I do not perform my oath,
then the blame is upon me. An economy in our livelihood is
better for me than praise, so take it and go."

It is not strange, then, when the public monies were conserved and paid out only to those who had a rightful claim to
them, that contemporary accounts should represent the people
as being so satisfied under Umar II that in many districts there
were no recipients for alms. The majority of the tribes were
so content with the payment of their other claims that they
made no call on the alms money. On this subject we have the
testimony of Yahya ibn-Sa'id, as follows:

"Umar sent me to collect the alms in the province of Africa. This accomplished, I started to look for the poor to
whom to give the money. But we could find no poor there, nor
could we discover anyone who would accept the money. Umar
had so satisfied the people that I had to use the money to buy
slaves and manumit them."

Poverty and need are the fruits solely of vast and concentrated wealth, and the poor in every age are the victims of
the rich. And the rich are produced generally by stipends and
assignments, by partiality, by injustice, and by exploitation.

* * * * * * *

Thus in the times of the Umayyads, and later in the days
of the Abbasids, the public treasury was open to the ruler, as
it had been his personal possession. And that too despite the
fact that there were two treasuries, one public and the other
private. In the first of these it was laid down that the revenues
and expenditures should be from and on behalf of society; in
the second the revenues and expenditures were to be the private
affair of the ruler. Yet we find occasions when the public
monies were taken straight to the private treasury, and other

occasions on which the ruler's private expenses were met
direct from the public treasury.

"Pensions and all expenses connected with the office of
the caliphate were taken from the public treasury. We have
a statement dating back to the beginning of the fourth (tenth
A.D.) century, which details the sources of income which
were available to the private treasury.

"1. The private resources of the Caliphs, which were
passed on from father to son in the treasury. It is said
that Al-Rashid left the greatest amount of money, totalling
forty-eight million dinars. Al-Mu'tadid (279-289 A.H.
/892-902 A.D.), after paying all his expenses, increased
the contents of the private treasury by a million dinars
every year of his caliphate, until he had acquired nine
million in his coffers. He desired to make this up to ten
million dinars, and then to melt it down to form one ingot;
he intimated that when he had achieved this, he would remit to the people one third of the land-tax payable for that
year. His intention was to leave the ingot in public view,
so that all corners of the world might learn that he had
ten million dinars which he did not need. But fate prevented the fulfillment of his desires. He was succeeded
by al-Maktafi (289-295 A.H./902-907 A.D.), who raised
the treasure to fourteen millions.

"2. Income from the land-tax and the public estates
in the provinces of Faris and Karman, after local expenses
had been deducted. The value of this reached an annual
level of twenty-three million dirhams between 299 and
320 A.H. (911 and 932 A.D.). Of this total only four million went direct to the public treasury; the remaining nine-
teen million went straight to the private treasury. From
this we must deduct the constant expenditures necessitated
by the country itself; thus in 303 A.H. (915 A.D.) the
Caliph spent seven million dirhams in the pacification of
the country.

"3. Income from Syria and Egypt. The poll-tax from
the protected peoples was one example of what went direct
to the Caliph's treasury, as pertaining to the Commander
of the Faithful, rather than to the public treasury. This
theoretically was all that the Caliph required.

"4. Income arising from the seizure of the wealth of
ministers, officials, or governors who had been deposed,

or from the proceeds of the sale of their lands; or income deriving from the estates of men deceased. The Caliph was in the habit of inheriting the possessions of his servants, and those of the clients of his family who died without an heir. Since such men were generally eminent personalities and in a good financial position, this produced a comfortable income of considerable proportions flowing constantly into the Caliph's treasury.

"5. There went direct to the private treasury a portion of the estate taxes and the land-taxes from Lower Iraq and Al-Ahwaz, and from the Eastern and Western provinces.

"6. The surplus which each successive Caliph amassed. Each of the two last Caliphs of the third (ninth A.D.) century, Al-Mu'tadid and Al-Muktafi, had had an annual surplus of a million dinars; the purpose of Al-Muqtadir was to have a similar surplus, so that after twenty-five years he would have twenty-five million dinars, or approximately half of what Al-Rashid left."[63]

From all this it is apparent how much in error are those who give the name of "Caliph" to those who exercised such power over the public funds. It is also apparent what a gulf lay between this form of economic theory and the principles of Islam. It is clear to what an extent wealth and luxury increased on the one hand, and on the other misery and destitution. It is obvious how far these results led the Islamic community away from the true path of Islam, and how contrary were these things to Islamic principles.

* * * * * * *

Yet in spite of all this, the historical experience of Islam can prove a number of the fundamental principles of economic theory, and can provide confirmation of most of the theories and principles of Islam. And this despite the reverse which it suffered in the course of time at the hands of the Umayyads to the great misfortune of all mankind.

The historical experience of Islam can prove these points.

1. That the poor have a better right to the public monies than those who were merely converts to Islam. We find in the Musnad of Ahmad ibn-Hanbal: Adi ibn-Hatim[64] related this story. I came to Umar ibn-al-Khattab along with a num-

ber of my people, but he allotted to another man of Tayy
the sum of two thousand dirhams, and he turned away from
me. So I said to him: "Commander of the Faithful, do
you know me?" He smiled broadly and said: "Yes, by
Allah, I know you. You were a Believer when these were
unbelievers, you came into us when they turned their backs,
you fulfilled all your obligations when they defaulted. The
first tax money which came in to cheer the hearts of Allah's
Messenger and his Companions was that of Tayy, which you
brought to the Messenger." Then he started to apologize,
saying: "I have allotted to people who have been ruined by
destitution, to people who are the noblest of their tribes,
only as much as will meet their needs."

And this, be it noted, refers to Umar who gave preferential treatment to those who had been early converts, when
he was making up the stipends; therefore it is surely valuable
and significant evidence. Necessity is the first justification
for making a claim on Islamic society. This is a deep-
seated principle which indicates the horror in which Islam
holds need and destitution, and which demonstrates the Islamic insistence that these things should be removed first
of all, before attention can be given to any other matter.

2. That Islam is opposed to excessive wealth on the one
hand, and to privation on the other. In an effort to put an
end to any such state of affairs it will grant to the head of
the state a freedom of action which is in proportion to the
conditions which obtain. The historical experience of Islam
draws this principle from the account of Allah's Messenger
distributing the whole of the Banu Nadir booty to the poorer
Emigrants as their private property, and to the two poor
Helpers, in an attempt to restore a measure of equality to
the Muslim community at the first possible opportunity. And
the Qur'an adds its ratification to this historical precedent:
"In order that it may not be passed around among the rich
among you."

This precedent is intensely significant. The head of the
state always has the right to give the poor a share in the
public money; thereby he restores a measure of equality to
the Islamic community, and reasserts the desire of Islam
that there shall be no great gulf between the classes to destroy that general equality.

3. The principle of pro rata taxation, according to the

amount of one's means, much or little. When the poll-tax
was imposed on protected peoples, it was imposed on the
following scale:

    a. The rich had to pay forty-eight dirhams per head
per year.

    b. The middle class had to pay twenty-four dirhams.

    c. The poor who were yet earning had to pay twelve
dirhams.

No poll-tax was taken from the destitute who were in re-
ceipt of alms, from those who were incapacitated for work,
from the blind, the crippled, the insane, or the deformed.
This obtained throughout all countries. Poll-tax was not
imposed on anyone save free and sane men; there was no
tax on women or children.

When the Muslim community was overtaken by the "Year
of Ashes" in consequence of a drought, Umar did not send
out his collectors to take in the poor-tax; he left the people
alone until the year of drought had passed. Then, when conditions were normal and prosperity had returned, he sent
out his governors to collect a double due from the rich; one
part for the "Year of Ashes," and the other for the current
year. Others he excused payment altogether. Then he commanded that these others be given one half of what had been
collected, while his governors brought the second half to
him.

    4. The principle that there must be no sequestration of
the staple commodities in order to pay the taxes, and that
taxes must not be exacted by force. Ali once said to one of
his governors: "When you collect their taxes you must not
force them to sell an article of clothing, in winter or in
summer, the food which they must eat, or the beasts which
they must use for work. You must not strike anyone even.
once over a dirham, nor must you bastinado anyone in search
of a dirham; and you must not sell anyone's goods to pay
his taxes. For our business with them is simply to admit
their excuses."[65]

    5. The principle of the care of the family, and of enabling
a man to meet his needs. Thus the Prophet allotted to a
single man one share, and to a married man two shares, of
the plunder. In this allotment it is indicated that need as
well as effort put out by the married man is just the same
as that put out by the single man, but the former has double

the need of the latter; therefore his share should be double. Thus need alone is a satisfactory justification of possession according to Islam; hence the emphasis of Islam on social security.

6. The principle of universal social security for all who are disabled, and for all who are in need. Thus Umar allotted a hundred dirhams to every new-born child; when the boy grew up he was given two hundred, and when he came to manhood, the allowance was further augmented. A foundling was allotted a hundred, and his guardian received a monthly provision allowance specifically for him; his nursing and expenses were chargeable upon the treasury; then, when he grew up, he was treated as the equal of the other children. This humane treatment by Umar inspired a similar humanity throughout Islam, so that a foundling is always regarded as guiltless, and does not have to bear the weight of his parents' sin. We have already noticed what allowance Umar made for the blind Jew and the Christian lepers. This is the essential humanity of Islam represented through the mind of Umar towards all people, and not merely to Muslims. It means social security against the misfortunes of need, disability, and privation.

7. The principle of "Where did you get this?" A governor has no means of preventing society calling him to account for the money which he has acquired, and making him prove whether it is his money or theirs. The application of this principle runs out in the fact that the governor must promise to repay twice the value of any disputed money before he is given control of the disposal of public monies. Such a principle was adopted by Umar in the case of all his governors, and by Ali in the case of some.

8. The principle of universal liability to pay the poor-tax. This has never been dropped except in times of intense oppression or corruption of the Islamic spirit. No one has ever objected to it, either in theory or in practice, since the Wars of Apostasy at the beginning of Abu-Bakr's caliphate. But in our present age, when Western civilization has become paramount, this last living principle of Islam has fallen into desuetude.

9. The principle of universal mutual responsibility. This makes the people of every town generally responsible for any of their number who die of starvation. This is a criminal

responsibility for which the blood-money is payable; for the townspeople are regarded as having killed any man who dies of starvation while living in their midst. This principle runs out in a kind of economic socialism which is supported by the fact that it is the established right of any man who is hungry or thirsty to use force on anyone who has food or water, if the needy man fears that he is in danger of death. If the result is the death of the man who has the food or water, then no blood-money and no punishment attach to the other.

10. The principle that usury is forbidden because of the hardship which it imposes on the debtor. Usury was always forbidden until material Western civilization made it legal when it was imported by French law, and made one of the general principles of economic life. The sole and inevitable result was the checking of the moral element in life, and the destruction of the spirit of helpfulness and charity in men's hearts. But it was this spirit which Islam took as the basis of society; and as the foundation for man's dealings with man.

All of this takes no account of the duties of charity, equality, and mutual responsibility within society--outside of purely legal considerations. Evidence of the spirit of Islam in Muslim societies has been provided in the recent past, even in our fathers' times, not to mention our grandfathers, and in all parts of the Muslim world; a remnant of this spirit will still be in evidence after material Western civilization has ceased to make havoc of the Islamic world, for it has been sufficiently abundant to dispense with laws and with compulsion. The numerous bequests and the various charitable foundations, which today are diverted from their true purposes and plundered by sundry persons under a variety of excuses and pretexts, testify to the forces of benevolence and charity, responsibility and social security which existed in the hearts of Muslim peoples, both far and near, before they were corrupted by this rigid material civilization which hardens the heart and the feelings.

The aim of social security has today become limited to the poor, and has even begun to ignore man and deal only with animals. For some of the charitable foundations are restricted to the care of ailing animals, to provide homes for them, and to ensure to them a safeguard against homelessness and starvation.

* * * * * * *

This is Islam, in spite of the thwarting of its first practical steps by the victory of a family whose hearts were un-
familiar with its spirit, but who looked forward to a time
when they would be able to overcome Islam itself. They kept
dreaming of an hereditary tyrannical monarchy until at length
they achieved it, and they led it along a path not sanctioned
by Islam.

VIII.   The Present State and the Prospects of Islam

Our mission is to preach a renewal of Islamic life, a life
governed by the spirit and the law of Islam, which alone can
produce that form of Islam which we need today, and which
is in conformity with the genuine Islamic tradition. We have
already examined the theoretical bases of society as they
are outlined in the Qur'an and the Traditions, and we have
looked briefly at Muslim society as it evolved in the course
of history. It now remains for us to ask: Is it possible today to renew something similar to that form of Islamic life
for the present and for the future?

It is not sufficient that Islam should have been a living
force in the past; it is not enough that it has produced a
sound and well-constructed society in the time of the Prophet
and in the age of the caliphate. Since that distant time there
have been immense changes in life, mental, economic, political, and social; there have even been material changes in
the earth, and in its powers relative to man. All these
things must be carefully considered before an answer can be
given to our question.

There is also a further consideration which cannot be
overlooked in any discussion which is directed to a practical
and particular end, rather than to a theoretical and general;
we must discover why it was that the spread of the Islamic
spirit came to a halt in matters of political and economic
theory only a short time after the age of the Prophet. Was
this the longest possible span of life which the inner spirit
and resources of Islam could command?

Before dealing with these two considerations we must emphasize the two following truths:

1. That Islamic society today is not Islamic in any true
sense. We have already quoted a verse from the Qur'an
which cannot in any way be honestly applied today: "Whoever
does not judge by what Allah has revealed is an unbeliever."[1]
In our modern society we do not judge by what Allah has revealed; the basis of our economic life is usury; our laws
permit rather than punish oppression; the poor-tax is not

obligatory, and is not spent in the requisite ways. We permit the extravagance and the luxury which Islam prohibits;
we allow the starvation and the destitution of which the Messenger once said: "Whatever people anywhere allow a man
to go hungry, they are outside the protection of Allah, the
Blessed and the Exalted." The Imam Ibn-Hazm also delivered
a fatwa[2] on the same subject, to the effect that if a man dies
in starvation in any town, the people of that town are regarded
as having killed him, and the blood-money may be demanded
of them. We permit this and similar things which have long
been the subject of vain protest. Yet the Qur'anic text is undeniably applicable to such things; it refers to the existence
in our modern society of such laws as those which permit
usury, adultery, and refusal to pay the poor-tax, which
thereby prove themselves to be in opposition to the divine
laws laid down in the Qur'an.

2. So long as Muslim society adhered to Islam it manifested no weakness and no tendency to abdicate its control of
life. It was when it fell away from Islam that these things
took place. Emphasis on this fact will compensate for the
idle aspersions which Western scholars have cast on our faith,
and which they have evidenced from history. These aspersions have been taken up by some in the East who were either
gullible or mercenary, and have been the cause of the sully-
ing of hundreds of pages by such men, under the claim of being liberal thinkers and accurate scholars. This is nonsense,
and can only serve as a pretext for the false, the gullible, or
the mercenary mind.

We may now return to treat of the two considerations whose
discussion we deferred until we had noted the above points.
We may start by answering the second question: Why did the
spread of the Islamic spirit come to a halt a short space after the time of the Prophet?

Here again we must emphasize two historical facts:

1. This halt was only partial, never complete. It took
place only in a limited sphere, that of politics. The tolerant
caliphate became a tyrannical monarchy; the public funds
were made accessible to the monarch, his relatives, his
courtiers, and his flatterers, while they became inaccessible
to those who had a true claim on them by the laws of Allah
and His Messenger. But the remainder of the teachings of
Islam remained in force; the charity and benevolence, the

mutual help and responsibility, the tolerance and freedom of conscience and human equality, the payment of the poor-tax and the alms, and all the other positive and negative ordinances of Islam--all these continued in force to a greater or a lesser extent in many Muslim communities. The shari'a even continued in force as the system of civil law until the nineteenth century, when we introduced French law, thus giving the coup de grace to another tie which bound us to the beliefs of Islam.

2. The change which overtook the system and the development of politics--a partial change, as we have just said-- was the product of an unfortunate mischance, as we have already contended. The mischance was that control should fall into the hands of the Umayyads, first in an indirect way in the reign of Uthman, and latterly quite openly in the reign of Mu'awiya. If we are to be fair to Islam we cannot hold it responsible for the Umayyads; for it was injured far more by this clan of the Quraish than by the fiercest of its enemies.

I am certain that, if the life of Umar had lasted several years longer, or if Ali had been the third Caliph, or even if Uthman had become Caliph when he was twenty years younger, then the course of Islamic history would have been very considerably changed. For the policy which Umar enunciated was: (a) to take excessive wealth from the rich and give it to the poor; and (b) to equalize the stipends assigned to the people, as had been the practice under Abu-Bakr. If Umar had done this, there could have been no opposition to a policy so consistent with Islam. Umar's conscience was above all question, as was his zeal for the faith; the reverence in which he was held for his fidelity to the faith was similarly above the attacks of jealousy and doubt. So if this program had been carried out by Umar, it would have restored economic and social equity to the Islamic world, and the civil war would have been averted at its very beginning, or, at the least, would have been postponed for a long time.

Or if Ali had succeeded Umar, he would have guided the people in Umar's policy, whatever might have been the position of the Quraish, who had more self-confidence in dealing with Ali than they had in dealing with Umar. In that case the matter would not then have come to the stage of rebellion or civil war. The Umayyads would not have later aspired to power; for their nobles had no high standing in Islam because of their early conversion or their renown in the early wars; they were only among the "forced" converts who embraced Islam at the conquest of Mecca, when the success of the new faith was already assured. Under such circumstances they could have held office in the army or in provinces, but with no special reason for holding or being kept out of office, such as they gained in thirteen years under the reign of Uthman.

But it will be asked: How were the Umayyads able to effect such a speedy revolution during a period of turmoil in Islam? Does not this indicate that the Islamic system is unsteady by nature, or at least unsuited to permancy? Does it not indicate that by nature Islam provides no adequate safeguards against such revolution?

We must here take account of the condition of the Islamic state in that age, and we must reckon not only with factors of external power, but also with those of internal agitation.

The truth is that at that stage Islam was in a ferment, and the really strange thing is that the Umayyads did with it only as much as they did. For the fact is that the astonishing speed of the conquests, to which history can produce no parallel, added to Islamic society a huge territory, teeming with various races and skills, intellects and languages, systems, traditions, and heritages. However strong the spirit of Islam may have been, and however powerful in suppressing all these heritages, an element of time was essential before all this new material could be homogenized, before a change could be wrought in the old moral ideas, the rooted traditions, the cherished social systems and customs. Thus the Umayyad attack on the spirit of Islam just at this juncture took place at a unique point of time; if it had been stayed for a space, it could never have accomplished all that it did.

We have seen that the bulk of Mu'awiya's support lay in Syria, a conquered country, rather than in Arabia itself. Those of his supporters who did hail from the Peninsula, such as Amr ibn.al-As, were of a nature akin to Mu'awiya himself, men who trampled down the moral element in their reckonings, who justified the means by the end, and who justified the end simply on the grounds that they desired it.

As for the suggestion that the Islamic system does not provide by nature adequate safeguards against revolution, for one thing we must bear in mind that this system was assailed by revolution before it had properly struck roots; and for another thing we must remember that in practice no system has any real such safeguards. Where, for example, are the safeguards of democracy in Europe? This is a strongly entrenched system, which has achieved a definite form, and which has had time to establish itself and to spread its influence over a long period into every quarter of life. Yet where were its safeguards at the time of the Nazi revolution, or the Fascist, or the Spanish? Or again take the institution of free speech in the United States, whose people fled from Europe to form a free society--where are its safeguards? Today a few newspaper and radio companies can hold a monopoly of both information and opinion, and can forbid any contrary opinions to find their way to the eyes, the ears, or the thoughts of the people.

The truth is that any suspicion that the Islamic system does not afford safeguards against revolution is due to ignorance of what is practically feasible in any system. It betrays also an ignorance of the true facts of Islamic history; we have the evidence of the minor rebellion in the Hejaz, and of the great rebellion against Uthman; we have the evidence of the Qarmatian rebellion, [3] and of many others, all of which were directed against exploitation, arbitrary power, and class distinctions. The spirit of Islam has continually and successfully resisted all such things, in spite of the grievous injuries which it has suffered at their hands throughout thirteen hundred years.

The spread of the spirit of Islam, then, was not halted because that spirit was unable to establish itself, nor because it was found inadequate to cope with the demands of life. As we shall shortly see, this spirit has been continuously operative in many of the aspects of life and society. The halt in its spread was the product of an unfortunate mischance at a unique point of time. And it was when that mischance brought to Islam a Caliph who retained something of the true spirit of the caliphate in the person of Umar II, that the spread of Islam became again apparent, and the government again truly Islamic. But then the times were not propitious for such a truly Muslim Caliph to restore what had been destroyed, or to establish the roots of Islamic traditions in the political system.

But none the less the attempt of Umar II does give us a clear indication that the inner power of Islam was really strong and capable of application in very different times. For his attempt followed the oppressive and evil age of the Umayyads, and it indicated clearly that a renaissance of Islamic government was possible, and not out of the question.

But we must repeat our contention that even when the spread of the Islamic spirit came to a halt in the realm of politics-- though even here it was only a partial halt--it still continued to operate in other aspects of both social and individual life. It continued to realize many of its ideals, and to achieve many of its aims; indeed even to the present day it is still effective in such spheres as are not strongly under the influence of politics.

As the Frenchman, Gouilly, says in "Islam and the Great Powers":[4]

"The number of Muslims in Madagascar is not less than three quarters of a million. Most European authorities explain the spread of Islam in the native villages by the fact that it is a unifying religion which ensures for the negro an equality and justice for which he longs; it emancipates him finally from the bondage of priesthood and superstition, and even from the nightmare of evil spirits."

Or H.A.R. Gibb in "Whither Islam?":

"Islam still has it in its power to render a conspicuous service to mankind. There is no other society which can show such a record of having united various races in one unity based on equality. The great Islamic community in China, and the still smaller community in Japan, all show that Islam has still the power completely to reconcile such divergent elements as these of race and class. If ever the opposition of the great states of the East and West is to be replaced by understanding, this can only be done through the medium of Islam."

The conduct of the Muslims during the Crusades showed the full inspiration of the strong spirit of Islam, as it rose superior to worldly considerations, treachery and ruthlessness. It showed a belief in the unity of mankind and the relationship of humanity beyond all differences of faith, and above all temporal and ephemeral enmities. Saladin was not the only one whom the history of the Crusades has recorded as being of the true and lofty Islamic spirit; rather would this description apply to all the Muslim armies which took part in these long and bitter wars. And this remained true

despite the foul deeds of the Crusaders. These may be ex-
emplified in the fall of Jerusalem on the fifteenth of July,
1099 A.D. (492 A.H.), during the first Crusade. The Muslims sought refuge and sanctuary in the Aqsa Mosque, but
the Crusaders followed them inside and despatched them with
their swords, so that blood flowed through the sacred pre-
cincts in a flood. In this act the Crusaders violated a solemn
treaty which their leader had made with some of the Arabs.[6]
This was only one example of the barbarity of the Crusaders,
involving as it did a violation of their honor, punishment of
the living, and retaliation on the infirm and the children.

Yet even after that, when fate turned against the barbari-
ans, their treatment at the hands of the Muslims was imbued
with the Islamic spirit, which was strong enough to check
the desire for vengeance in Muslim hearts, and to keep them
within the bounds of humanity and religion.

Again, within our own times, the recent war against the
Jewish settlers in Palestine has revealed the penetration of
the Islamic spirit. For even after the long interval during
which Muslims have been divorced from the spirit and traditions of their faith, these have proved effective in keeping
the Arab forces from taking vengeance for the most horrible
and inhuman crimes committed by the Zionists in the Holy
Land. They have been effective in keeping Muslim armies
true to the lofty traditions which their religion has maintained
for fourteen centuries, and that in the midst of a constant
record of inhumanity.

While we are discussing the inner vitality of Islam, we
must not overlook the succession of disasters and calamities,
both internal and external, to which Islam has been subjected
throughout its long history. Yet to this day it is still a powerful element in human history, and commands the attention
even of some Occidentals as a means of saving humanity from
its present dilemma, as we have already seen in the quotations
from Gouilly and Gibb. And this despite the fact that such
men are unable fully to comprehend the Islamic spirit, but
confine themselves rather to a review of its practical profit
as it now exists, than to an appreciation of its profound
spiritual content. For it is difficult for Occidentals who have
been brought up in the shadow of a deeply rooted materialistic civilization--and such we shall later see that it is--to appreciate this subtle spiritual element.

We have already indicated the first internal disaster which overtook Islam, namely its subjugation by the Umayyads. This was an interlude which neither permanently affected the practical traditions of Islam, nor altered its spiritual exhortations and laws. It did not produce any permanent social principles, any accepted practical traditions, or any rooted practices.

We must now examine quickly the more important developments which befell Islam, and mark their influence through the following centuries.

The first of these is to be found in the rise of the Abbasid state, with its reliance on racial elements newly converted to Islam. The attitude of these peoples to their new religion was never whole-hearted, because of the national loyalties whose roots remained strong within them. But as time went on the Abbasid state deserted these elements on which it had been founded, and which were now beginning to acquire a tincture of Islam, for others whose nucleus was a body of Turks, Circassians, Dailamites and such like. So this dynasty continued to find its support in elements which were opposed to the spirit of Islam, and to which it gave a favored position because it relied on them. There was nothing to withstand these racial elements--and hence to withstand the power of the dynasty--except the spirit of Islam, with all the inner force and vitality which it could muster.

Then followed the destructive raids of the Tartars, bursting with savage ferocity on the Islamic world. Without delay Islam turned aside the force of the onslaught, swallowed it up, and assimilated it. Yet this was not accomplished without causing in the spirit of Islam itself a profound upheaval in which the practices and traditions of this religion were forcibly modified. None the less, in spite of the humiliation of the state by the Tartar onslaught, the Islamic community continued powerful and loyal to its ideals, and constant in the fundamentals of its religion, no matter how far it may have wandered from them in a few purely official aspects.

We must also bear in mind here that the Roman Empire, the building and growth of which had occupied almost a thousand years, was cut off and fell to pieces in a single century, as a result of the incursions of the Huns and Goths; nothing was left of it except a few scattered traces. But the Islamic state remained in occupation of a wide territory, although its building had occupied little more than half a century, and though it had had to contend with a number of internal struggles between ruling families, as well as the external attacks of the Tartars, and others. Such factors demonstrate the intense vitality of Islam, in that it was able to meet these circumstances.

As we trace the development further, in the West we find the war in Spain, and in the East the disaster of the Crusades. In the first of these Islam was worsted, in the second it was victorious. But from that time to this it has had to contend with ferocious enemies of the same spirit as the Crusaders, enemies both open and hidden.

But the final overthrow of Islam took place only in the present age, when Europe conquered the world, and when the dark shadow of colonization spread over the whole Islamic world, East and West alike. Europe mustered all its forces to extinguish the spirit of Islam, it revived the inheritance of the Crusaders' hatred, and it employed all the materialistic and intellectual powers at its disposal. With these it sought to break down the internal resistance of the Islamic community and to divorce it gradually over a long period from the teachings and the heritage of its religious faith.

When we speak of the hatred of Islam, born of the Crusading spirit, which is latent in the European mind, we must not let ourselves be deceived by appearances, nor can we let their hypocrisy blind us to the fact that they deny to us any freedom of religion. They say, indeed, that Europe is not as unshakably Christian today as it was at the time of the Crusades, and that there is nothing today to warrant hostility to Islam, as there was in those days. But this is entirely false and inaccurate. General Allenby was no more than typical of the mind of all Europe, when, entering Jerusalem during the First World War, he said: "Only now have the Crusades come to an end." Similarly the governor of the Sudan was no more than typical of the European mind when he placed all governmental power at the disposal of missionaries in the Southern Sudan, while forbidding any Muslim trader even to enter the country. It happened once that a certain official was stationed for a rather long time in the South, and so asked for a transfer to the North; it was not granted. He then bethought himself to try lifting up his voice in the Muslim call to prayer; that single act sufficed to ensure his transfer the following day.

And England is, of all the European countries, the most
tolerant and patient and skillfull in reconciling questions of
religion.

People sometimes wonder how this obstinate spirit of resistance to Islam can persist so strongly and to such a pitch
in a Europe which has discarded Christianity, and where the
exhortations of preacher and monk no longer fill European
ears as they did in the age of the Crusades. But this fact
ceases to be surprising when we take account of two facts:

1. "The enmity which the Crusaders stirred up was not
confined to the clangor of arms, but was, before all else and
above all else, an intellectual enmity. The European mind
was poisoned by the slurs which the Crusaders' leaders cast
on Islam as they spoke of it to their ignorant Western com-
patriots. It was in that age that there grew up in Europe the
ridiculous idea that Islam was a religion of unbridled passion
and violent sensuality, that it consisted merely of formal
observances, and that it had no teaching of purity or of re-
generation of heart. And this idea has remained as it started.
It was in this age also that the Messenger, Muhammad, was
contemptuously known as 'My Dog,'7 (Mahound).

"This loathing spread apace. The ignorant mass of Crusaders had dependents in many places throughout Europe;
and the process was hastened by the Spanish Christians in
their war to deliver their country from 'the yoke of the
idolaters.' But the downfall of Muslim Spain was to require
many centuries before it was completed; when this protracted
struggle and the constraint which it involved grew too great,
a hostility to Islam started to take root in Europe, and ultimately became permanent. Finally it took the form of a complete extirpation of Islam throughout Spain, after a conflict
which reached a pitch of ferocity and bitterness hitherto unknown. The cries of joy which all over Europe greeted this
event were unfortunately uttered in ignorance of the consequences which would arise; for the result was that science
and learning were blotted out, and in their place came the
ignorance and the barbarity of the Middle Ages.

"But before the echoes of these happenings in Spain had
died away, there took place a third event of immense significance, which was to hasten the breaking of the ties between
the Western world and Islam. This was the fall of Constantinople to the Turks. Europe had always looked to Byzantium
as a relic of the glory of ancient Greece and Rome, and had
regarded it as the fortress of Europe against Asiatic barbar-
ism. Hence with the fall of Constantinople the gate was thrown

wide open to the flood of Islam. In the centuries which followed, and which were filled with wars, the hostility of Europe to Islam was no longer a question of merely academic importance; it was now a question of political import also. And this fact further increased the violence of that hostility.

"In addition to all this, Europe derived great profit from this cleavage. The Renaissance or rebirth of European arts and sciences in the widest sense arose particularly from an Islamic and Arab source; in most cases it can be traced back to material contacts between the East and the West. Europe profited more than did the Muslim world, but it did not acknowledge the gift, because it was blinded by its loathing of Islam. Or, more correctly, the reverse is true, that that loathing increased with the passage of time, until it was second nature. At this point loathing swamped all understanding whenever the word 'Muslim' was mentioned; it entered into all their thoughts until it came to form a permanent part of the thinking of every European, man or woman. And still stranger than this is the fact that this feeling continued to flourish even after all the movements of intellectual exchange. Then followed the age of the Reformation, during which Europe was divided into various sects, each continually employed in arming itself against every other; yet hostility to Islam was the common feature of all of them. This in turn was followed by an age when religious feeling started to subside, but the hostility to Islam continued unabated. One of the clearest proofs of this is that the French philosopher and poet, Voltaire, was one of the bitterest critics of Christianity and of the Church in the eighteenth century; yet he was at the same time violently hostile to Islam and to its Messenger. A few score years later came the age in which Western scholars commenced to study foreign learning and to regard it with a measure of sympathy. Yet in all matters connected with Islam the traditional dislike began to creep in under a form of partisan spirit which was not conducive to academic study. Thus the gulf which history had dug between Europe and the Islamic world remained still unbridged. Dislike of Islam thus became a fundamental part of European thinking; and the fact that the first Orientalists of the modern age were Christian missionaries who were working in Muslim territory meant that the picture which they formed of the teachings and the history of Islam was distorted; for it was founded on an axiomatic con-

ception that Europeans were superior to 'idolaters.' And
despite the fact that Oriental studies have now been liber-
ated from missionary influence, this intellectual bias has
persisted, although any mistaken view can no longer claim
the excuse of ill-informed religious zeal. Hence the attacks
made by Orientalists upon Islam betray an inherited characteristic, and a peculiarity of nature; they are based on an
impression created by the Crusades, and shaped by all the
mental influences of these on the early Europeans.

"But it will immediately be asked: How does it happen
that an ancient antipathy such as this, which was originally
religious in its basis, and which in the period of its birth
owed its inception to the spiritual mastery of the Christian
Church, can persist in Europe in an age when religious convictions are no more than a matter of antiquarian interest?

"There is never anything surprising in such a situation;
for it is well known to psychology that men may lose all the
religious beliefs which they held in their youth, and at the
same time retain some of their personal idiosyncrasies, even
those which formerly centered upon the very religious beliefs
which they have now discarded. It is these idiosyncrasies
which provide the intellectual motivation for every act of such
men. This is the state which obtains in Europe regarding
Islam. Despite the fact that the religious convictions which
gave rise to European hostility to Islam have now lost their
power and been replaced by a more materialistic form of
life, yet the ancient antipathy itself still remains as a vital
element to pour a secret poison into the European mind. So
far as the strength of this antipathy is concerned, it undoubtedly varies from one individual to another, but that it exists is
indisputable. The spirit of the Crusades, though perhaps in
a milder form, still hangs over Europe; and that civilization
in its dealings with the Islamic world still occupies a position
which bears clear traces of the early Crusader spirit."[8]

2. European imperial interests can never forget that the
spirit of Islam is firmly opposed to the spread of imperialism.
Such an opposition must either be crushed or at least diverted.
No weight need be attached to the contention of gullible or mercenary writers that religion is of no concern to Europe, that
the source of European power is not religious, and that the
only thing about the Muslim world which Europe fears is its
material power. Fundamentally religion is a spiritual power

which is always effective for the provision of material powers.
Besides, Islam is essentially different from Christianity; it
encourages the fostering of material powers, it enjoins self-
defense and defensive war, and it warns the weaklings who
tamely submit that theirs will be an evil fate in this world and
in the next. "Prepare for them as much as you can in the way
of forces and cavalry, with which you may overcome Allah's
enemies and your own."[9] "Do not take unbelievers for your
friends in preference to Believers."[10] "So let those fight in
the way of Allah who would exchange the life of this world for
that of the next."[11] "Do not grow weary or grieve now that
you have the upper hand, if you are true Believers...etc."[12]

So Islam is at once a spiritual power and an incentive to
material power; it is at once a form of opposition in itself,
and an incentive to a still more forcible opposition. Therefore European imperialism cannot but be hostile to such a
religion. The only difference lies in the fact that the form
of that hostility varies according to the imperialistic methods
of each nation, and according to local conditions. Thus, for
example, France declared open war on Islam in the Western
Arab world, under the name of "protecting the Berbers," or
some such phrase. But England took a more devious and
tortuous road to the same end in Egypt, that of education.
Her aim was to encourage the growth of a general frame of
mind which would despise the bases of Islamic life, and even
of Eastern life; when this was accomplished there would be
a generation educated into this frame of mind, ready to go
out into the schools and educational offices to imbue the coming generations with the same ideas. These would set a
fashion in manners and customs which would ultimately lead
to the permanent establishment of the desired frame of mind,
and would emphasize the difference between the basic elements
of Islamic education and the policies of the Education Ministry.
Thus England could dispense with open hostilities as a means
of opposition to religious convictions. And this objective was
actually ascribed by a large and influential party to a desire
to establish a pan-Egyptian mentality. In the Southern Sudan,
again, there was no call for such guile; the position there
was simply that which we have already described in speaking
of the Christian missionaries and the Muslim merchants.

Thus each imperialist state has proceeded by one means
or another to oppose and to throttle Islam since the last cen-

tury, and even before that. And that they still proceed to do essentially the same thing in concert is obvious from the position taken up by the United Nations on the question of Indonesia and Holland, on that of Kashmir, India and Paskistan, and on that of Hyderabad, India and the Nizam. Finally the same thing is supremely evident in the position of the United Nations on Palestine.

There are those who hold that it is the financial influence of the Jews in the United States and elsewhere which has governed the policy of the West. There are those who say that it is English ambition and Anglo-Saxon guile which are responsible for the present position. And there are those who believe that it is the antipathy between East and West which is responsible. All these opinions overlook one vital element in the question, to which all other elements are subordinate, the Crusader spirit which runs in the blood of all Occidentals. It is this which colors all their thinking, which is responsible for their imperialistic fear of the spirit of Islam, and for their efforts to crush Arab strength. For the instincts and the interests of all Occidentals are bound up together in the crushing of that strength. This is the common factor which links together communist Russia and plutocratic America.

The truly remarkable thing is that the spirit of Islam has survived all these attacks which have been launched against it from the earliest period of its life right up to the present. It has persisted, in spite of sudden assaults and the effect which these have had on its life; it has lasted out, in spite of the modern conquest by Western civilization with its material and educational weapons, from which some Muslims have borrowed the means of breaking down and destroying Islam at the direction of imperialistic powers.

Despite all these things, the spirit of Islam has remained essentially sound, and its inner force has left clear imprints on the course of human life in the broadest sense. Islam has left its marks on the forms and objectives of civil government throughout fourteen centuries to the present day. There is no political or military institution in the world but owes something to Islam; and this has been true even in those ages when the Muslim world has been weak and divided, when it has seen its spiritual, social, and economic life disturbed.

But the period of obscurity and weakness is now at an end, and the tide of Islam has commenced to rise. In East and

West alike the Arab world is gaining unity, and two great Islamic blocs have made an appearance in Pakistan and Indonesia. These are portents which cannot be overlooked, significant of the underlying vitality of Islam. They are significant also of the massive resources of Islam, sufficient to bring about a complete renewal of Islamic life. Such a renewal need not be based merely on wishful thinking or on good fortune; rather it may be based on actual concrete facts which are apparent to the sight.

I personally, quite apart from my religious faith, have an absolute belief in the possibility of a renewal of Islamic life within the Muslim world; I believe in the soundness of Islam as a world-wide, rather than a local, system for the future. I have no desire to take refuge in vain speculation, but I do believe this to be not only possible, but even easy.

Not that there will not be various and vast difficulties; there will also be great tasks which must be accomplished before the complete renewal of Islamic life can take place with any facility within Muslim society. The assessment of these vast obstacles, and the inspiration to undertake the tasks involved is something which is necessitated by any true understanding of the immensity of the goal at which we are aiming, and of the weight of responsibility awaiting any man who aims at that goal. It is something which is necessitated also by an understanding of the importance of public opinion in such vast undertakings.

But it is not enough for any one man to issue a ringing call for hope to become actuality, and expectation reality. The results and the consequences must be assessed, and the man who exhorts others must equally offer to them the same vast effort which he demands of them.

In the very nature of the case the wide divergence between existing political theory and the spirit of Islam, which has arisen over a long period and has hence become deep-seated, will make it a matter of some difficulty to return to a theory which is truly based on that spirit. For the machinery of the state and of society, the foundations of life in all its aspects, the spiritual and intellectual background are all so built up on specific bases that they are difficult to change without the application of vast energy over a long time. And the longer the time, the greater the difficulty, and the greater the need for yet vaster and longer enduring effort.

The time factor is linked up with another consideration in
the present age. We do not live only in this world, but we
cannot live in isolation from it. Thus our interests and our
needs are interwoven with this present world, which is governed by a certain form of civilization, involving an outlook
completely contradictory to that of Islam. This we shall see
later. In one respect this fact will slow down our progress
along the path of renewing the true Islamic form of life, and
in another respect it will lay additional responsibilities upon
us.

The importance of this last consideration is enhanced by
the fact that this Western world with which our interests are
interwoven is at the present moment stronger than we; we
do not have today the control over it, or the strength equal
to its strength, that we had in the first age of Islam. At the
same time it is hostile to us, and in particular hostile to our
religion. Therefore it will not permit us to produce a new
Islamic system, or to renew a truly Islamic form of life,
however great the effort we put forth. This result we could
hope for only if we had control of the Western world, if our
strength were comparable to its, or if it were honest with
us and with our religion to which we seek to return.

But all this does not mean that return to the Islamic system is impossible. All that it means is that this is a great
and difficult task, requiring unremitting effort. Above all it
demands courage to believe in it, boldness to face the inevitable results, patience to endure the hard work demanded,
and faith to believe that this is necessary for Islamic society
and for mankind as a whole. It demands the fostering of a
new mentality, whose task will be not simply to elevate the
existing state of things, but rather to produce a new and perfect state.

This is our task. We have already seen the foundations on
which the system must be built; thus we can now balance the
profits which we shall enjoy if we return to it against the labor
and sacrifices which we must make in order to realize it.
When our faith in these profits reaches the point at which they
outweigh the sacrifices, then let us settle the matter, make up
our minds, and leave the result with Allah.

Perhaps one valuable aspect of the present situation might
be here pointed out. The great Western civilization has led
the world into two global wars within a quarter of a century;

after the second of these it has led it to a complete division into two blocs, an Eastern and a Western, and to the constant threat of a third war. It has brought about a state of hostility in every quarter, it has produced starvation and destitution and adversity throughout three parts of the world. It should be pointed out also that the social fabric of the whole world today is in that state of insecurity and instability where it must look for new foundations and search for some spiritual means of restoring to man his faith in the principles of humanity.

We must not, however, read more than is legitimate into this readiness of the Western world to accept the foundations of our Islamic civilization; this is another matter. Although be it noted that such a man as Bernard Shaw says that the West has already started to turn in this direction, and even prophesies that it will come to it eventually, in these words:

"I forecast that the religion of Muhammad will be accepted in Europe in the near future, for it has already started to gain some acceptance. The priests of the Middle Ages insisted on portraying Islam in the darkest colors, either out of ignorance, or from criminal bigotry; but they were led to excess by their hatred of Muhammad and his religion; indeed they held him to be the anti-Christ. For myself I find it preferable to call Muhammad the savior of mankind, and I believe that if such a man were given authority over the modern world, he would succeed in solving its problems and giving it peace and happiness. And how great is the world's need of these things.

"There were some impartial thinkers in the nineteenth century who discovered how much value there is in the religion of Muhammad, among them Carlyle, Goethe, and Gibbon. From this fact there has arisen a salutory change in the attitude of Europe towards Islam; thus Europe has seen a great advance in the past years of the twentieth century, and has even started to respect the faith of Muhammad. It may be that in the century that lies ahead Europe will make further progress, and will acknowledge the contribution of this faith towards a solution of its problems. Many among my own nation and among all European nations already belong to the religion of Muhammad, a fact which enables us to say that the conversion of Europe to Islam has already begun."[13]

But so far as we can see Shaw's prophecy is still no more than a prophecy--if, indeed, it is not intended to drug the senses of Muslims and to make them content to wait idly for Europe to embrace their faith. But however, this may be, we must at least wait until time has proved such a statement, for two principal reasons:

1. There is this deep-seated and inherited hostility to Islam in the very European nature itself. This is at present augmented by the opposition of imperialistic interests to the very existence of our faith, as being an obstacle in their path.

2. European culture is rooted in material foundations, and the influence of intellectual and spiritual interests is very weak; such has been the case from the time of Roman civilization to the present day. This matter requires detailed consideration, and a full treatment, rather than merely a brief mention. So we must here make an extended study of this important question: Is it possible for Islamic and Western civilization to work together in partnership? And if so, then what are the limits of that partnership?

We have already asserted at the beginning of this book that Europe was never at any time truly Christian, because by its very nature its peoples had to fight over their meagre territories. Thus the tolerant principles of Christianity could gain no footing in such a stubborn ground. In addition to this, Christianity is essentially an asceticism, a refusal to live, or to take an interest in, a practical worldly life. To these two factors we must now add a third, to which we have already made a passing reference. This factor was the existence of the Roman Empire, and its position athwart the path of Christianity, together with the permanent influence of that Empire on the bases of European civilization even today. And that despite the infusion of Christianity which the Roman Empire received in its last days.

We may quote here some passages from "Islam at the Cross-roads," which we find completely satisfactory:

"The doctrine on which the Roman Empire was founded was to destroy by force, or to exploit other peoples for the sole benefit of the mother country. In order to indulge this privileged body the Romans saw nothing wrong in their violence and nothing humiliating in their oppression. The famous Roman justice was a justice for Romans only. It is apparent that such a tendency as this is possible only on the basis of a materialistic ideal, which is wholly devoted to worldly life and civilization--though it may be an ideal promoted and shaped by a philosophical taste. In any case it was far removed from any appreciation of spiritual values. The Romans did not really understand religion; their traditional gods were only variant forms of the Greek myths which, as being mere shades, were never believed to have any connection with social affairs, and which were never permitted to interfere in any way with the real business of life. Their duty was to speak in metre through the agency of their attendant priests, when questions were asked of them; but no one ever expected them to enunciate laws for the guidance of mankind.

"Such was the soil in which modern Western civilization grew up, though during the period of its growth it undoubtedly came under many other influences. Thus in the very nature of the case it changed and thereby modified the legacy which it had received from Rome in more than one way. Nevertheless the fact remains that all that is truly great in the modern West, whether of life or nature, owes its origin to Roman civilization. Hence since the intellectual and social environment of ancient Rome was always secular rather than religious--and that not ex hypothesi, but in actual fact--so the same environment persists in the modern West. There is to the European mind no possible argument against the complete futility of religion, nor will it even admit the need for such an argument. For modern European thinking in general leaves the absolute outside its scheme of practical considerations --although it does tolerate religion, and even at times may assert that it is a social virtue. Western civilization does not irrevocably disown God, but it can see no place and no significance for Him in its present intellectual system. It has made a virtue out of a philosophical inability on the part of man, that is to say, out of his inability to take a comprehensive view of the whole field of life. Hence it is that modern Europe tends to attach the greatest practical importance to the values deriving from the experimental sciences, or at least from those sciences from which may be expected some perceptible influence of human social relationships. And because the question of the existence of God does not fall into either of these categories, the

European mind tends to drop the concept of God out of the sphere of practical considerations.

"A question emerges here: How is this tendency to be reconciled with Christian thought? Is not Christianity a faith founded on the Absolute, as is Islam? And is it not ostensibly the spiritual background of Western civilization? There is no doubt that all these things are true. But there could not be any greater mistake than to imagine that Western civilization is the outcome of Christianity. The true philosophical basis of the Western system is to be sought in the ancient Roman view of life as a matter of advantage, quite independent of absolute values. It is a view which can be summarized thus: Because we have no specific knowledge, either in the way of practical experience, or in that of proof, about the fundamentals of human life, or about its destiny after physical death; therefore it is best for us to confine our powers to those material and mental fields which are accessible to us, rather than let ourselves be tied-down to metaphysical and moral questions arising from claims which can have no intellectual proofs. Such an argument as this, which is characteristic of modern Western civilization, will certainly not find acceptance in Christian thought, as it will not in Islam or in any other religion, simply because it is essentially irreligious. Thus to try to establish a causal relationship between Christianity and modern Western civilization, is a gross historical error. Christianity may indeed have played a very small part in the rise of intellectual materialism which today dominates modern Western civilization, but the truth is that the growth of this spirit has been the product of Europe's prolonged struggle against the Christian Church, and against its supervision of life. In its general aspect Christianity today is a purely spiritual thing, as was the case with the Roman deities, which were neither permitted nor expected to exert any real influence on society. No doubt there are in the West individuals who are still prepared to judge and to think on a religious basis, prepared to fight a last ditch action to reconcile their beliefs with the spirit of their civilization; but they cannot be more than isolated cases. To Europe as a whole it is a matter of indifference whether the political system is democratic or fascist, plutocratic or bolshevist, technical or intellectual; Europe knows but one necessary religion--the worship of material prosperity; the only belief that it holds is that there is but one goal in life--the making of that life easier and easier. It is, as the definition has it in significant terms, 'an escape from the tyranny of nature.' The shrines of such a culture are huge factories and cinemas, chemical laboratories and dance-halls and power stations. The priests of such a worship are bankers and mathematicians, cinema stars and scientists and aviators. The inevitable result of this state of affairs is that man strives to gain power and pleasure; this brings into being quarrelsome societies, all armed to the teeth and intent on mutual destruction whenever their conflicting interests come into active opposition. On the intellectual side the upshot has been the evolution of a humanism with a moral philosophy confined to purely scientific questions, in which the highest criterion of good or evil is whether or not any given thing represents material progress."

The sum and substance of all this is that the present-day European conscience is not ready to accept the spirit of Islam, or to seek in it a solution of human problems. But even so, it is not impossible that even this may take place after a number of other changes and developments in the West, and after the Islamic world itself has entered upon a clearly defined and independent renewal of Islamic life. In this the West may find philosophical realities and practical truths which will attract its attention and balance its thinking. But it is my personal belief that many generations must elapse before the West will be able to appreciate the spirit of Islam in any real sense.

Again the substance of this argument is that the mode of the Muslim doctrine that work must serve moral ends cannot be reconciled with the mode of the modern Western doctrine that morals must serve some material advantage. We must reckon with this fact, and hence we must work to establish a sound form of Islamic life; this cannot be achieved by the importation of elements borrowed from abroad, since such elements will not fit into the texture of our native beliefs.

The Muslim world will have to admit defeat on the first occasion on which it seeks to renew its own life by borrowing

Western ways of thought, life, and custom. Such an experiment can only result in the suffocation of that very form of life which it seeks to revive; for from the very first step the Muslim world will be departing from its own true and natural path. This path involves a belief based on Islam that the moral element is fundamental to the structure of life; it regards work as a means to moral ends, and it will not make material advantage the highest aim of morals.

We have already seen in an earlier chapter of this book that Islam satisfies all the highest aims of life, among them the moral consciousness. We have also seen that Islam's supreme virtue is that it preserves the unity of life, and that it makes no distinction between means and ends. It will not lend its authority to any idea that there is an opposition between material and spiritual in the substance of life or in the nature of the universe or of mankind; rather it emphasizes that the whole of life is a unity which must make an orderly progress towards the highest objectives.

Islam, then, enunciates for men a complete theory of life. This theory is always liable to growth by development or by adaptation; it is not open to change or to adulteration, either in its fundamentals or in its general aims. Therefore, in order that this complete theory may bear its full natural fruits, it is necessary to make a complete application of it. Otherwise, even the slightest change in its fundamentals or its aims will produce a disorder, because it will no longer be in conformity with the Islamic conception of life.

The continual growth of this universal theory by development or by adaptation is a natural product of the nature of Islam; it is encouraged by Islam, the institutions of which are adapted to recognize it. Analogy, interpretation, and the wide powers entrusted to the head of the state--all these are living methods of ensuring growth through development and adaptation, in order to keep pace with life and to meet its needs as they emerge. But there is one thing which must be kept in mind: these developments must not pass out with the roots of the fundamental Islamic theory, nor must they be allowed to serve any foreign aim; they must not betray the spirit of Islam or give allegiance to any other spirit in preference to it.

The criterion by which we may accept or reject any development is first to compare it with the basic theory and

the general spirit of Islam. Anything that is in agreement
with this theory and this spirit we may accept, and anything
which is contrary to these we must reject. Thus we may
profit by all the fruits of human labor within the bounds of
our basic philosophy of the universe, man, and life; we need
raise no barriers between ourselves and human endeavor,
nor need we stand in isolation from the continuous business
of living. Above all we must be firmly convinced of the value
of faith and enthusiasm; we have a scheme of life greater
than any possessed by the followers of any religion or school
or civilization which has yet been born. And that is to say
the least of it.

＊ ＊ ＊ ＊ ＊ ＊ ＊

However this is only a general statement; it requires a
detailed discussion of the practical methods of attaining this
great objective. It requires also a detailed discussion of
the specific question of social justice, which is the primary
interest of this book. May the blessing of Allah be with us,
then, as we start this discussion.

＊ ＊ ＊ ＊ ＊ ＊ ＊

No renaissance of Islamic life can be effected purely by
law or statute, or by the establishment of a social system on
the basis of the Islamic philosophy. Such a step is only one
of the two pillars on which Islam must always stand in its
construction of life. The other is the production of a state
of mind imbued with the Islamic theory of life, to give permanence to external forces leading to this form of life, and
to give coherence to all the social, religious, and civil legislation. Social justice is an integral part of this Islamic life;
it cannot be realized unless this form of life is first realized,
and it cannot have any guaranteed permanence unless this form
of life is built up on solid foundations. It is in this similar
to all other social systems; it must have the support of public
belief and confidence in its merits. Failing this, its foundations will be purely spiritual, and its establishment will depend on the force of religious and social legislation; these
are too weak to sustain it, in which case it may easily mis-
carry.

Hence Islamic legislation is more akin to ecclesiastical
ordinance because it depends on religious belief. Thus we
must always keep in mind the necessity for a renaissance

of our religious faith; we must cleanse it of all accretions, such as alterations and interpretations and ambiguities; only thus can it be a support for the necessary social legislation which will establish a sound form of Islamic life. This form of life will depend upon legislation and exhortation, those twin fundamental methods of Islam towards the achievement of all aims.

We must, then, establish our Islamic theory in individuals and societies, at the same time as we set up the Islamic legislation to regulate life. And the natural method of establishing that philosophy is by education.

But how can we possibly induce Islamic theory by education? For educational methods and modes of thought are essentially Western and essentially inimical to the Islamic philosophy itself; first, because they stand on a materialistic basis which is contrary to the Islamic theory of life; and second, because opposition to Islam is a fundamental part of their nature, no matter whether such opposition is manifest or concealed in various forms.

As we have already maintained, we shall advertise our defeat the first time that we adopt a Western theory of life as the means of reviving our Islamic theory. So primarily we must avoid the ways of Western thought; rather we must choose the ways of native Islamic thought, in order to ensure pure results, rather than mongrel.

The import of these words is not that we should adopt a position of isolationism in regard to thought, education, and science; all these are a common heritage of all the peoples of the world, in which we among the foremost have a fundamental part. We shall continue to take our rightful share in the furthering of these things, even if it should become apparent that we are far removed from the influence which they exert. For the only true and permanent form of cooperation is that between all the nations of the earth.

Isolation from human life, then, is not our aim; rather what we seek is to build up a characteristically Islamic theory of life, and to renew that form of life now, when it is apparent even to some of the more enlightened Occidentals that the philosophy of materialistic Western civilization is a danger to the continued existence of man. It breeds in human nature a ceaseless anxiety, a perpetual rivalry, a continuous strife, and a weakening of human ties to the breaking point. And this in spite of all the triumphs of science which could have tended to human happiness and peace and content, had it not been that the bases of the Western philosophy of life were purely materialistic and hence unsuitable to guide men along the path to perfection.

As long as our aim is the building up of this Islamic theory along these lines, we must make a distinction between things which we may profitably accept, and those which we may profitably reject, out of Western society. Only thus may we complete the building of an Islamic society out of sound materials which will produce a structure secure against co-operation and opposition alike, against both borrowing and giving. From another point of view we must ensure to the theory of life which we establish a safeguard in the form of a period of fostering--fostering, that is, in our own minds rather than in its own essence. For Islamic life in itself is a strong and definite thing when it does not stand in awe of any other Western form. Rather it is we who need to be fostered and nurtured, as we are living on a strange diet; hence we must be on our guard while we are engaged in the establishment of our new system.

In the case of the pure sciences and their applied results of all kinds, we must not hesitate to utilize all things in the sphere of material life; our use of them should be unhampered and unconditional, unhesitating and unimpeded.

Similarly we must be careful to derive the fullest profit from other things also; from philosophy, which is the intellectual treatment of the universe and life; from literature which is the emotional treatment of these things; from history, which is a factual treatment, and from legislation, which is a treatment of the relationships between individuals and societies.

It will do us no harm to make use of the pure sciences in all the spheres of life; but on the other hand it will do us harm to account these the sum total of life; for such a view involves a philosophy which is not ours. It tends to establish a conception of the universe and of life which is at variance with the Islamic conception of these things; ultimately it would lead us along a path which is not that of Islam. It is this path which has produced the present ailments of mankind, and which is responsible for their present troubles.

It is sometimes objected that even if this be so, the pure

sciences themselves cannot be held responsible, because essentially they cannot be divorced from the method of Western thought. The experimental method rests on the basis of a definite philosophy which is neither intellectual nor spiritual; if this had never established itself in favor, science would never have followed the course which latterly it has taken. In the same way science can never remain in isolation from philosophy, nor can it be content to be influenced by philosophy without in turn influencing it. For philosophy benefits by the experimental results of science, and is influenced by it in aim and method. Thus a study of pure science involves a study of philosophy, which is influenced by that science, and which in turn exerts an influence on it. All this is over and above the fact that the applied results of science must influence all material life, methods of gaining a living, and the division of wealth. All this will in due time produce new forms of society based on a new philosophy, or at least based on a theory of life which must be influenced by these developments in the course of life.

All this is very true. But what must be must be. There is no possibility of living in isolation from science and its products, though the harm that it does may be greater than the good. There is no such thing in this life as an unmixed blessing or an unalloyed evil. Thus Islam does not oppose science, or the utilization of science; there is nothing contrary to the spirit of Islam in culling the fruits of science from all the sources of the world. But while we may acknowledge the universal influences of philosophy and culture, history and law, together with all their consequences in the way of educational methods and modes of thought and logic, we must set all of this in its proper place on a spiritual Islamic foundation. We must hold to the guiding principle that all the results and material consequences of science do not essentially affect our universal philosophy of life and custom.

When we mention educational methods we might well bear in mind here that these are indivisible and inseparable from the general philosophy of the community. Thus when we borrow Western methods of education, systems of training and curricula, we borrow also a general scheme of philosophy and a mode of thought which underlies these methods and systems and curricula, whether we like it or not.

There is a belief that these are questions of pure "pedagogy, and therefore universal and identical throughout all countries. This is a naive and shortsighted belief, encouraged by the delusion of the psychologists, who give an undue weight to their own subject; despite the difference between psychology and philosophy, such men believe that they can master their own subject, and through it can answer the philosophical questions of education also.

That claim is one thing, but the actual fact is quite another. Psychology may perhaps be a pure science to be studied in the laboratory. But the trend of its results and the use to which these are put, such as educational techniques and curricula--all these things are still influenced by the general philosophy of life, still accept the dictation of that philosophy, and still form an integral part of it. More; the very fact that psychology is ruled by the laboratory is one of the influences exerted by experimental philosophy, or by the experimental method. It is this same method which in latter years has governed all materialistic Western thought. The only type of independence which psychology can expect from the philosophy which is its mentor is that superficial independence which cannot influence the final result.

For an example of this we may look to the American curriculum, their methods of education and instruction. These are more akin to vocational training than to any system of thorough and systematic study; they have as their objective the promotion of technical skill based on theoretical principles. The reason for this tendency is to be sought in the philosophy of Pragmatism, founded by Charles Pierce in 1878 which was advanced by William James and applied by John Dewey, the modern educational philosopher. This school of thought represents a reversal of the accepted terms of thought and study; bare ideas and theoretical principles are abandoned, as is the study of things according to their logical class and nature. According to Pragmatism all study should be confined to the practical effects and results of objects.

"According to Charles Pierce and according to Pragmatism the idea is no more than a secondary product of some act or activity; it is not in itself a reality. For example, I may have the "idea" of the horn of an automobile passing in the street; this "idea" gains no meaning by my study of its nature, its origin, and the method of its production. It may be a reality or it may be a figment of the imagination; it may be produced

by the ear and the nervous system, or it may be produced
by the horn, the automobile is turning to right or to left,
and that a path must be cleared for the vehicle and its driver.
It means only: 'I am about to change the direction of my
vehicle and to proceed in a different direction.' Hence Pragmatism argues that the idea is secondary to the act, or the
product of certain conditioning circumstances. This is the
first step along the path of Pragmatism in which all the remaining steps must follow. "[14]

It has been the rise of this theory or this method of thought
which has produced the educational techniques of America.
It has been responsible for a teaching curriculum and a system which will encourage the mind to take this view of things
and to rationalize life along this line. More; it is this which
has given American life its most characteristic mark, which
has directed it towards technical production, and which has
to a large extent diverted it from academic and theoretical
education.

Accordingly we must reckon with this general philosophy
of life; if we borrow educational techniques, teaching systems,
and curricula, this philosophy underlies all of them. This
philosophy shapes and forms them, assisted by the results
of pure psychology. Such an influence is inevitable, though
this same science in its methods and in its results is itself
influenced by that very philosophy.

* * * * * * *

From the theoretical point of view, then, our method of
establishing an independent Islamic scheme of thought is to
proceed readily but cautiously in the matter of borrowing
such a philosophy along with its concomitants, such as educational techniques, teaching systems and curricula, literature, history, and law. But we shall deal now with all these
subjects together.

* * * * * * *

So far as the study of philosophy is concerned, we have
already indicated the universal theory of Islam on the universe,
life, and mankind. This is essentially different from the nature of other universal philosophies which have obtained in
the West from the days of the Greeks to the present. This
is not the place to discuss this difference, and it will suffice
to recognize merely that there does exist a radical divergence.[1]

A petition of peculiar importance was once addressed to the Azhar University concerning a matter which was not favorably regarded in this quarter. It requested that study be directed to this universal Islamic theory of life and that a full and clear treatment of it be given in modern terms and applications; also that it be compared with other schools of philosophy. But the Azhar, instead of responding to this petition, continued to teach in its Faculty of Theology what it called the errors of Islamic philosophy, taken from the writings of Ibn-Sina and Ibn-Rushd. This is, of course, a reversion to Greek philosophy, which has no real connection with the universal philosophy of Islam. Thus in effect the petition sent to the governors of the Azhar was neglected, and a spiritual and intellectual defeat was acknowledged in our primary seat of learning, a defeat for the Islamic theory of life.

If, then, we are to establish a sound Islamic theory of the universe, life, and mankind, it is essential that Western philosophies and their moral corollaries should not be studied at all in our secondary schools, and that they should be studied in the university only after at least two years in the department of philosophy. And by the very nature of the case they should not be studied in the Azhar colleges until the very end of the course. In every center of study such Western philosophies should be preceded by a course in pure Islamic thought, as distinct from the so-called "Islamic philosophy," in order to emphasize the true Islamic viewpoint.

Thus, the minds and thoughts of the students will assimilate the native bases of the spirit of Islam, together with its ideas on the universe, life and mankind, good and evil, work and reward, and all the other philosophic aspects of pure Islamic belief. This having been assured, we may in the later years of university study proceed to give some account of the other philosophies; these would include Greek philosophy and its opposition to Islamic, modern European and American philosophy; these should be compared in every case with Islamic philosophy. In this way we can ensure that the student mind and conscience will not be too much influenced; we can ensure also a minimum influence on student ideas and thoughts, because by then they will be equipped for critical appreciation. They will have the requisite knowledge to reject all that does not agree with the fundamental modes of thought of a Muslim

people. Under these circumstances their new knowledge
will not harm, but will rather benefit students; for it will
be purely academic knowledge, largely independent of any
influence on their conscience or on their conception and understanding of life and its requirements.

We have already given one example of pragmatism in its
view of things. But in this example there was no indication
of the dangers inherent in that philosophy or in its method;
so we must now follow out this philosophy in its further results, in order to note the dangerous influences of its intellectual system on any nation which follows such a mode of
thought.

"Most people believe in God. This is an idea which logically may be either false or true. Intellectual theory says:
If God really exists, then His existence must be logically
demonstrable. Pragmatism on the other hand attacks the
problem from a different angle, and lays the emphasis on a
different aspect. In its view the truth of the idea of God does
not depend on logical necessity; it depends solely on the profit
of this idea to our well-ordered life, in our daily activity and
in our experiences. If the idea tends to produce a profit in
life, then it is sound and therefore true. Hence God does
exist. Apart from this test, pragmatism claims, in the first
place we cannot judge of this idea; and in the second place
we cannot trust our own judgment."[16]

The Islamic line of thought differs to a greater or lesser
extent from that of pure intellectual theory, insofar as it
does not entrust the whole question to human logic alone, but
relies also upon revelation. But it is in complete opposition
to pragmatism; for when we follow out its logic to a conclusion
we find that the idea of God must disappear if the outward
benefits of material life are not forthcoming. When this
happens the idea of God loses its existence because it cannot
control its instruments and set the machinery in motion.

In consequence material profit becomes the sole criterion,
not only of the acceptance or the rejection of things, but also
of existence or non-existence. This implies a state of affairs
in which man loses all nobility, where he is neither more nor
less than an instrument.

Policies in this world cannot be divorced from such philosophies. Thus perhaps we are not far from the truth when
we say that the policy of the United States on the Palestine

question and its stand in the United Nations on the question of Egypt were merely the results of its intellectual background of pragmatism--in conjunction, of course, with other factors. The idea of right and justice has little effective place in materialistic American life; and hence it has little chance of permanent acknowledgment in international policies. This idea is perhaps the most satisfactory comment on these puzzling policies.

What we do not want is to establish such an intellectual background as this in our Islamic society. We must therefore be cautious about the study of Western philosophy until we have first established in adolescent minds a firm, strong, and clear pattern of thought which is founded on the universal Islamic theory. Similarly we must be cautious about borrowing educational techniques, curricula, and systems of teaching; for all of these are ruled by the general field of philosophy in their native lands; they subserve the aims which that philosophy assigns to them, whether immediate or remote.

* * * * * * *

Literature, again, is the emotional response to life. It issues from the same well-spring whence flow in any culture all the philosophies, the religious beliefs, the experiments and the influences.

Literature is the most important factor in the establishment of a moral philosophy of life, and in the production of any specific influence on the human mind. Hence we must exercise care in the choice of Western literature which we make available to our youth, alike in their Arabic and their foreign studies.

It is not necessary to take this as meaning that our youth are to be prohibited from reading European literature; what we have in mind here is simply a process of choice and selection. For in this literature there are elements, the spirit of which is at one with the spirit of Islam. By this we do not mean that such books encourage goodness and reprobate wickedness; for literature is no preacher to exhort and to direct. Rather we mean that such books have a view of life which is spiritual and moral, rather than materialistic, and that they acknowledge the spiritual values of life. This type of literature agrees in spirit with the general teachings of our Islamic theory; it can therefore do no harm to the moral consciousness of our youth, nor can it upset their emotional and mental development at a dangerous stage. This dangerous stage lasts at least until the third year of university work, if not until the time of graduation. There is no harm, but rather great benefit, in having private reading include all types of the literatures ot the world, without restraint or exception. But the prime aim of a process of choice and selection is to safeguard the period of adolescence from being defiled and led astray.

History is a branch of literature; but it is one which has its own characteristics, and which therefore has also its peculiar dangers. For history is a presentation of the events of life, and it is necessarily influenced by the materialistic background of the West. Even if it is by intellectual theory that it is influenced, it will still ignore the spiritual powers and their effect on the course of events, together with the spiritual explanation of facts. It will give its own interpretations, designed to establish a philosophy of life independent of the spirit and unconnected with moral aims. Here it is opposed to Islamic theory.

Beyond this, historians, who have been for the most part Europeans, have made the history of Europe the focal point of world history. In view of the nature of man this is excusable, and we have borne it with patience as a characteristically Western and European delusion. Yet if our youth are to study history in this spirit and by this method, then they will finish with two false beliefs:

1. That spiritual factors have no influence on the course of events in time, or at least that any such influence is very weak.

2. That Europe is the mistress of historical events, and that the influence of the East and of Islam is exiguous.

Both these ideas have harmful and dangerous results; they establish a false general idea of life, of the world, and of events, and they endanger our patriotic pride and our pride in Islam, which is so necessary in face of the sweeping pride of Europe.

In order to guard our youth from this evil we must take the two following steps:

1. We must begin by putting general world history, as Islam views it, in perspective, in the form of events and happenings. We must not be concerned solely with the European point of view in this present dangerous fashion. In such a his-

tory we must give Europe its rightful place and no more, and we must emphasize the part played in world history by the East in general, and by Islam in particular.

2. We must change the present curriculum of history teaching in our schools and colleges. We must start by teaching primarily the history of Islam throughout the Muslim world, and by expounding it from the Islamic point of view. It is not enough to teach our children the history of Islam as written by Western authors, or as expounded by Western philosophies. When their minds are filled with the history of their own country, then we can give them world history as written by ourselves, to form the next stage of study. And when they have completed that, then we can give them in successive stages the remainder of the developments of history.

* * * * * * *

The study of law is similarly influenced by the Western point of view, by Western philosophy, Western history, Western law, and Western society. For law is a reflection of society, or is produced by it; and society is the offspring of all these factors.

Thus, in order to build up a sound Islamic doctrine, we must teach Islamic law in a broad general way before beginning to teach any specific legal system. The teaching of Islamic law must be firmly in the control of Muslim professors, and the Western point of view must not be allowed to obtrude, except in the later stages. And similarly the study of law in general must not be opened up till that same later stage.

It is one of the requirements of Islamic life that the religious law shall occupy a paramount position; and that very fact will make necessary such a study of Islamic law as we have indicated. The great necessity which faces our professors of Islamic law in this field is to follow the authoritative path traced out by the Imams and their students at the time of the first growth of Islamic law.

* * * * * * *

When we have disposed of this theoretical question of the objective, we are still confronted by that of the specific constitutional enactments which will ensure a sound form of Islamic life and which will guarantee social justice to all. In this question it is not possible to take a stand purely on the form of the original Islamic life; rather we must utilize all possible and permissible means which fall within the general principles and the broad foundations of Islam. Nor must we be afraid to use also all the discoveries which man has made in the way of social legislation and systems, so long as the principles of these do not run counter to the principles of Islam, and so long as they are not opposed to its theory of life and mankind. We must include these in our legislation so long as they conduce to the true welfare of society, or so long as they ward off any impending evil. In the two principles of "public interest" and "blocking of means" we have two clear Islamic principles which give wide powers to the temporal ruler to ensure the general welfare at all times and in all places.

Before we go on to deal with the application of these two principles it might be well to quote a short passage in explanation of them.[17]

Public Interest. "Any welfare measure which has no specific detailed authority to support it is known as a measure of public interest. The question of whether or not it is a root of jurisprudence is a matter of dispute among the jurisconsults. Al-Qarafi has argued that all the jurisconsults have used it or have admitted it as a proof at one time or another, even though in lecturing most of them deny it the status of a root. He says in regard to this point: 'Other people loudly deny the validity of public interest. But when the case is closely examined, they are found to refer to the word in its absolute sense. They do not trouble to take any account of the evidence offered by the reference of the term in its synonyms and contexts; they hold that it means merely "convenience," and that such is the sole meaning of the phrase, "public interest.'"

"No matter whether this claim is true or false, it is certain that the validity of any measure of welfare which lacks a specific validating authority is a matter on which the ulama may well disagree. And even if public interest is not one of the accepted roots of jurisprudence, at least it has the status of a custom, as Al-Qarafi indicates.

"The opinions of the ulama on this matter can be divided into four main views, as follows:[19]

"1. The Shafi'ites and those who share their opinions do not believe in any form of public interest whose validity is unsupported by legal evidence; for they only admit legal pre-cedents and the treatment of these by analogy, based on the existence of a solid connection between the root and its deriv-atives, that is to say, between a case governed by a precedent and another analogous to it. If we follow Al-Qarafi we must admit that it is strange that they should deny public interest while they admit analogy.

"2. The Hanafites and others of similar opinions main-tain the principles of preference and analogy, but their in-terpretation of preference is sometimes almost indistinguish-able from public interest. A fair estimate would say that in their system they make a greater use of interest than do the Shafi'ites. But even so, the extent to which they do use it is negligible, and hence we cannot say that this principle is one of the roots of their system; not, at least, on any grounds of the use which they make of it in itself.

"3. There are those who attach an excessive importance to public interest, even to the point of making it stronger than precedent in their dealings with cases; they regard it as a form of precedent, or rather, as a form of concensus. Thus where the ulama are agreed on a point turning on prece-dent, but some aspect of that point runs counter to public interest, then the validity of the latter is the stronger. This applies also to specific cases, as Al-Tufi has maintained.

"4. There are those who hold a middle course, which is the soundest of all. Here validity is granted to public in-terest, but it is not derived from precedent, which is held to be entirely different. To this view most of the Malikite rite adhere.

"Malik held that public interest was an independent root of the system of jurisprudence, but that it was a derived, rather than an original root; and that, for the following reasons:

"1. The Companions of Allah's Messenger found that ques-tions arose after his death which had not been apparent during his lifetime. Thus they collected the noble Qur'an in book form. This had not been done in the time of the Messenger, but now such a collection was in the public interest; for they feared that the Qur'an might be forgotten because of the deaths of those who had memorized it. Umar saw such men dying in numbers during the Wars of Apostasy, and, fearing that through their death the Qur'an might pass from memory, he advised Abu-Bakr to have it collected in book form. To this the Companions gladly assented.

"2. After the death of Allah's Messenger his Companions agreed that the punishment for wine-drinking should be eighty lashes. Their reason for this was the public interest or general inference; for they saw that drinking tended to produce lying and the slandering of chaste women because of the wild talk in which drinkers indulged.

"3. The orthodox Caliphs agreed upon imposing conscription on craftsmen, although the root principle was that the exercise of their craft was a matter of good faith. But it was found that unless they were conscripted they would neglect the care of the people's belongings and wealth. There was great need of craftsmen, and therefore it was in the public interest to conscript them, that they might perform the duties which they had. Thus Ali, when he prescribed the conscription, said: 'The people's interests cannot be served otherwise.'

"4. Umar ibn-al-Khattab used to claim half of the wealth of those governors whom he suspected of having increased their resources by extortion. This also was a form of public interest, because to his mind it was in the interests of the governors to prevent them capitalizing on their power to amass money and heap up illegal plunder.

"5. It is told of Ali that he poured out on the ground milk which had been adulterated with water, as a lesson to the man who had done it. This act also was akin to public interest, to show that people were not to adulterate goods.

"6. There is a tradition that Umar put a whole community to death for the murder of one man, for which they had been jointly responsible. This he did because the public interest demanded it. There was no precedent for the case, but the public interest demanded that the case be considered as one of premeditated murder of a sacrosanct individual. To let the murder pass unavenged would have been to deny the root principle of 'an eye for an eye'; while to choose one out of the many who had had a hand in the business would have made the whole matter ridiculous. For the man chosen would know that in his case it was not a case of retaliation. Or if it were said that this was an anonymous murder, a killing without a killer, on the grounds that every single individual could not be said to be the murderer, then the guilty party was the

community itself. The whole of a community can commit a
murder in exactly the same way as an individual criminal.
And murder can be charged against a community just as it
can against a single person, and the members of the community stand in the same relation to the act of murder as
does an individual. Hence the community furthers the public
interest when it prevents blood-shed and guards communal
life.

"Another general aspect of public interest is the power
which is granted to the Imam to levy upon the rich whatever
toll he thinks that the circumstances warrant. This he can
do when the public treasury is empty, or when the army has
extraordinary needs, while there are no funds to meet those
needs. Toll may be levied until the treasury is replenished,
or until the needs are sufficiently met. Further, the Imam
has the duty of instituting this levy at times of bountiful harvest and plentiful crops, so that the rich will not be overburdened by the fact that it is they alone who pay it. The
public interest here lies in the fact that if a just Imam did
not do this, his power would be vain, and wealthy establish-
ments would provide an incentive to civil war, and to attacks
by envious persons. It is sometimes said that the Imam,
instead of enforcing the provisions of the levy, borrows
money for the public treasury. To this Al-Shatibi retorted
that: 'Borrowing in time of need is allowed only when the
treasury has the prospect of more revenue. Otherwise, or
alternatively when the revenue is too small to be sufficient,
then recourse must be had to the principle of a levy.'"

Means. "A means is that which leads to an end, and to
'block the means' is to remove it. The sense of the phrase
is that anything which conduces to a forbidden end is itself
forbidden, while anything conducive to a desirable end is itself desirable. Thus, for example, adultery is forbidden,
and therefore to admire the charms of a strange woman is
also forbidden, as being a means towards aultery. On the
other side, attendance at prayers is compulsory, and therefore an effort to attend prayers is also compulsory, as is
leaving one's business to make that effort. To make the pilgrimage is compulsory; therefore an effort to visit the
sacred House and to perform the other rites of pilgrimage
is also compulsory.

"The fundamental reason for the validity of 'blocking the

means' is a realization of the repercussions and final results of all actions. If they are conducive to those public
interests which constitute the aims and objectives of the
dealings of man with man, then they are as desirable as those
aims themselves. But it they are not equally desirable, or
if their results might be evil, then they are forbidden just
as that evil is forbidden, even though the means may be somewhat less objectionable.

"In considering the results of actions the matter of interest is not the purpose or the objective of the agent; rather
it is the result and outcome of his action. The individual
will be rewarded or punished for his intention in the next
world; but in this world it is according to its result and
outcome that an action is good or bad, desirable or undesirable. For this world must take its stand on the welfare of
mankind, on judgment and justice, and these things require
a scrutiny of results and outcomes rather than of estimable
aims and worthy intentions. A man who out of a sincere
love for the worship of Allah reviles idols has gained the
approval of Allah by the formulation of his purpose; and yet
He has forbidden such reviling in cases where it would result in the rage of the idolaters, who would then revile Allah
the Great, Himself. So His exalted words run: 'And do not
revile those who invoke deities other than Allah, lest in response they revile Allah without knowledge.'[20] In this noble
prohibition regard is had to the actual consequences, rather
than to the commendable religious aim. Hence it appears
that in cases which tend towards crime or evil, the veto is
directed not towards the aim itself, which is sincere, but
towards the consequences which will arise; thus an act may
be forbidden because of its consequences, even though Allah
may be aware that the intention underlying it is sincere.

"Sometimes also a man may seek an evil end through a
legal act, in which case he is guilty in his own conscience
and in the sight of Allah. But no man may take measures
against him, nor may any legal penalties be invoked upon
him. Such is the case of a man who cuts the price of his
goods in order to injure a business rival. This is undoubtedly
a legal act; yet it is a means towards a crime, that on injuring
another. This crime is the man's object, but in spite of that
his action cannot be punished by the power of the law, nor
does it fall under any penalty which the law of the land can

impose. His action, from the point of view of intention, is
a means to evil, but externally it is a means to public and
private benefit. Undoubtedly the seller benefits by selling,
by the circulation of his goods, and by the good-will which
he gains; equally certainly the public benefits by the cut in
price, by which a general lowering of prices is encouraged.

"The principle of blocking the means has regard not only
to individual aims and intentions, as we have seen, but also
to the encouragement of public welfare and to the prevention
of public evil. Thus it must take account of the consequences
along with the intention, or even of the consequences alone.

"The principle of 'means' is firmly established in the
Qur'an and the Sunna. In the former there is the verse: 'And
do not revile those who invoke gods other than Allah, lest
in response they revile Allah without knowledge.' Of this it
is related that the idolaters said that they were content to
have their gods reviled if they in turn could revile Muhammad's God. Thus again: 'O you who believe, do not say
Ra'ina; say Unzurna and hearken. This was because the
Muslims used the former word with good intention, but the
Jews took it as implying a derogatory sense to the Prophet.[21]

"In the Sunna there are many stories of the Prophet and
many decisions of his Companions; among them is that of his
refusal to kill the hypocrites, lest the unbelievers should
have a pretext for saying that Muhammad killed his companions.

"There is also the story that the Prophet forbade a man
who had loaned money to accept a gift from the debtor, unless the gift was counted as part repayment of the loan. The
reason was simply that the gift was a means of postponing
payment, and was therefore a form of interest. For the
lender would get his money back and extra also in the form
of the gift. We have also the account of the Prophet's having
forbidden that men's hands should be cut off in time of war;
the purpose was to stop this practice leading to an illegal
treatment of fighting men which would inevitably ensue.
Similarly laws should not be intermitted in time of war, lest
freedom become license; the two are closely related. And
there is the account of the earliest Believers, both Emigrants
and Helpers, having on their death-beds appointed their
divorced wives as their heirs; this they did because there
was a suspicion of a plot to debar such wives from inheriting.

It was not even certain that such a plot existed, but divorce was a 'means' which might have produced injustices.

"Again the Prophet forbade monopolies, saying: 'Only sinners hold monopolies.' For a monopoly is a means to oppress the people in all things which are considered to be essential. But there is no law against a monopoly in any article which cannot injure the people by being withheld, such as cosmetics and the like; for these things do not come under the heading of necessities.

"The Prophet also forbade any man who had given alms to buy them back, even though he might see them displayed for sale in the market. Thus he sought to check the means to recover what had been given to Allah, even by purchase. Thus any one who gives alms is forbidden to repossess them by purchase, and is yet more stringently forbidden to repossess them by any other means. To permit repossession by purchase might be a means of cheating the poor; the rich out of his wealth would give alms to the poor, and might then buy them back from him at less than their value. The poor man, on the other hand, would see some profit to himself, and thus his conscience would not oppose the sale.

"Thus there are many indications of this principle, deriving from the Messenger and his Companions. Ibn-Qiyam has collected some ninety such examples from actual occurrences, in all of which the principle of blocking the means is clearly illustrated.

"Means are counted to be half of the legal principles of Islam."

These two principles, that of public interest and that of blocking the means, both run back to a common root, that of ensuring the welfare of society. They are integrally connected with the established laws of Islam and with its general purposes. It is these two principles which can guide us towards the legislation necessary to ensure a sound form of Islamic life and to include in its scope a comprehensive social justice.

This last must be our concern in a general work dealing with social justice in Islam; yet it is desirable to mention some of the things which Islam is able to ensure in this sphere for the present and the future. We must also deal with the legislation necessary to produce these things, so that it may be used as a pattern for analogous treatment in

other cases. We cannot deal with all possible developments
but these may be safely left to the dictation of circumstances,
times, and conditions.

* * * * * * *

1. <u>Laws governing the Poor-tax</u>. This tax was a compulsory duty in Islam, levied on all possessions according
to a sliding scale of one-tenth, one-twentieth, and one-fortieth.
In all cases it represented a very small fraction, and hence
it is but natural that the question should arise: How could
such a small sum be of assistance to all the Muslim poor?
To answer this question we must consider the following facts:

a. The small amount of capital on which the tax had to
be paid made the greater part of the community liable to it.
The exemption value for the poor-tax was fixed at six pounds,
which meant that practically all the population had to pay the
tax; thus the income from it was relatively great.

b. Disbursements from the tax money were confined to
specifically limited classes of people. For their livelihood
the great majority had to rely on work, which has always
been reckoned by Islam to be the primary source of a living.

c. Most important of all, the livelihood of the very poor
did not depend solely upon this source of income. There
were also the vast sums acquired as booty during the war
days, sums which lasted for more than half a century. In
this booty all the fighting men shared, and most of them were
of the poorer classes. They received four-fifths of the booty,
while the other fifth was turned into a charitable foundation
for the benefit of all classes of necessitous persons, relatives,
orphans, the destitute, and the wayfarer. And when Umar
resolved not to take the booty away from the conquered countries, but to leave it for the benefit of the native peoples, he
instituted the land-tax in its place; then this latter was sufficient to provide for all the poor.

Today this last primary source of revenue is no longer
available, and the poor-tax in itself is not sufficient. Therefore we must consider alternative sources to take the place
of booty and plunder , in order to provide an ample living for
the generality of men.

But before we consider new sources we must first exhaust
the poor-tax as a source in itself. It is a compulsory duty,
and it must be paid if the community is justifiably to be de-

scribed as Islamic. For the payment of the poor-tax is a
spiritual duty as well as a financial one. Again we must
consider the sources of the poor-tax as including all types
of property, some of which are not at present included because they were not familiar in the early days of Islam.

That is to say, we must bear in mind those forms of wealth
which are liable to the poor-tax but which are not mentioned
in the Qur'an except generally in the verse: "O you who
have believed,. expend of the goods which you have acquired,
and of that which We have provided for you from the earth.
And do not purpose any evil in thus expending it; for you got
it yourselves only by connivance."[22] The fact that the poor-
tax was prescribed as a duty only upon such types of property
as were familiar in the time of the Prophet does not prevent
its being prescribed today as a duty on all that is known as
property or wealth, and on all that produces an income. It
makes no difference that such things may not be of the kind
on which the tax was originally imposed.

Similarly we can control the outlets for the tax money,
just as Umar exercised the same control when he stopped
payments designed to convert unbelievers. It must not be
given in any form of money to those who are eligible for it;
rather it must be given them in the basic form of goods or
services, or it must be used to buy for them some part of
their basic necessities. The source of their livelihood must
be fixed and unconnected with any kind of temporary or hap-
hazard charity; for these things are not in accord with the
needs of modern life.

But in any case such detailed considerations have no place
in this book. The scope of our thinking here is the broad field
of the promotion of social justice and equity, as the Muslim
world gives its attention to a renaissance of the true Islamic
life.

2. Laws Governing the Mutual Responsibility of Society.
The Prophet said: "Any household which suffers a man to remain hungry among them is outside the protection of Allah,
the Blessed and the Exalted." In this brief sentence he emphasized the principle of mutual responsibility in society, a
principle which most of us must recognize from the prece-
dents and the examples provided by our study of the Qur'an.
This principle was authoritatively imposed on both the individual and the social conscience. Today the law must again
enforce it as an essential root of Islam.

This means that the law can enforce that which Umar intended to enforce: "If I had known earlier what I now know, I would have taken the excess of their wealth from the rich and given it to the poor." Thus the law can impose taxes, the only limit of which is the establishment of equality in the social sphere, the removal of crime and oppression from the community in general, and the ample provision of food and drink, clothing and housing, medical treatment and skill for every single individual in the country. It does not matter how much tax is placed upon capital so long as the latter is not thereby made incapable of work and of reasonable increase; this condition must be observed because the steady turning of the wheels of labor brings other benefits which cannot be overlooked.

Thus the law can put into the hands of the poor with perfect justification a stretch of funded property which they may use without paying any basic rent, or at a nominal rent, that they may from it obtain a means of life. For this constitutes a source of livelihood and is the only means of work within their power. By this act the law will fulfill the Messenger's words: "Any one of you may permit to his brother the use of his land as a gift, without exacting for it any agreed rent."[23]

The law may also with justification fix the wage of the factory or the farm worker at a stipulated proportion of the production or of the harvest. The lowest limit of this wage must be a competence to cover food and drink and clothing, and medicine and medical care to a certain extent. The standard is to be taken as that of a moderate living, determined by the proportion of the inhabitants of the country to its general wealth.

3. <u>Laws governing General Taxation</u>. Every individual in the Muslim community has the duty of taking a share in the general expenses of the state according to his ability. We have already noticed the opinion of the Imam Malik on what may be done when the treasury is empty, or when the needs of the army are increased; the law has the power according to need to levy a toll on the wealth of the rich. Similar to the needs of the army are the other needs of the state, such as improvements in public services, irrigation of waste lands, the education of the people, and the medical treatment of the sick. All these things are communal duties which must be met and satisfied just as much as the needs of the army; they

must be preserved as strongly as frontiers and defense posts
must be guarded. This is particularly true today when wars
make demands on all the resources and services of the bel-
ligerent nations. In modern war everyone may be said to be
in the army, and thus should be capable of taking responsibility in time of peace.

4. Laws governing Public Resources. Monopolies on the
necessities of life are forbidden by Islam. A monopoly on
food is forbidden, for example, since Islam has always asserted the communal ownership of water, pasturage, and
fire, as being the primary needs of life. But the needs of
life are not unchangeable, varying as they do from age to age.
Consequently the preservation of this general Islamic principle demands what is known today as the nationalization of
natural resources. It is essential not to have in the hands of
private individuals or companies the resources of water,
light, heat, electricity, coal, and oil, or the resources of
public transport and public food supplying, and other such
things. For private ownership gives the power of monopoly,
imposes upon the general public the will of the monopolists,
and permits them to indulge in that disgraceful exploitation
which we witness today.

The head of the state has the power to make all these
things state-owned, and to fix prices and costs of them so
that they will be within the reach of the poorest, and so that
they may be bought or rented at equitable rates without excessive prices. By these means Islamic aims for the checking of monopolies can be realized.

5. Laws governing the Public Interest and the Blocking
of Means. Everything which tends to advance the public welfare or to retard oppression of the public is a duty laid upon
the law, and everything which tends towards a prohibited end
is itself prohibited. The application of these established
principles of Islam lays on the law today several duties.

a. The taking of excessive wealth out of the hands of
bloated capitalists. The fact that such excessive wealth is
in their possession tends towards a number of crimes. In
the first place it tends to produce that luxury which is forbidden by Islam. Luxury is a relative matter, which can
be defined only in terms of the general condition in each age
and country. The permanent rule is that luxury shall not increase beyond the mean struck by the national wealth in pro-

portion to the population. One result of luxury is the iniqui-
tous rise in prices which springs from the fact that one section of the populace has an unlimited power to buy, while
the goods available for sale are not equal to the demand.
Another result is the rise of social vices, springing from
the fact that some people possess more money than they
need; to dispose of this they look for illegal outlets and seek
sensual and corrupt pleasures; through these their morals
and their standards are degraded, and on the other hand their
victims are the needy men and women who always exist in
an unbalanced society.

b. The removal of extreme poverty, because of its results in the way of crime and evil. These results include a
great number of social evils which can only exist in surround-
ings of privation and destitution, theft, infamy, and moral
degradation, a general atmosphere of corruption, and so
on.

This is over and above the vast differences which are set
between those who have and those who have not, the hatreds
and the social disturbances which the law must prevent before they occur by removing their causes.

If it be asked how this extreme poverty is to be removed,
it is by the ample provision of work for every able-bodied
man, and by the provision of an adequate wage, by social
security for all who are disabled, and by speedy relief. This
is the method in general outline; the specific applications are
easy once the general aim is established.

c. The struggle against disease and ignorance. Because
of their evil effect on the individual and the community these
weaken the general strength of the community and afford a
footing to its enemies. This condition is forbidden, as is any
factor which leads to it. Nothing can oppose disease and ignorance successfully except a rise in living standards and in
general wealth; but the laws of charity and such other things
are only palliatives to soothe the sore, not to heal it. The
real treatment is that every individual should be possessed
of private means for medical and educational purposes. Or
alternatively that medical care and education should be provided free to every individual in the country on a common
basis and to a common level. The rich must not be able, by
money, to get more than the poor in schools or hospitals.

6. Laws governing Legacies. "When there are present

at the division of the estate relatives, orphans, and poor people, give them a provision out of it and speak them fair."[24] Thus runs the Qur'anic precept. It clearly means that out of every estate there must be a share for relatives, orphans, and the poor. The law has the power of disposal according to the nature of the case; it may change the beneficiaries, or it may leave them unchanged. So Umar did in the case of paying out money to convert others to Islam. The law also has the power to apply the regulations according to the needs of the estate or according to those of the community. And we must remember that the meaning of being "present" can legitimately be extended to cover virtual presence, that is to say, existence. In every community there are orphans and poor, and there is no necessity for them to be present in person when an estate is being divided; they are already present in time and space. So by the power of the law all duties must be enforced which are not enforced by the power of conscience.

7. <u>Laws governing Mutual Help and Usury</u>. Islam rooted out usury, and fought it in all its forms and appearances; hence it is impossible for any form of Islamic life to exist on an economic basis which includes the principles of usury. We have already discussed the causes which made Islam unable to countenance usury, but they may be summed up by saying that it is the negation of the spirit of mutual help and friendliness. If usury obtains, then it is to the benefit of the capitalist who can thus increase his wealth without working and without the risk of loss.

The national economy must be set on a basis of mutual help rather than of usury. All the faults which can be alleged against the latter system have been summed up to justify its rejection by Maula Muhammad Ali in his book, "Islam and the New World Order," from which we may quote the following passage:

"It is objected that to forbid interest on money will hinder business and commercial transactions, and will hinder the accomplishment of important domestic projects. We may grant the truth of this, but on the other side we have the far greater advantage that to proscribe interest will prevent world wars, which can only end in misery, and which are kindled and inflamed only by loans and debts governed by interest. And if we examine the facts of the case, we shall find that, from the very first, trade followed its natural course and spread over more and more widely as important national projects were maintained and as ever

wider limits were brought within the Islamic sphere. So
that today the Islamic states are still among the greatest
of the old-established countries of the civilized world.

"This prohibition of usury cannot in any sense be reconciled with the conditions of the new world which ma-
terlialistic Western civilization is bringing into being.
The social system most like to that which Islam today
has in mind is that practical system which was successfully applied in practice by Islam at its inception centuries ago. As for the capital sums, without which business cannot be carried on, there was little difference between the gains which they made under the Islamic system and those which they made by ordinary lending; for
the Islamic system was in effect one of partnership between capital and labor. Such a partnership is not impossible, for the Islamic system holds that capital and
labor should share together in all profit and loss; whereas the result of paying a steady rate of interest is that
capital makes a continual profit, even when labor has to
work at a loss.

"It is sometimes objected that the partnership of capital and labor in both profits and losses is not practicable,
because it means that regular accounts have to be kept,
since this is one of the necessities of trade; and further,
because trading records have to be available for the asses-
sing of taxes which have to be paid. But all the share-
issuing companies which take part in trading on a large
scale have to keep accounts. And indeed this partnership
system is more to the public advantage than that of giving
all the dividends to capital; for it is the latter system
which produces most of the evils of capitalism, and which
is the source of the oppression of the workers. And the
loans which are floated by governments or companies to
carry out immense projects such as railroads or canals
or such things have done no more than prove this point.

"But since the system of state banking depends on the
principle of mutual help, which is approved by the Islamic social system, it must be of great benefit to mankind."

This is a general statement, the particular details of which
are too lengthy for a book dealing with general ideas. At the
same time there can be no harm in giving an example as a
guide to the general objective which we have in mind.

Suppose that the state decrees the abolition of interest on funds in banks, companies, public enterprises, and private loans, what will happen then?

What will happen will be that capitalists will find themselves unable to increase their wealth except by two general methods. First they may put it to some profitable use themselves in manufacture or trade or agriculture. Or second, they may put it to a profitable and helpful use by investing it in share-issuing companies, where the share values may rise or fall. Both these methods are sanctioned by Islam, and neither of them will work the slightest injury to economic life.

It is sometimes feared that the rich will refrain from depositing their money in the banks, which generally finance the large public projects. This is an imaginary danger which gains currency among us because we are familiar only with European methods of using money. In Europe the primary natural impulse is to make money increase; this can be accomplished only by using it for some means of exploitation, and so this natural impulse is a guarantee that money will not be kept out of circulation. But when we desire to take in hand some large project to justify what is known as the great era of production, we have the power to create legislation covering various kinds of industry; this legislation enacts that no new enterprise may be set up except on the basis of capital over such and such a sum. On that, capital sums flow in to take up shares and to become liable to profit and loss on the market. Thus there is no more need for banks, except for the issuing of currency. If other banks wish to make a profit, then they must buy shares with their own and their depositors' funds--the latter only with permission--in some profit-seeking enterprise, where the shares are liable to fluctuation on the open market. But the banks' guaranteed rate of interest is undoubtedly usury. This system will not stop the flow of capital, either domestic or foreign; for the greater proportion of capital wealth is not deposited in banks, but is put out to profit in enterprises.

As for insurance companies, it may be that their basis is Islamic, inasmuch as the funds which are deposited with them are liable to profit and loss, to fall or rise. Funds deposited in these companies are put to work in profit-seeking enterprises, subject to fluctuation. Every time a beneficiary receives more than he has paid in, the amount of the company's loss is deducted from the remainder of the depositors in proportion to the funds which they have invested. Thus insurance companies' members form a body united for mutual help; in effect they pay out of their own pockets to support any unfortunate one of their number, when need arises. They have a form of security from which they can benefit in time of hardship or need. This can be applied also to savings banks and similar institutions, all of which rest on the basis of mutual help in one way or another, and from which funds are employed in profit-seeking enterprises, always liable to fluctuation. Such institutions have no fixed rate of interest, and hence our economic system here can be free from the taint of usury; hence also all capital is compelled to work as the only method of achieving profit and increase.

8. Laws governing Gambling. Gambling is a dishonest practice, both in act and in spirit, for it represents an effort to make money without working. In addition it produces enmity and hatred among its adherents, and gives rise to laxity and insecurity in the fabric of society. There are many forms of gambling, of which lotteries are but one. It is not any spirit of charity which prompts people to buy lottery tickets, nor is it any desire to assist works of healing and charity. It is merely the desire to gain more money without working. This is at once practically and spiritually dishonest, as we have said; it hinders and retards the feelings of mercy. There is no need to mention the disgraceful foreign race-meetings which draw their immense crowds; this is merely the outcome of luxury, and the corrupting result of luxury-loving natures with their aversion to virtue and their love of vice, with their avarice except when money is lavished on sensual pleasures and coarse enjoyment.

We must halt the practice of gambling altogether, with its green tables, its tempting lottery tickets, and its late hours. Islamic life has need of none of these things, and Islam will never admit that relations between man and man should ever stand on such a basis, or that charity should spring from such impure desires.

9. Laws governing Prostitution. Prostitution is the product of spiritual degradation and material destitution, sometimes together and sometimes separately. Islam prohibits illegal sexual intercourse in all its forms, and the most de-

graded of these is prostitution. Lewdness is the poison
characteristic of an unbalanced community, for the two factors which produce prostitution are excessive wealth and
humiliating necessity. It was once said: "A well-born woman
cannot feed from her own breasts because she is hungry;
but she may do so if she is in danger of death." We must
not expose people on the one hand to the trials of need, and
on the other to the temptations of wealth and other things,
and then expect them to be models of self-control and virtue.
The principle of blocking the means demands that the law
give attention to check this thing at its root. The laws af-
fecting prostitution must be established without delay.

10. Laws governing Alcohol. The nature of these laws
needs no discussion. Alcohol is undeniably forbidden, and
the Islamic community can never countenance its use. It is
closely related to prostitution in most cases, and is especially
allied to it socially; similarly it is related to luxury and to
the destitution which arises from luxury. For luxury produces a spiritual weakness and a need for inhibiting thought
and vital activity by means of some intoxicant. Whereas
the life, the work, and the watchfulness which Islam prescribes can never be reconciled with alcohol or with any other
drug.

* * * * * * *

Islam forms a plastic social system, capable of adaptation
to all times and all circumstances; it is preserved by its
general spirit and principles. Its duty is to ensure a form
of life which will be virtuous, sound, productive, and strong;
to ensure a comprehensive social justice based on all the
foundations of human nature, and aiming at giving every man
his due. But it must never stand in the way of fruitful individualism, nor must it permit that individualism to become
a harmful egotism.

The Islamic theory of life is the finest that the world has
known because it brings together the material and the spiritual elements of life, making out of them a unity directed
towards the highest standards and aimed at patterns which
can be actually achieved. It does not envisage objectives
which are woven only of the imagination.

But the perplexed and disturbed world, fearful and cautious,
can only be brought to Islam and to peace, can only be given
complete security and justice, when it returns to this perfect
social system, under the will of Allah.

IX. The Parting of the Ways

Now where are we to go?

We must pause for a moment and ask ourselves this question; for we have the power to direct our lives in any direction which we wish.

The world today, after two wars in close succession, is divided into two main camps: That of Communism in the East, and that of Capitalism in the West. That is what appears on the surface; it is what everyone says, and what everyone thinks. But it is our belief that this division is merely superficial, rather than real; it is a division based on interests rather than on principles; it is a fight for goods and markets rather than for beliefs and ideals. The nature of European and American philosophy does not differ essentially from that of Russian; both depend on the preponderance of a materialistic doctrine of life. But while Russia has already become communist, Europe and America are as yet merely going the same way, and will ultimately arrive at the same position, barring the occurrence of any unforeseen happenings.

There is but one thing behind the materialistic philosophy which the West holds, which makes morals a matter of advantage and advocates grabbing markets and benefits. There is only one thing behind this philosophy which denies the spiritual element of life, which denies the existence of faith apart from trial and experiment, which despises the loftiest objectives, and which rejects the existence of any reality in things, save only their usefulness--even to the point where it can conceive a philosophy such as pragmatism. There can be only one thing behind such a philosophy, and that is Communism, with a change of some of its economic teachings in the case of the West.

No essential difference is to be found between the American and the Russian philosophies, though some differences do exist in the economic and social aspects. What keeps the ordinary American from becoming a communist is not a philosophy of life which rejects any materialistic explanation

of the universe, of life, and of history; rather it is the fact
that he now has the opportunity of becoming rich, and the
fact that a worker's wages are high. But when American
capitalism reaches the end of its tether, when the restraints
of monopolies are tightened, when the ordinary man sees
that he has no longer the opportunity of himself becoming a
capitalist, when wages drop because of the tightening of
monopoly control or for any other reason, then the American
worker is going to turn right over to Communism. For he
will not have the support of any stronger philosophy of life
than the materialistic, nor will he have the support of any
spiritual faith or moral objective.

We need not be deceived by the apparently hard and bitter
struggle between the Eastern and Western camps. Neither
of them have anything but a materialistic philosophy of life,
and in their thinking they are closely akin. There is no difference between their principles or their philosophies; their
only difference lies in their worldly methods and in their
profitable markets.

The real struggle is between Islam on the one hand and
the two camps of East and West on the other. Islam is the
true power which opposes the strength of the materialistic
philosophy professed by Europe, America, and Russia alike.
It is Islam which stands for a universal and articulated theory
of the universe, life, and mankind, and which sets up the
idea of the mutual responsibility of society in place of the
idea of hostility and struggle. It is Islam which gives to life
a spiritual doctrine to link it with the Creator in His Heaven,
and to govern its direction on earth; and it is Islam which is
not content to allow life to be limited to the achievement of
purely material aims, even although material and productive
activity is one of the Islamic modes of worship.

The truth is that all spiritual religions--and Christianity
most of all--are opposed equally to European and Russian
materialism, and to Russian communist materialism; for
both of these are of the same nature, and are equally at odds
with any spiritual philosophy of life. But Christianity, so
far as we can see, cannot be reckoned as a real force in opposition to the philosophies of the new materialism; it is an
individualist, isolationist, negative faith. It has no power
to make life grow under its influence in any permanent or
positive way. Christianity has shot its bolt so far as human

life is concerned; it has lost its power to keep pace with
practical life in this and the succeeding generations, for it
came into being only for a limited and temporary period,
between Judaism and Islam. When it was embraced by Europe
owing to specific historical circumstances, and when it proved
incompetent to keep pace with life as it developed then, Christianity confined itself to worship and to matters of the individual conscience, ceasing to have any control over the practical
affairs of life; for it had not the power to persevere, to
develop, or to grow.

Christianity is unable, except by intrigue, to compete with
the social and economic systems which are ever developing,
because it has no essential philosophy of actual, practical
life. On the other hand Islam is a perfectly practicable social
system in itself; it has beliefs, laws, and a social and economic system which is under the control of both conscience
and law, and which is open to growth through development and
application.

It offers to mankind a perfectly comprehensive theory of
the universe, life, and mankind, as we have shown, a theory
which satisfies man's intellectual needs. It offers to men a
clear, broad, and deep faith which satisfies the conscience.
It offers to society legal and economic bases which have been
proved both practicable and systematic.

Islam bases its social system on the foundation of a spiritual
theory of life which rejects all materialistic interpretations;
it bases its morals on the foundation of the spiritual and
moral element, and it rejects the philosophy of immediate
advantage. Thus it is very strongly opposed to the materialistic theories which obtain in both the Eastern and the Western camp. It raises life to a higher level than such petty
standards as those which claim observance in Europe, America, and Russia.

* * * * * * *

From this brief conspectus it will be apparent that in the
Islamic world we are in need of a return to our true position,
where we will hold actively a universal theory of life far
higher than any held in Europe or America or Russia. We
can offer to mankind this theory whose aims are a complete
mutual help among all men, and a true mutual responsibility
in society. This theory professes as an aim the raising of
the value of life to a level compatible with a world which has

emanated from Allah. So our true place is not at the tail of the caravan, but where we may grasp the leading rein.

But it will not be easy for us to take our rightful place; we can reach it only by making great and ineluctable sacrifices, for our own sake and for the sake of all mankind. Heavy burdens will fall on capitalists and profiteers who are accustomed to enjoying plenty, but these burdens are inevitable. We may go the Islamic way, or we may go the communist way; one of these two we must inevitably follow in the end. Or there are also Europe and America; we may adopt their social systems and choose these in preference to our own Islamic social system. But finally these systems also run out into Communism, over a short or a long period; because their doctrines are by nature the same as those of Communism, their philosophy of life is the same, and any differences are superficial rather than real.

The capitalists and the profiteers realize what Communism means, and they shrink from its very name as a superstitious man shrinks from genii and demons. Let them understand, then, that neither they nor humanity as a whole can have any defense against Communism except Islam; the true, real Islam, the principles of which we have outlined here, in giving examples of its social system and its demands on life and property.

We are indeed at the cross-roads. We may join the march at the tail of the Western caravan which calls itself Democracy if we do so we shall eventually join up with the Eastern caravan which is known to the West as Communism. Or we may return to Islam and make it fully effective in the field of our own life, spiritual, intellectual, social, and economic. We may draw our strength from it, and we may promote its growth through development and legislation within the limits of its universal and comprehensive theory of life, and we may fulfil its demands on life and property.

And certainly if we do not do this today, we shall not do it tomorrow. The world is broken by two consecutive wars, disturbed in faith and shaken in conscience, perplexed among varying ideologies and philosophies. It is today more than ever in need of us to offer to it our faith and our social system, our practical and spiritual theory of life. But we cannot offer these things to the world at large until first we have applied them in our own life, so that the world may see their truth demonstrated in practice, may understand that this is not merely an imaginative and theoretical scheme.

Conditions today are favorable because of the birth of two great new Islamic blocs in Indonesia and Pakistan, and because of the awakening of the Arab world, both in East and West. The ultimate issue is with Allah; our duty is to trust in Him, and to have faith.

A Short Bibliography for the Interested Reader

Antonius, G. The Arab Awakening. London, 1938.
Bodley, R.V.C. The Messenger. New York, 1946.
Brockelmann, C. History of the Islamic Peoples. London, 1949.
Gibb, H.A.R. Mohammedanism. Oxford, 1949.
Hitti, P.K. History of the Arabs. (Third Edition) London, 1946.
Jones, L. Bevan: The People of the Mosque. London, 1932.
Lammens, H. Islam, Beliefs and Institutions. New York, n.d.
Nicholson, R.A. Literary History of the Arabs. (Fourth Edition) Cambridge, 1941.
Tritton, A.S. Islam, Beliefs and Practices. London, 1951.

(Note.   This is but a very small selection of the
          available works, and has been chosen
          mainly on the grounds of providing simple
          and attractive reading for those without
          previous knowledge of Arab and Islamic
          affairs. Fuller bibliographies will be
          found in the works listed here, especially
          in Brockelmann.
                              --Editor.)

NOTES

Chapter I
1. Matthew, 5:38-41.
2. I cannot find the explanation of this word, but perhaps it is
a term of abuse or condemnation. (Raca of A.V. is generally
taken to be the transliteration of the Aramaic reqa'   one lacking in intellect. Compare the use of the word in II Samuel 6:20;
Judges 9:4.--Trans.
3. Mt. 5:21-37.
4. Sura 4:68.
5. Sura 59:7
6. Sura 5:48.
7. (The reference here is to the qibla or orientation of all
Muslim worshippers towards Mecca. The original qibla was towards Jerusalem, but the direction was changed by the Prophet
in A.D. 623 (A.H. 2)--Trans.)
8. Sura 62:9-10.
9. Sura 78:10-11.
10. (Anas was one of the Companions of the Prophet, and his personal attendant. He is frequently quoted as an authority for Traditions.
--Trans.)
11. (The point of this story is that such exemplary piety leaves no
time for work, and therefore the brother has to provide for both men.
--Trans.)
12. (This story is typical of the temper of Umar who was a close
friend of the Prophet, and later the second Caliph.--Trans.)
13. Sura 28:77.
14. Sura 22:41.
15. Sura 2:186.
16. Sura 2:172.
17. Sura 19:95.
18. Sura 2:159.
19. Sura 30:18-23.
20. Sura 35:25.
21. Sura 39:12.
22. Sura 4:99.

Chapter II
1. (Ibn-Sina, known to the West as Avicenna, was born in Bokhara
in 979 A.D. and died in 1039. He is known as the outstanding Arab
philosopher of the classical school, and, after the fashion of his time,
as the outstanding physician. His philosophy was that of Aristotle, his
medicine that of Galen and Hippocrates.--Trans.)
2. (Ibn-Rush or Averroes lived nearly a century and a half after Ibn
Sina, and at the other end of the Muslim world. Born in Cordova, Spain,
in 1126, he also was an Aristotelian in philosophy; and, though he left

comparatively little impress on Arab thought, he was exceedingly influential on the development of Mediaeval European philosophy. He died
in 1198.--Trans.)

3. Sura 36:82.
4. Sura 13:2.
5. Sura 22:64.
6. Sura 36:40.
7. Sura 67:1.
8. Sura 67:3, 4.
9. Sura 41:9.
10. Sura 67:2.
11. Sura 30:47.
12. Sura 16:15.
13. Sura 55:9.
14. Sura 67:15.
15. Sura 2:27.
16. Sura 67:5.
17. Sura 78:6-16.
18. Sura 11:8.
19. Sura 50:15.
20. Sura 40:62.
21. Sura 6:152.
22. Sura 49:13.
23. Sura 5:37.
24. Sura 49:9.
25. Sura 2:252.
26. See the chapter on 'History in the Qur'an' in my book, "Literary
Artistry of the Qur'an."
27. Sura 23:54.
28. Sura 100:8.
29. Sura 4:127.
30. Sura 17:102.
31. Sura 49:13.
32. Sura 58:12.
33. Sura 18:44.

Chapter III
1. Sura 112.
2. Sura 3:57 ("People of the Book" or "Scripturaries," as Lammens
translates the phrase, is the Muslim expression in the Qur'an for religions
which possess a body of Scripture, and particularly for Jews and Christians. The verb sharaka rendered "associate" characterizes the darkest
crime in Muslim theology, that of placing other objects of worship alongside Allah, and thereby compromising His unity and His uniqueness.
This verse dates from a period of Muhammad's life soon after the Hegira
when he still believed it possible to make some accomodation with the
Jews and Christians.--Trans.)
3. Sura 3:138.
4. Sura 3:123.
5. Sura 17:76-77.
6. Sura 72:20-23.

7. Sura 5:19.
8. Sura 43:59.
9. Sura 5:116-118.
10. Sura 42:18.
11. Sura 2:182.
12. Sura 12:87.
13. Sura 39:54.
14. Sura 107:4-5.
15. Sura 3:139.
16. Sura 9:51.
17. Sura 10:50.
18. Sura 6:14.
19. Sura 13:26.
20. Sura 29:60.
21. Sura 10:32.
22. Sura 35:3.
23. Sura 6:152.
24. Sura 9:28.
25. Sura 2:271.
26. Sura 3:25.
27. Sura 23:90-91.
28. Sura 3:154.
29. Sura 35:11.
30. Sura 63:8.
31. Sura 6:18.
32. Sura 49:13.
33. The Noble Traditions.
34. Sura 34:34-36.
35. Sura 18:44.
36. (The usual Muslim formula to express wonder.--Trans.)
37. Sura 18:31-41.
38. (The legend here referred to runs that Joseph concealed three treasures in Egypt, one of which fell to Korah. The keys of the treasure-chambers are said to have been a sufficient load for 300 white mules. The Biblical account of Korah is in Num. 16.--Trans.)
39. Sura 28:76-82.
40. Sura 20:131.
41. Sura 18:27.
42. Sura 9:55.
43. (I.e., by giving alms.--Trans.)
44. Sura 80:1-10. (The story here in question is best introduced to the English reader in the form in which it is given by Baidawi in his commentary on this passage. "It is related that Ibn-Umm Maktum came to the Messenger of Allah while he was in company with some of the prominent men of Quraish, whom he was seeking to convert to Islam. Ibn-Umm Maktum said to him, 'O Messenger of Allah, teach me something of what Allah has taught you.' This he repeated, not knowing that the Prophet was busy with other people; so Allah's Messenger, unwilling to rebuke him, frowned and turned away from him. Then this passage was revealed to him, and ever after Allah's Messenger honored the blind man, saying to him whenever he saw him, 'Welcome to one on whose account my Lord

remonstrated with me.' And he made him his regent in Medina on two occasions." -Trans.)

45. Sura 9:24.
46. Sura 3:12-13.
47. Sura 7:30.
48. Sura 28:77.
49. Sura 64:15.
50. Sura 2:274.
51. (The "poor-tax" is the zakat, one of the practical obligations of Islam. By the end of Muhammad's life it appears that this tax was a fixed contribution made by all Muslims to a common fund which was used for the relief of certain classes of the community, specified in Sura 9:60. These include the poor, slaves, debtors, travellers, and those who suffer loss in the "way of Allah." To the true Muslim the zakat is not so much a tax as it is a loan made to Allah, which He will repay many-fold. In the later books of jurisprudence the amount is fixed, generally at one-fortieth of a man's possessions. A full account of the institution will be found in L. Bevan Jones: "The People of the Mosque," p. 115.--Trans.)
52. Sura 51:19.
53. Sura 112.
54. Sura 19:91-95.
55. Sura 77:20-23.
56. Sura 86:5-7.
57. Sura 35:12.
58. Sura 23:12-14.
59. Sura 4:1.
60. Sura 49:13.
61. Sura 4:94.
62. Sura 24:32.
63. Sura 4:123.
64. Sura 16:99.
65. Sura 3:193.
66. Sura 4:8. To this day French law grants to women fitness to possess property, but not to administer it.
67. Sura 4:36.
68. Sura 4:38.
69. Sura 2:228.
70. Sura 2:282.
71. Sura 4:28.
72. Sura 2:231.
73. Sura 4:23.
74. Sura 6:152.
75. Sura 17:33.
76. Sura 81:8-9.
77. Sura 7:189.
78. Traditions.
79. Sura 57:17. (The almsgiving of this quotation is the sadaqa or freewill offering, and is independent of the zakat or poor-tax mentioned above. Sadaqa, which in the Qur'an is sometimes used as the equivalent of zakat, later came to refer to almsgiving or charity in general.--Trans.)

80. Sura 17:72.
81. Sura 49:11.
82. Sura 24:27-28. (It was the custom of pre-Islamic Arabia to enter any house announced--with regrettable moral results. Hence the Qur'anic prohibition of the practice.--Trans.)
83. Sura 49:12.
84. Sura 79:37-41.
85. Sura 91:7-10.
86. Sura 2:191.
87. Sura 28:77.
88. Sura 7:29.
89. The Noble Traditions.
90. Sura 74:41.
91. Sura 53:37-42.
92. Sura 2:286.
93. Sura 39:42.
94. Sura 4:111.
95. Sura 17:24-25.
96. Sura 31:13.
97. Sura 33:6.
98. Sura 2:233.
99. From "Children Without Families" by Anna Freud and Dorothy Burlingham. (Published in London by Allan and Unwin in 1942, under the title, "Small Children in Wartime."--Trans.)
100. Sura 4:12-14.
101. Sura 4:175.
102. Sura 2:176.
103. Traditions of the Prophet.
104. (The story here quoted in abridged form will be found in the Qur'an, Sura 18:59-81, where this incident is linked with two others of a similar tenor. The unnamed servant of Allah is generally taken to be Al-Khadr, the Green One, so called either by reason of his eternal youth, or, more probably, because of the green garments which he is said to wear when he appears to Muslims in distress. He is variously indentified with Elias (i.e., Elijah), St. George the patron saint of England, and the prime minister of Alexander the Great. The origin of the legend is unknown.--Trans.)
105. Traditions of the Prophet.
106. Sura 9:106.
107. Traditions of the Prophet.
108. Traditions of the Prophet.
109. Traditions of the Prophet.
110. Sura 5:3.
111. Sura 3:100.
112. Sura 69:30-37.
113. Sura 107:1-3.
114. Sura 17:17.
115. Sura 8:25.
116. Sura 5:82.
117. Sura 9:72.
118. Sura 5:104.

119. (Abu-Bakr was one of Muhammad's most intimate friends, an early convert to Islam, and the first Caliph or successor of the Prophet. He was renowned alike for his mildness, in sharp contrast to Umar, and for his uprightness and mental integrity. From this comes his appellative, "The True."--Trans.)

120. Sura 4:77.

121. Sura 4:5-7.

122. (The virtue here in question is that of the careful observance of the fast of Ramadhan. As is well known, during this month Muslims neither eat nor drink from sunrise to sunset; those who keep the fast very strictly will in addition rise from sleep several times during the night in order to repeat extra prayers. This is regarded as a highly meritorious custom; hence the comparison here.--Trans.)

123. Sura 89:18-26.

124. Sura 2:173.

125. Sura 4:95.

126. Sura 17:35.

127. Sura 5:49.

128. Sura 2:175.

129. Sura 24:2.

130. Sura 24:4.

131. Sura 5:42.

132. Sura 5:37.

Chapter IV

1. Sura 50:37.

2. Traditions.

3. Sura 49:12.

4. Sura 24:27.

5. Sura 49:11.

6. Sura 17:39.

7. Sura 68:4.

8. Sura 24:4.

9. Sura 24:6-9.

10. Sura 2:282.

11. Sura 2:282.

12. Sura 2:283.

13. Sura 58:8.

14. Sura 50:15-17. (It is a Muslim belief that every man throughout the course of his life is attended by two angels; one on his right side records the good that he does, and the other on his left records the evil. This is the reference here to the two who meet and sit one on either side of the man. This verse is also sometimes interpreted as being a reference to the meeting of the angel of life with the angel of death, but this seems less satisfactory.--Trans.)

15. Sura 20:6.

16. Sura 21:48.

17. Sura 99.

18. Sura 23:1-4.

19. Sura 27:1-3.

20. Sura 41:5-6.

21. Sura 24:55.
22. Sura 22:41-42.
23. Sura 19:55-56.
24. Sura 21:72-73.
25. Sura 60:8.
26. Sura 22:35-36.
27. Sura 32:15-17.
28. Sura 59:9. (The reference of this whole passage is to the Hijra or Emigration of Muhammad from Mecca to Medina in the year 622 A.D. It is from this date that the Muslim era is reckoned, as it is with good reason held to be the turning point in Muhammad's career as a prophet. At the time of the Emigration the Prophet already had some converts at Medina, and it was these who received the Emigrants with such grace, literally sharing with them all that they possessed.--Trans.)
29. (Ali was a first cousin to the Prophet through his father Abu-Talib who, though he never embraced Islam, extended his protection to Muhammad throughout a difficult period of the latter's mission in Mecca. Ali himself was an early convert to Islam, and through his marriage to Muhammad's daughter, Fatima, became the Prophet's son-in-law. After the death of the Messenger, Ali was the fourth Caliph, though owing to the civil war he never was the sole ruler of the Muslim world. He met his death by assassination in 661 A.D. The connection of this Qur'-anic passage with Ali and his family is given by Baidawi on the authority of Ibn-Abbas in the following story. "Hasan and Husain--the two sons of Ali--fell ill, and the Messenger of Allah went to visit them with a company of people. They said to Ali, 'O Abu-al-Hasan, if you had made a vow over your two sons, all would have been well.' Then Ali and Fatima and Fidda, a slave-girl belonging to them, vowed that if the boys recovered and got well they would keep a fast for three days. So they had nothing in the house, and Ali borrowed three measures of barley from Simeon of Khaibar, and Fatima ground up one measure and baked five loaves which she put before them to break their fast. Just then a poor man arrived at their house, and they gave him what they had, and themselves spent the night without tasting anything save water. So the next morning they were still fasting, and when again food was placed before them, an orphan arrived and they gave him what they had; then on the third day a prisoner arrived, and they did the like again. And Gabriel revealed this sura to Muhammad."--Baidawi on Sura 76. --Trans.)
30. Sura 76:7-22.
31. Sura 57:11.
32. Sura 57:17.
33. Sura 35:26-27.
34. Sura 2:274.
35. Sura 3:127-128.
36. Sura 9:103-105.
37. Sura 13:19-25.
38. Sura 2:191.
39. Sura 50:23-24.
40. Sura 68:10-12.
41. Sura 90:12-16.

42. Sura 74:43-48.
43. Sura 3:175-176.
44. Sura 9:34-35.
45. (I.e., they did not add the phrase "If Allah will."--Trans.)
46. Sura 68:17-33.
47. Sura 14:36.
48. Sura 63:10-11.
49. Sura 64:15-16.
50. Sura 4:40-41.
51. Sura 2:211.
52. Sura 24:22. (The story of Mistah is connected with the well-known misadventure of A'isha. Having been lost in the desert during one of the Prophet's expeditions she was brought in to Medina under compromising circumstances. A tempest of scandal at once assailed her reputation, and one of the foremost in spreading the scandal was Mistah, a poor relation of A'isha's father, Abu-Bakr. The latter in his anger vowed that Mistah for this ingratitude would no longer enjoy his generosity to which he was accustomed. The forbearance which is indicated in the verse of the Qur'an here quoted is the most notable since Muhammad himself must have deeply resented the calumny of Mistah, A'isha being his favorite wife.--Trans.)
53. Sura 2:263-268.
54. Sura 2:273.
55. Sura 4:127.
56. Sura 3:86.
57. Sura 17:35.
58. Sura 9:112.
59. Sura 22:41.
60. Sura 4:77.
61. Sura 2:276-277.
62. Sura 2:278-279.
63. Sura 5:92-93.

Chapter V
1. (This is the translation of ahl al-dhimma given by Sir William Muir, and seems best to render the phrase. The "People of protection" are those who adhere to their Christianity and stay in their villages under the protection of the Muslims. So Wellhausen in "The Arab Kingdom and Its Fall." The true distinction is here preserved in the text, between the "scripturaries" who may enjoy protection, and the infidel peoples, with whom only a "compact" may be made.--Trans.)
2. Sura 22:40.
3. Sura 2:186.
4. Sura 8:73.
5. Sura 34:27.
6. Sura 21:107.
7. Sura 33:40.
8. Sura 5:5.
9. Sura 17:9.
10. Sura 2:257.
11. Sura 16:92.

12. Sura 4:61.
13. Sura 6:153.
14. Sura 5:11.
15. Traditions.
16. Sura 4:62.
17. Traditions.
18. Sura 3:153.
19. Sura 42:36.
20. (Badr was the scene of the Prophet's first major victory over the Quraish. It took place in 624 A.D. [2 A.H.]--Trans.)
21. (In 627 A.D. [5 A.H.] the Muslim forces were besieged in Medina by Quraish troops. On the advice of "Salman, the Persian, the Prophet defended the city by a ditch, a novelty in Arabia.--Trans.)
22. (After Badr there was considerable dispute about what was to be done with the prisoners. Abu-Bakr is said to have counselled clemency, while Umar advocated inflexible slaughter. When the generality of the Muslims were consulted, their advice was to save the prisoners alive and hold them to ransom. The Qur'anic reflection of the matter will be found in Sura 8:68-72.--Trans.)
23. (After the death of Muhammad all Arabia threw off the yoke of Islam, and the common sign of this rejection of allegiance was the re-fusal to pay the poor-tax. These so-called "Wars of Apostasy" lasted only through the first year of Abu-Bakr's caliphate, and it was very largely owing to his firmness of spirit that the outcome was favorable to Islam.--Trans.)
24. (In 633 A.D. [12 A.H.] Abu-Bakr resolved on a campaign in Syria; the army was under the command of Khalid ibn-Sa'id, of whom Umar did not approve, and accordingly the Caliph took counsel with the people of Mecca.--Trans.)
25. (In 639 A.D. [18 A.H.] plague broke out in Southern Syria, the so-called "Plague of Amwas or Emmaus," the village where it originated. Umar's decision was to withdraw from the affected area; though he was reproached with "fleeing from the decree of Allah," his retort was that this was merely "to flee from the decree of Allah to the decree of Allah." His argument was, as is here mentioned in the text, by a saying of Muhammad: "If plague break out in a country, go not thither; if thou art there, flee not from it."--Trans.)
26. ("Poor members of the community" is a paraphrase of the Ara-bic phrase, ahl al-suffa, literally "people of the bench." The reference is to the stone benches outside Arab houses, which formed the only home of the destitute members of the community.--Trans.)
27. Sura 24:27.
28. Sura 2:185.
29. Ibid.
30. Sura 49:12.
31. Traditions.
32. Sura 22:77.
33. Sura 2:184.

Chapter VI
1. (Uhud, the site of a famous Muslim defeat at the hands of the Mec-

cans in the year following Badr, was the district where, according to
the traditions, the flocks and herds which the Prophet possessed were
pastured. --Trans.)

2. Sura 4:36.
3. Sura 4:2.
4. Sura 18:81.
5. Sura 5:42.
6. Sura 57:7.
7. Sura 24:33.
8. Sura 16:73.
9. Sura 4:4.
10. Sura 59:7.

11. (The Banu Nadir were a Jewish tribe inhabiting Medina and hostile to the Muslim community. It is said that Muhammad, on a visit to
them, got wind of a plot against his life, and promptly roused his followers against them. The Jewish tribe retired to their fortresses, but
were compelled to capitualte after an investment of some three weeks,
during which the Muslims cut down the cherished date-palms of the Jewish community. A peace was negotiated on terms which permitted the
Banu Nadir to withdraw from Medina, taking with them only such of
their possessions as they could transport. The affair is the subject of
most of the revelation in Qur'an, Sura 59. --Trans.)

12. Sura 59:7-8.

13. From "Possession and Religious Theory in Islamic Law" by
Prof. Muhammad Abu Zuhra, Professor of Islamic Law in the Faculty
of Law, Fu'ad al-Awwal University.

14. Sura 8:42.
15. Sura 9:106.
16. Sura 67:15.
17. (Cf. p. 13 supra.--Trans.)

18. (The Umayyads were the first dynasty to hold power in the Muslim world after the four Orthodox Caliphs, Abu Bark, Umar, Othman,
and Ali. Under them the center of the Muslim world moved away from
Arabia to Damascus, where lay their chief strength.--Trans.)

19. Sura 9:60.
20. Sura 5:92.
21. Sura 5:93.
22. (Vd. supra, p. 78 and Qur'an, Sura 4:12-14.--Trans.)
23. Sura 3:125.
24. Sura 2:276 and cf. p. 112 supra.
25. Sura 2:278-9.
26. Sura 2:280.
27. Sura 17:31.
28. Sura 7:29.
29. Sura 7:30-31.
30. Sura 9:87.
31. Sura 34:33.
32. Sura 23:34-36.
33. Sura 33:67-68.
34. Sura 25:18-19.
35. Sura 28:58.

36. Sura 56:40-47.
37. Sura 17:17.
38. Sura 33:62.
39. (The Ka'ba is the supremely sacred building of the world to Muslims. It is a small cube-shaped building in Mecca, in one corner of which is set the Black Stone, which is kissed by all Muslims who perform the hajj or pilgrimage to Mecca. By Muslim custom the Ka'ba is covered every year by a rich curtain or robe which is carried in a special litter known as the mahmil in the pilgrimage. This curtain, or kiswa, is provided annually today by Egypt.--Trans.)
40. Sura 17:72.
41. (After the death of Muhammad the tribes of Arabia which had accepted his suzerainty during his lifetime, threw off the Muslim yoke. The first Caliph, Abu-Bakr, resisted all attempts at compromise, and, at grave risk to the infant religion, despatched all his available men for the reconquest of Arabia. The resultant campaigns, in which the Muslims were conspicuously successful, are known as the Wars of Apostasy. --Trans.)

Chapter VII
1. (The "Orthodox Caliphs"--al-Khulafa al-Rashidun--were the first four who held the office of Caliph, Abu-Bakr, Umar, Uthman, and Ali in that order, all having been among the Companions of the Prophet. --Trans.)
2. Denison, V. H.: Emotion as the Basis of Civilization. Published by Scribner, N.Y., 1928.
3. We have already seen that Europe was not at any time truly Christian. The destruction and division to which the author here alludes arose, not from the nature of Christianity, but from the reaction of the peoples of Europe against Christianity.
4. Quoted in Maula Muhammad Ali: Islam and the New World Order.
5. (The story of Khalid ibn-al-Walid forms an interesting commentary on the manners and customs of the early Islamic period. Khalid, the "Sword of Allah," was the main military support of the early caliphate, but, being a man of haughty spirit and unbridled passions, he fell foul of Umar on two important occasions which are discussed later in this chapter. During the Wars of Apostasy he was instrumental in the killing of Malik ibn-Nuwaira, after the latter had submitted to him and declared his reconversion to Islam. The usual account is that Khalid order the prisoners, Malik among them, to be "wrapped up," but that he used an ambiguous word which in another dialect meant to kill. This is the "error of speech" to which reference is made below. Khalid's enemies thereupon denounced him as the murderer of a Muslim, and the charge was given additional weight by the fact that Khalid had married the dead man's widow, the beautiful Laila on the same day, and had actually consummated the marriage that night. On a later occasion in the same campaign Khalid did the same with the daughter of Maja'a, a chief of the Yarbu' tribe whom he had captured. It was on this occasion that Abu-Bakr wrote him the famous letter "sprinkled with blood." The upshot was that Umar had no love for Khalid, and is said to have relieved him of his command at the earliest opportunity when he became Caliph. There

is, however, considerable uncertainty about the whole matter.--Trans.)

6. (The 'idda or legal term is that period which a woman must observe unmarried after being divorced, or after the death of her husband. The period is three months, as in Qur., 2:228.--Trans.)

7. If this had been so, he would have punished him for it when he came to the caliphate.

8. (Mu'awiya was the first of the Caliphs belonging to the family of Umayya, of whom more will be heard later. The reference here is to the shrewdness for which he was famous, but at the same time he was by no means devoid of personal courage.--Trans.)

9. (The currency mainly in use in the early Islamic world took two forms. The dirham--Greek drachme--was the smaller unit of exchange, being worth approximately ten cents; the dinar--Latin denarius-- was valued at twenty times the dirham.--Trans.)

10. From Abd al-Halim al-Jundi: Abu Hanifa, the Champion of Freedom and tolerance in Islam.

11. (The form "Beduin" generally used in English is properly a plural of Bedu, the true Arabic form in the singular.--Trans.)

12. From Abd al-Rahman Azzam: The Eternal Message.

13. (The word "client" here and throughout the translation is used to render the Arabic, maula, a freed slave who at his emancipation attached himself to the family of his emancipator.--Trans.)

14. (Usfan is a township some thirty-six miles from Mecca.--Trans.)

15. (Salim had been killed in the battle of Yamama in 632 A.D. [11 A.H.]. Tradition relates that Abu-Hudhaifa died, carrying as a banner some leaves of the Qur'an stuck on his spear shaft; when he fell, Salim seized this improvised banner and, exclaiming, "If I feared death I would be but a craven bearer of the sacred text," plunged into the thick of the battle and was there killed.--Trans.)

16. Taken from Abd al-Halim al-Jundi: Op. Cit.

17. Ibid.

18. (Abu-Yusuf was also a disciple of the famous Abu-Hanifa. For some account of him, vd. Hitti: History of the Arabs, p. 397.--Trans.)

19. (Amr was another of the influential figures of early Islam. We have already had mention of him in the account of the emigration to Abyssiania mentioned above. In his heavenly days he had been familiar with Egypt, and in the caliphate of Umar he begged for the opportunity of reducing that country to the rule of Islam. His request was granted, and Amr carried out a brilliant conquest of the Nile lands, in which he then became governor. In later days he became the friend and the lieutenant of Mu'awiya.--Trans.)

20. (Burd, plural abrad, is a large square piece of cloth which is used as a wrapper, but is not large enough to make a cloak or outer garment for an average man.--Trans.)

21. (Al-Mansur was the second of the Abbasid Caliphs. He followed Al-Saffah, the "shedder of blood," and ruled 754-775 A.D. [136-158 A.H.] --Trans.)

22. Al-Jundi: Op. Cit. (Haman is represented as the wazir or prime minister of Pharaoh in Qur'an, Sura 28:5, 29:38--Trans.)

23. (Abbasid Caliph 842-847 A.D. [227-232 A.H.].--Trans.)

24. (Sura 4:88.--Trans.)

25. From the Musnad, part I, edited by Prof. Ahmad Shakir.

26. (Ruled 785-786 A.D. [169-170 A.H.].--Trans.)

27. (Successor of Al-Hadi, the famous Harun al-Rashid, ruled 786-809 A.D. [170-193 A.H.]--Trans.)

28. Al-Jundi: Op. Cit.

29. (Founder of the so-called Tulunid dynasty, ruled himself in Egypt 868-883 A.D. [254-270 A.H.]. Ahmad made himself independent of the now weak Abbasid dynasty in Baghdad under Al-Mu'tamid, and extended his conquests into Palestine and Syria.--Trans.)

30. Al-Jundi: Opt. Cit.

31. Ibid. (The most famous member of the Ayyubid dynasty was Saladin or Salah al-Din, born 1138 A.D. [534 A.H.] died 1193 A.D. [591 A.H.]--Trans.)

32. (Isma'il Pasha, born 1830, died 1895, was the grandson of Mehemet Ali, and became Wali or governor-general of Egypt on the death of his uncle Sa'id in 1863. In 1867 the incident related in the text book place when Isma'il was made Khedive, an ancient Persian title meaning "ruler," and in fact implying almost independence of Turkish sovereignty. --Trans.)

33. (Tawfiq or Tewfiq was the son of Isma'il, and was Khedive of Egypt from 1880-1892.--Trans.)

34. Sura 2:257.

35. Sura 16:126.

36. Sura 22:40.

37. Sura 2:186.

38. Sura 3:86.

39. (Husain was the second son of Ali, and therefore a grandson of the Prophet. He was killed at Karbala by Umayyad forces in 680 A.D. [61 A.H.].--Trans.)

40. Sura 59:7.

41. (The fifth year of Umar's caliphate, 639 A.D. [18 A.H.], was marked by the double calamity of famine and pestilence. The soil of the Hejaz is said to have been so dry that clouds of dust incessantly obscured the sky; hence the name of "The Year of Ashes."--Trans.)

42. (The story of Joseph is to be found in Sura 12 of the Qur'an, and the commentators refer this expression of Muhammad to verse 31 of this Sura, where the Egyptian women are said to have cut their hands at the sight of Joseph's beauty.--Trans.)

43. (Owing to the hostility of the Quraish Muhammad's Hegira to Medina had to be taken secretly. With Abu-Bakr as his only companion he took refuge in a cave on Mount Thaur, where they stayed for three days until the hue and cry had abated. The experience is referred to in Sura 9:40, where Abu-Bakr receives what was to be his proudest title, the "second of the two," or, in ordinary English, "the sole companion."--Trans.)

44. (Yazid was the son and successor of Mu'awiya. After the death of his father he reigned from 680-683 A.D. [60-64 A.H.] His reign was chiefly notorious for the killing of Husain at Karbala.--Trans.)

45. (Immediately after the capture of Mecca, when Abu-Sufyan embraced Islam, the Muslims fought against the Hawazin tribe at the battle of Hunain. The battle was bitterly fought, and fortune wavered more

than once, but finally the Muslim forces gained the day. --Trans.)

46. (This oath of fudhul, or things which are over and above what is necessary, was a confederacy of three of the principal Quraish families for the purpose of securing justice for the weak and the helpless. The date is relatively uncertain, but as the Prophet appears to have been present on the occasion it may be placed somewhere around the turn of the century, circa 590-600 A.D.--Trans.)

47. (Umayyad Caliph 717-720 A.D. [99-101 A.H.].--Trans.)

48. (The khutba or sermon here referred to is the public address at Friday prayers in the mosque or on any other solemn occasion. It corresponds in large measure to the sermon in Christian worship, but was more largely used for statements of policy on the part of the head of the state. --Trans.)

49. From Prof. Al-Aqqad: The Valour of the Imam.

50. (Al-Walid, the fifth Umayyad Caliph, ruled 705-715 A.D. [86-96 A.H.]. Under him Umar ibn-Abd al-Aziz was governor of Arabia. Al-Walid was Umar's cousin. --Trans.)

51. (Sulaiman, the brother and successor of Al-Walid, was Umar's immediate predecessor in the caliphate. --Trans.)

52. From Ahmad Zaki Safut: Umar ibn-Abd al-Aziz.

53. (Arabic fai', to be distinguished clearly from the following category, ghanima; for the latter "plunder" seems a more appropriate word, since it is the fruit of war, whereas "booty' is the general word for what is gained with or without fighting. --Trans.)

54. (Sura 9:60. Cf. supra, pp. 150, 148 ff.--Trans.)

55. Haikal: Al-Faruq Umar, II.

56. Ibid.

57. (The verb used here, aslamu, is the technical word for embracing Islam; indeed the name of the faith is the verbal noun of this form, aslamu. --Trans.)

58. We have already said that the spirit of Islam destroyed the influence of this kind of aristocracy. Until the time of Uthman this older kind had not revived, so that there was only an aristocracy based on early conversion and on sufferings for the faith; and this was a milder form of aristocracy.

59. (Quoting Sura 9:35. --Trans.)

60. (Ka'b was a learned Jewish convert to Islam. --Trans.)

61. (Ali ibn-Husain, known as Al-Mas'udi, is chiefly famed for his great historical work, the Muruj al-Dhahab, the Golden Meadows. The French translation by Barbier de Meynard is published under the title "Les Prairies d'Or." A native of Baghdad, Mas'udi flourished in the first half of the tenth century, and is known as the "Herodotus of the Arabs"; Ibn-Khaldun calls him the "Imam for all historians." --Trans.)

62. (Jarir ibn-Atiya was a contemporary of the famous poet, Farazdaq, both of them dying in 728 A.D. He was as famous for his vituperation as for his eulogies. Vd. Nicholson: Literary History of the Arabs, 244 ff.--Trans.)

63. From Adam Mez: Islamic Civilisation in the Fourth Century of the Hijra. (I have not had access to this work, but I believe it to be published by Mez in 1922 at Heidelberg under the title of "Die Renaissance des Islams," of which an English translation was published in London in 1937 under the same name. --Trans.)

64. (Adi belonged to the famous tribe of Tayy, whose former chief Hatim, the father of Adi, was, and is to this day, a proverb for generosity. --Trans.)

65. Abu-Yusuf: The Book of the Land Tax.

Chapter VIII

1. (Sura 5:48. Cf. supra, p. 10--Trans.)

2. (A fatwa is the decision of a Mufti, based on the Islamic law. --Trans.)

3. (The Qarmatians, thus named from Qarmat, the dwarf, which was the nickname of the original leader, were Isma'ilis who raised a dangerous rebellion in Iraq and Syria during the reign of Al-Muktafi. They were defeated in the latter province in 901 A.D. [288 A.H.], but their fierce risings continued to trouble the Abbasids for at least fifty years. --Trans.)

4. (Alphonse Gouilly: L'Islam devant le Monde Moderne. --Trans.)

5. (H.A.R. Gibb: Whither Islam? p. 379. --Trans.)

6. From Prof. Hasan Habashi: The First Crusade.

7. This takes place through equating the form "Mahomed" and the form "Mahound." "Ma," which is the first person possessive pronoun, "my," and "hound," from the German "hund," a dog. This is a play on words between the forms "Mahumad" and "Mahund."--From Leopold Weiss: Islam at the Cross-roads. (This work was originally written by Muhammad Asad, and published by Ashraf, 1937, Lahore. It was translated into English in 1938 by Weiss, and thence retranslated into Arabic by Umar Farrukh. --Trans.)

8. Ibid.

9. Sura 8:62.

10. Sura 4:143.

11. Sura 4:76.

12. Sura 3:133.

13. Quoted from Haikal's Life of Muhammad, where he quotes from an article in the magazine Nur al-Islam, No. 40, page 5720, dated 1934 A.D. [1353 A.H.].

14. Jacob Fahm: Pragmatism, or the Philosophy of Means.

15. The present author hopes in the near future to produce for the Arab reader a complete study on "The Islamic doctrine of the Universe, Life, and Mankind."

16. Jacob Fahm: Op. Cit.

17. Quoted from "The Imam Malik" by Prof. Muhammad Abu Zuhra, professor of the Shari'a in the Faculty of Law in the Fu'ad al-Awwal University.

18. ("Public interest" is an arbitrary but convenient translation for a phrase which means literally a measure of welfare for society which lacks a precedent in the primary authorities. --Trans.)

19. (Reference is here made to three of the four schools into which Muslim jurisprudence is divided; these are the Shafi'ite, the Hanafite, the Malikite, and the Hanbalite schools. The roots by which the system of jurisprudence is governed, being also mentioned here, may be said to include: nass or precedent, drawn from the Qur'an or the Sunna; these two authorities are in theory the sole root of jurisprudence (fiqh); ijma'

or concensus of opinion; qiyas or analogy. Other principles in use but
more dubious of acceptance are ray, or independent critical opinion, and
istihsan, or preference. Vd. Lammens: Islam, pp. 82 ff.--Trans.)

20. (Sura 6:108--Trans.)

21. (Sura 2:98. Baidawi in his commentary on this verse gives the
explanation that the Jews of Arabia took the form ra'ina, look at us, or,
better, pay attention to us, as connected with a similar word meaning
"evil." Muhammad therefore, disliking their ridicule, proscribed the
use of the word, which was to be replaced by another which did not lend
itself to such paranomasia. Vd. Jeffery: Foreign Vocabulary of the
Qur'an, 136, and Palmer: Koran, 13.--Trans.)

22. Sura 2:269-270.

23. Tradition No. 2541 in Prof. Ahmad Muhammad Shakir: Musnad,
iv, published by Dar al-Ma'arif. (The isnad, or chain of transmitting
authorities, which has been omitted in the body of the translated text,
follows the tradition. It runs as follows: Related by Ahmad on the
authority of Affan, from Humad ibn-Zaid on the authority of Amr ibn-
Dinar, who quoted it from Tawus, who had it from Abdullah ibn-Abbas.
--Trans.)

24. Sura 4:9.